Viticulture

Viticulture

An introduction to commercial grape growing for wine production. Written for Master of Wine candidates, students taking the WSET Diploma, and anyone else who wishes to know more about the subject.

Stephen Skelton MW

Published by the Author
2020

Copyright © Stephen Skelton 2020

1B Lettice Street, London, SW6 4EH.
E-mail: mail@stephenskelton.com
Telephone: +44 7768 583700

First published in paperback in Great Britain in 2007. Second edition first published in Great Britain in 2020

Edition: 2-005f

A CIP catalogue record for this book is available from the British Library.

ISBN Lulu: 978-0-9931-2357-3

ISBN KDP: 978-0-9931-2355-9

ISBN Ingram-Spark: 978-0-9931-2354-2

Designed by Geoff Green Book Design, Cambridge

Cover: A young Chardonnay vine, just before flowering at Breaky Bottom Vineyard, Lewes, East Sussex, Great Britain.

Acknowledgements

This book is a compilation of my personal knowledge, experience and research gained by working with vines since 1975, plus a huge amount of delving into the published works and internet postings of others. Chief amongst these published works, in alphabetical order, are:

Grapevine, The – Patrick Iland, Peter Dry, Tony Proffitt, Steve Tyerman
Oxford Companion to Wine – Jancis Robinson (Editor)
Pruning and Training – David Jackson
Sunlight into Wine – Smart and Robinson
Venture into Viticulture – Tom Crossen
Viticulture 1 and 2 – Dry and Coombe (Editors)
Wine Science – Jamie Goode

Full publishing details of the above, together with a complete list of publications consulted, will be found in the bibliography at the end of this book.

Thanks

I would especially like to thank a fellow Master of Wine, Nova Cadamatre MW, Senior Director of Winemaking, Robert Mondavi Winery for Constellation Brands, for her help and advice. She reviewed the whole book for me, making many suggestions about content and organisation and contributed substantially to the re-writing of Chapter 1. She also supplied the illustrations in that chapter.

I would also like to thank the following who over the years have given me their comments, constructive criticisms and help with writing both editions of this book: Antony Moss MW, Jill Norman and Monty Waldin. Thanks also to Geoff Green for his book designing skills, Lynne Sharrock for proofreading and the indexer, Dr Laurence Errington.

Picture Acknowledgements

Cabernet Sauvignon leaf – Pancrat, Wikimedia Commons
Channel irrigation – Professor Peter Dry, University of Adelaide
Chardonnay leaf – Karl Bauer, Wikimedia Commons
Double-sided leaf trimmer – Spezia Technovit, Pianello Val Tidone, Italy
Frost irrigation – Stephen Farquharson of Wooing Tree Vineyard, NZ
Frost windmill – Hawkes Bay Wind Machines Ltd
Leaf stripper – Pellenc, Pertuis, France
Pruning cart – Constructions Humeau, Montrevault-sur-Evre, France
Quebec, vines in the snow – Julie Peglau
Vines in China being earthed up – Peter Hayes AM

Contents

Units of measurement

Area:	1 hectare (ha) = 100 ares
	1 are = 100 square metres
Therefore	1 ha = 10,000 square metres
1 acre =	43,560 sq. feet, 4,840 sq. yards, or approx. 4,047 sq. metres.
	Approx. 2.471 acres = 1 ha
Weight:	1 tonne = 1,000 kilograms (kg)
	1 ton (Imperial) = 2,240 lbs or approx. 1,016 kg
	1 ton (US) = 2,000 lbs or approx. 907 kg
Volume:	1,000 litres = volume of 1,000 kg (1 tonne) of water at sea-level at 20°C
	1 hectolitre (hl) = 100 litres
Yields:	1 tonne per hectare = approx. 7 hl/ha (see note below)
	1 tonne per acre = approx. 17 hl/ha

Note:

The volume of juice/wine produced from 1 tonne of grapes will depend on several factors: the type of press, degree of pressure, grape variety, whether pressed pre-fermentation (white grapes) or post-fermentation (red grapes), whole-bunch pressed, crushed and not de-stemmed or crushed and de-stemmed, machine harvested etc. The output of liquid from 1 tonne of grapes for still wines will vary between 775 litres (extreme) and 650 litres (low).

For sparkling wines using the *official méthode Champenoise*, 4,000 kg of grapes may yield 2,050 litres of *cuvée* juice and another 500 litres of *taille* – a total of 2,550 litres or 637.5 litres per tonne. Any additional juice pressed (known as the *rebèche*) is used for table wine or distillation. The best champagnes and sparkling winemakers only use the *cuvée*.

Introduction

The foundation of this book is the four-hour lecture on viticulture that I used to give to Diploma students at the Wine and Spirit Education Trust (WSET) in London, other parts of the UK, as well as Ireland, Canada and Norway. I started delivering this lecture in 1986 and gave up (more-or-less) in around 2005 when the WSET changed its ideas on using outside lecturers. I decided then to put pen to paper and write up the lecture as a short, all-encompassing book on the subject that would contain enough detail for students to pass the relevant papers in the Diploma and Master of Wine exams.

The first edition, published in 2007, was a modest affair, put together by myself in a very amateur way, although it received some kind reviews and started to sell. I self-published the book on what was then one of the better known 'publish-on-demand' websites, www.lulu.com and the book achieved modest sales. Once I realised that it was selling, I decided that it needed re-launching and together with the help of some professionals – book designer, proof-reader and indexer – republished the same text in its current format. I also bit the bullet and loaded it onto Amazon's publish-on-demand website, now called KDP (Kindle Direct Publishing) and was amazed when – with a little help to start with from Google AdWords – sales almost doubled overnight. To date, the book in both editions and an e-book has sold almost 10,000 copies and been bought by students and wine professionals in all four corners of the globe. As I write, this 2nd edition text is being translated into Chinese and Japanese where hopefully it will find a modest market.

This edition of Viticulture, although a few thousand words longer than the first edition, has stayed true to its remit: as an introduction to the subject, written in terms that an interested and committed laymen can understand and sufficiently detailed to be able to answer any viticulture question in the WSET and MW exams. It is not primarily a book for people in the vineyard industry or for those wishing to enter the industry (although plenty have bought it) and it is therefore concise so that each chapter can be read in a relatively short time frame. What this book does not aim to be – and could never be given its size – is a complete guide to growing grapes in all regions of the world, for all types of wine and in every circumstance. Shortcuts and summaries have been made and for this I can only apologise in advance.

Viticulture, the growing of the grapes that every winemaker needs before he or she can make any wine, remains for me a fascinating subject even after 45 years of being involved. It still surprises me how some of those involved with wine, especially in wine marketing, fail to appreciate the importance of the decisions and actions taken in the vineyard, at all stages: from planning, through planting and establishment, via annual management to picking the grapes, every decision can affect the final outcome of what's in the bottle.

As with almost all agriculture, global warming has brought its up and downs. I work of course in a region which has massively benefitted from the rise in temperatures over the last half-century, but others have not been so fortunate and have had to change their farming practices as a result. Many regions are now seeing different grape varieties, different farming practices and of course irrigation, all because of global warming. The other game-changer in agriculture, slower to affect viticulture than other crops, is a combination of factors: GPS, automation, robotics and mechanisation. In viticulture the changes brought about by these factors is happening slowly, mainly because growers only get a chance to re-plan and re-plant their vineyards every 30–40 years, but happening it is. Self-steering and self-driving tractors are now, if not common, definitely on their way. Robots that can cut the grass and drones that can spray the vines are beyond the drawing-board and, if not seen much in actual vineyards, are being trialled and definitely here to stay. GPS and drones are starting to help with pest and disease control, silently flying along the rows of vines looking for abnormalities and changes in the canopy so that sprays can be more selectively (and hopefully less frequently) used.

I hope that you enjoy reading this book and look forward to hearing from you if there is something you don't quite understand. I also ask that if you notice any mistakes, errors or typographical upsets, please let me know. One of the benefits of publish-on-demand is that a new version can be uploaded at any time.

Stephen Skelton MW
London, October 2019.

Chapter 1
The grapevine

The grapevine

Grapevines are all members of the same genus (or family) of plants called Vitis and, in their natural habitat, are woodland plants that like to climb and clamber up convenient trees, putting out tendrils to attach themselves to branches, searching for the light. Their only aim is to produce grapes sweet enough to attract birds and animals who then eat the fruit and distribute the seeds. The seeds then fall to the ground where they eventually germinate, creating new vines. In this way, the future of a vine is assured. Because it often has to climb some distance and compete with trees for light, it has a natural propensity to grow fast and furious until it reaches its goal. It also has to compete, both at ground level and below ground level, with dense woodland for water and nutrients and thus it needs to have an extensive and deep root system if it is to survive. The natural tendency of many plants is to produce fruit which contain seeds. If the plant is not threatened, it will grow in a balanced manner, producing just enough fruit to ensure survival, and will expand its physical size to the limitations of its environment. If subject to adverse conditions however, its natural inclination is to increase the amount of fruit it produces, usually at the expenc maximise its chances of survival. These inherent traits and characteristics are present in all vines – wild or cultivated – and man's efforts to train and tame them and turn them to his financial gain, must take these natural tendencies into account.

The vine, like many types of fruiting plant that have a permanent woody framework (apples, pears, plums, cherries etc), produces its crop from wood that grew in the previous year. It is therefore, the growing conditions during the previous year that largely determine the quantity, and sometimes the quality, of fruit in the current year. Vine husbandry must therefore always look to the future, to prune and nurture the plant in the current year with an eye on the crop in the next year.

Most (but by no means all) vine varieties for winemaking belong to the species *Vitis vinifera*, known as the European Vine[1]. These are the varieties originally native to the Middle East which have, over the several thousand years that man has grown them, been developed into the individual cultivars[2] that we know today. *V. vinifera* varieties are now spread throughout the world wherever vines are grown. Vines for planting new vineyards (whether grafted or not) are always produced by taking hardwood cuttings from 'parent' vines and never grown from seed. Grape seeds (or pips) are never identical and each seed has the capacity to turn into a different new variety. However, many vine seeds, whilst they will often germinate and grow, are sterile and will never bear grapes. Other species of the genus *Vitis* used for winemaking (albeit in

1 According to *The Oxford Companion to Wine*, *Vitis vinifera* is, strictly speaking, a Eurasian species.

2 A cultivar is a just another name for what a layman would call a variety.

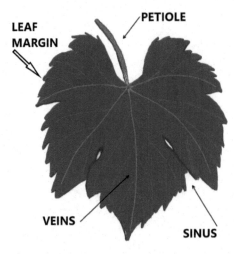

LEAF MARGIN

PETIOLE

VEINS

SINUS

BUD

INTERNODE

limited amounts) include *V. labrusca, V. rotundifolia, V. amurensis* and others. In addition, crosses of *vinifera* and non-*vinifera* varieties (known in viticulture as hybrids) are widespread, although not globally in large quantities. Rootstocks, used to counteract the damage caused by the root-louse *Phylloxera,* are usually the result of crossings of non-*vinifera* species of *Vitis.*

Vine physiology

One of the most essential parts of viticulture is to understand the growth habits and internal processes of the vine. Knowledge of how the vine functions allows a basic understanding of how all other decisions in the vineyard will impact the vine function and growth. While this subject can be daunting and is usually accompanied by a high level of chemical compounds and pathways which can be terrifying for people without scientific backgrounds, when broken down simply it can be quite easy to compare processes the vines use to processes which we ourselves use to survive daily.

Parts of the grapevine

All vines consist of two distinct halves: the above-ground system of trunk, canes, shoots, foliage (leaves) and fruit clusters; and the below-ground root system. In most vines, there is in fact more of the plant below ground level than above, something often not appreciated by the casual observer.

Leaves, shoots, and clusters

The 'green parts' of the vine are those that are the most rapidly growing during the season and generally encompass the leaves, shoots, and clusters (bunches of grapes) on the vine. Taken together, these are known as the 'canopy' or sometimes as the 'leaf-wall'. This area also makes up the microclimate of the vine since the air in this zone (including temperature and humidity) is highly affected by the plant itself.

Leaves

The leaves of the vine are like solar panels on a house. Their main function is to create energy for the rest of the plant to function. The underside of the leaf also contains special cells called stomata. These act as the 'nose' of the plant; inhaling carbon dioxide (CO_2) and exhaling water and oxygen (O_2). More information on these processes will be covered later in this chapter under Drinking and sweating.

Leaves of vines have a very similar structure to most deciduous plants (plants with broad leaves that go dormant in the winter). The part of the leaf that attaches to the vine is called a petiole. This primarily serves as support for the leaf and the main connection of the vascular system to the leaf blade. The main part of the leaf (or leaf blade), consists of veins of the vascular system and the leaf tissue where the majority of photosynthesis takes place. The miracle of photosynthesis will be explored later in this chapter.

The shape of the leaves, or morphology, is one of the key distinguishing features between different types of cultivars. The edge of the leaf is known as the leaf margin and it is common to see serrated margins on grape leaves. It is also common to see some type of leaf sinus in grapes. Sinuses are more pronounced in Cabernet than they are in Chardonnay for example. By understanding leaf morphology, it is easier to describe symptoms of disease or deficiencies since many affect only a specific part of the leaf such as marginal chlorosis (yellowing along the edge or margin of the leaf) or veinal chlorosis (yellowing only along the veins but not affecting the rest of the leaf tissue).

Shoots

The green stem structures that leaves are attached to are known as shoots as long as they are green. Once they have turned brown at the end of the season, a process known as lignification (or turning woody), they are referred to as canes. The shoots begin growing at budburst and extend throughout the growing season. They can be trimmed to keep them under control and growth will usually slow as the season progresses towards harvest. Lack of water will also slow their growth.

The structure of a shoot is relatively simple. It is a single structure made up of buds, or nodes (sometimes also called eyes), from which leaves, clusters, or tendrils appear. The space between nodes is known as an internode. The internal make-up of the shoots consists of support cells for structure and transport cells of the vascular system. Shoots do contain chlorophyll which mean that they can photosynthesize but this doesn't serve as the primary source of photosynthetic activity for the vine.

The distance between two leaf positions (the internode) determines how many buds occur on any given length of cane: the shorter the distance, the more buds; the longer, the fewer. Vines which are over-vigorous whether through climatic conditions, a high-vigour rootstock, or just because they are a vigorous variety, will tend to have fewer buds per metre of cane length. Conversely, vines on low-vigour rootstocks, or growing in dry years, when shoot growth is slow, will have more buds per metre length of cane. These differences will need to be taken into account at pruning time. On spur-pruned vines this is not so marked as the fruiting buds are not carried on canes, a factor in favour of this pruning system. As the season progresses and the main shoots continue to grow, side-shoots will emerge from the new buds and will add to the general mass of foliage that forms the leaf-wall. In very vigorous vines, these side-shoots will greatly contribute to the problem of overcrowding in the microclimate of the canopy.

Cabernet Sauvignon

Chardonnay

Clusters and tendrils

Either a cluster or a tendril will appear opposite a leaf on the shoot. Physiologically speaking a cluster and a tendril start as very similar structures. However, clusters have inflorescences (flowers) which eventually become bunches of grapes. The flower clusters in each node are determined by the conditions in the previous season so it is very easy to see them if a dormant bud is dissected. The part of the cluster directly connected to the shoot is called the rachis. The individual berries are attached to the rachis by a short stem known as the peduncle. The rachis and the peduncle, similar to the petiole of the leaf, offer support for the cluster and a vascular connection to the plant. Opposite the first two or three leaves, there will usually be no flower clusters. Opposite the next one, two and three, there

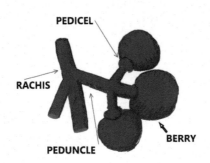

will be flower clusters (which reduce in size the further they are along the shoot towards the growing tip). After this point there are usually no more at this stage, although in many years secondary bunches will often appear which can be removed (or at least, not harvested). Most wine grape varieties bear three flower clusters per cane, although four is not unknown. Where there are no flowers there will be tendrils which will attach themselves to convenient wires or canes and provide support for the shoots as they grow.

The conditions in which buds develop, in terms of heat and light received and the general health and well-being of the vine, will determine the quantity (and often the quality) of the crop to come in the next year. The actual process by which this plant-matter turns into potential crop is compli-

cated and growth hormones called gibberellins play a role, as do the temperature and weather conditions at the time of 'flower initiation' as it is known. Vines growing in cool, damp, overcast conditions at this time of the year (which in Europe would be between mid-May and early July, depending on latitude), will be far more likely to produce small crops, than vines growing in warm, dry conditions.

Commercially grown vines are almost all hermaphrodite and therefore their flowers carry both the male and female parts required for successful pollination. Single sex varieties do exist (although usually for the production of table grapes or grapes for drying) and, in these instances, pollinator varieties will have to be grown amongst or alongside to provide pollen. Hermaphrodite flowers consist of five pollen-bearing stamens which, given the right conditions, transmit their pollen to the stigma which then travels down the style to reach the ovary where pollination takes place. Prior to flowering, the flower is covered by a cap, more correctly called a calyptra, which is in effect the petals of the flower. The cap is stimulated to open and lift off by a combination of time, temperature and hormonal signals generated by the vine. More about flowering can be found in **Chapter 8 – The Annual Cycle of the Vine—June and July.**

Woody parts – cordons, canes, and trunks

The woody parts of the vine consist of the trunk, cordons, and canes[3]. The trunk is the main support for the vine, outside of the trellis itself, and the vine's connection to the roots. In *Vinifera* vineyards, the base of the trunk is usually where the graft can be found. This is where the scion[4] is joined to the rootstock (in a grafted vine). A cordon is any length of wood on the vine that is older than two years but is not part of the trunk structure. Cordons typically have several spur positions from which the shoots

3 Every vine has a trunk of some sort. Cordons are typically only found on spur-pruned vines; and canes only on cane-pruned vines. See more in Chapter 7 – Trellising, training and pruning.

4 A scion is the term used to describe the top half of a graft i.e. the species of plant being grown.

and, later on, the canes grow from. Once shoots are lignified, they become canes. Depending on the pruning method, canes can either be selected and retained while the rest are removed for cane-pruned vines or shortened to spurs during the pruning process for spur-pruned vines. In cane-pruned systems, the trunk is usually vertical with the annual canes attached at the top of the trunk and (in a two-cane system) extending to either side in a T form. In spur-pruned systems, the trunk may well extend into a T or an inverted L shaped cordon, with the fruiting wood carried on spurs. In what might be termed 'extreme' pruning systems, the trunk might well be elongated and trained to an overhead pergola or extended cordon. In very extreme circumstances the trunk can be extended almost indefinitely and continue to provide moisture and nourishment to grapes many metres away from the plant's roots.[5] Pruning will be dealt with in **Chapter 7 – Trellising, training and pruning.**

Below the soil – the root structure

The rootzone of the plant starts just below the soil's surface. Grapevines have generally only a few roots which spread out in search of water and nutrients. These roots tend to grow in a more fibrous pattern rather than a taproot system similar to that of large trees such as oaks. However, they are not as fibrous as grasses. This makes them inherently weak scavengers of resources although it gives them the advantage of being able to thrive in poor soils. The vine typically has several 'main' roots which branch in different directions and from those main roots, smaller feeder roots grow, the number depending on the availability of water and nutrients. Through the feeder roots, the vine will seek out available water and nutrients and these smaller roots can die off once the resources in an area have been exhausted, while the main root will continue to produce smaller roots in other

Double Guyot cane-pruned vine in the winter

directions continuing the search. The roots are aided by root hairs which are covered in a mycorrhizal fungus (see later for more on this).

A vine's root system is often quite extensive and roots can penetrate the earth to a depth of 3 to 4 metres or even more although the size of the root system will depend on several factors: the type of rootstock, soil conditions, water supply and climate are the main ones. Roots are seeking moisture and nutrients and when their needs are satisfied, they will stop their search. In irrigated vineyards therefore, root systems are often smaller than in dry-farmed (i.e. not irrigated) vineyards. Shallow soils, especially those overlying an impervious layer of rock or compacted soil, will impede the progress of a vine's roots. Sideways growth is always possible, but competition from neighbouring vines will limit this.[6] Waterlogged soils will restrict the growth of roots, especially the small root-hairs (also called feeder roots) which grow from the established roots. Soils that have an imbalance of nutrients and minerals will also provide a barrier to extensive root growth.

The roots are there to perform several tasks: to anchor the plant in the soil; to

5 A single vine of the variety Black Hamburg, planted by Lancelot 'Capability' Brown in 1768 at Hampton Court Palace near London (and still fruiting) fills a greenhouse almost 37 m long.
6 The vine at the end of each row, which does not have any competition on one side, is often noticeably more vigorous than the other vines in the row.

provide a conduit for nutrients and moisture from the soil to the plant; and to store reserves of nutrients (mainly carbohydrates) and moisture as a buffer against variations in supply. When a vine is planted, the roots number about 3–5 and have typically been trimmed back to 100 mm long. In their first year, as the vine is making rapid growth above ground, the roots will be similarly busy and can easily expand to 500 mm long by the end of the first year if growing conditions (soil, nutrients and moisture) are ideal. As the vine enters its second and subsequent years and as the root system expands, extension growth slows, but the complete root system divides and expands until such time as it meets roots from its neighbours when competition for food supplies will force it to dig deeper.

A vine's roots start growing in the spring when the topsoil warms to around 10°C and a message is sent to the roots to start producing sap which travels upwards towards the plant. The energy for this activity is provided by the reserves of carbohydrates (starches and sugars) stored in the roots and in the above-ground fabric of the vine (the trunk and canes) and given stimulus by hormones called cytokinins which are produced in the root tips. Once green leaves are produced, sugars and starches are created through the process of photosynthesis. These sugars and starches are used to provide the motive power for the plant and are also stored for future use in the woody parts of the vine (both above and below ground) and of course in the grapes once they appear. The initial root activity is provided by the minute root-hairs which explore tiny cracks and fissures in the soil and which, with the help of mycorrhizal fungi (see below), extract nutrients and moisture as they grow. As the season progresses, some of these root-hairs turn into permanent roots which contribute to the expansion of the vine's root system.

The ability of the vine's root system to produce these fine root-hairs in the early part of the growing season is crucial if the vine is to get into leaf quickly and extend the growing season as long as possible. An early bud-burst is often associated with a successful year as flowering is earlier and ripening takes place in better and warmer conditions. Having said that, an early bud-burst means that spring frost could do more damage to buds and shoots as they are more advanced. A cold and wet spring, especially in vineyards which have poor drainage, does not allow a vine's roots to put out these root-hairs so easily with the result that bud-burst and subsequent shoot growth are delayed. A delayed bud-burst will mean a shorter growing season and one which, in temperate climates, is more likely to end in poorer weather for ripening.

Mycorrhizal fungi

Mycorrhizal fungi are beneficial organisms in the soil that exist by feeding off the carbohydrates in a plant's roots and, in exchange, increase a plant's absorptive capacity and enable the plant to access more nutrients and moisture in the soil than it would without the fungi. It is said that they increase a root's absorptive surface area by at least 100 times. They especially help in absorbing phosphorous from the soil, something a plant's roots cannot easily do on their own. Mycorrhizal fungi are also able to communicate between each other and, when the plant is put under stress by say drought, disease or insect attack, can pass on this information via their subterranean pathways from one plant to another. This enables the plant next door and further down the chain, to protect itself, for example, by closing down (to save water) or to increase levels of toxins in leaves (against diseases and pests). There is evidence to show that mycorrhizal fungi can redistribute water from a wetter area in a field to a drier area, thus allowing all plants to prosper. Research on mycorrhizal fungi is in its infancy and in future, may well become more important to hardwood plants such as vines in protecting them against a range of ailments and stress factors.

Internal processes of the vine

The circulatory system of the vine – Vascular system

The circulatory system of the vine (or any plant for that matter) is known as the vascular system. It is made up of two types of transport cells called xylem and phloem. Xylem (pronounced zi-lem) is responsible for transporting water and nutrients from the roots to the rest of the vine. The flow is one way only, bottom to top, known as 'root to shoot' transport. With the aid of mycorrhizal fungi, nutrients are drawn up into the vine together with water. The macro and micro nutrients needed by the vine ionize in the soil and can be drawn into the vine in a water and nutrient solution. It is worth pointing out that a vine (or any plant for that matter) will only take in the water and nutrients that it needs to support itself and its crop and will not normally take in more than it needs. It does not, for instance, seek out particular minerals because it likes the flavour!

Phloem (pronounced flo-em) serves as the carbohydrate transport within the vine and distributes carbohydrates (sugars and starches) produced by photosynthesis all over the vine, depending on where it is needed. This is called 'source to sink' transport. Early in the season, before the vine is able to produce sugar in the leaves, the phloem pulls sugar from carbohydrate reserves in the roots and woody parts of the vine and takes it to the developing shoots. Here it is used for cellular production and growth through respiration which will be discussed later. Once leaves reach 50 per cent of their full size, they become net producers of sugar and can contribute more sugar than they are using to grow back into the vascular system. At this point, the phloem moves the sugar away from the leaves and to other 'sinks' such as active shoot tips which are still growing, flower and fruit production, and carbohydrate storage replenishment.

A fun, easy to do experiment showing the difference between these cells is to take a stalk of celery and place it in a glass of water, dyed with food colouring. After a few days the dye will appear in the leaf veins and the stalk can be cut in thin slices. The vascular system will be clearly visible with the xylem dyed and the phloem, right next to the dyed xylem, un-dyed.

Drinking and sweating – the movement of water through the vine

The concept of 'root to shoot' transport comes in to play particularly when discussing transpiration and respiration. Think of the xylem cells as a straw with the roots being the part of the straw under water and the leaves of the vine being the top of the straw. When one sucks on a straw the water is drawn up through it to the top. This is due to a negative pressure being introduced to the system through the sucking action. The same thing happens in plants though instead of a mouth, they use the evaporation of water from the stomata in the leaves to create negative pressure through the xylem which then causes more water to be drawn in through the bottom. This almost continuous process is what is called 'evapotranspiration' and known as the 'ET' rate – the rate by which a plant loses water.

The negative pressure in the xylem is called 'turgor pressure' and is the source of water stress measurements when determining how much water stress a vine is under. The greater force (or sucking on a straw) the vine has to do, the greater the water stress. Think of the difference in force when sucking water through a straw compared to a milkshake. The milkshake takes much more negative pressure in the straw to draw it up since it is a thicker liquid. For vines, this happens when there is a lack of water in the soil. Eventually the pressure will be so great the vines will start to wilt and in extreme cases of stress, the xylem cells will collapse under the pressure. As a safety measure, the vines will trigger the stomata to close to conserve water and the increase in turgor pressure will slow considerably. This will happen as the temperature rises and stomata will typically close at temperatures of 30°C or higher. When water is available it will move up through the roots which will decrease the turgor pressure and trigger the stomata to reopen. This process is dealt with in more detail in **Chapter 9 – Irrigation.**

The Food Source – Photosynthesis
Unlike animals, plants don't need to travel to look for food as they have evolved to make their own. All they have to do to survive is to search for water and nutrients through their root system. The basic chemical equation for photosynthesis is quite simple:

$$CO_2 + H_2O + Sunlight \rightarrow C_6H_{12}O_6 + O_2$$

Carbon dioxide, plus water, plus sunlight converts to sugars (mainly glucose, fructose and galactose) and oxygen.

Photosynthesis takes place in very specialized cell structures within the plant that contain chlorophyll, the substance in leaves (and other parts of plants) which colours them green. The plant draws in CO_2 through the stomata. The chlorophyll then takes the CO_2 and water (H_2O) and using the energy in sunlight, converts them into sugars, carbohydrates and oxygen. Some of the oxygen is used for the respiration cycle, although much more is produced through photosynthesis than is needed for the plant so the excess oxygen is released back into the atmosphere through the stomata.

Once the plant has created its food from photosynthesis, it transports it through the phloem using the 'source to sink' idea explained above. Once where they are needed, the sugars and carbohydrates can be used to create energy through a process called respiration or they can be stored either in the woody structures and roots or in a fruit, in a vine's case, the grapes. There are apparently more than 70 chemical processes involved in this conversion of light to energy which Charles Darwin said was so complex that it alone proved the existence of a higher being.

Eating – Respiration
Respiration is the process by which the plant consumes the glucose to create energy for all manner of cellular functions. Respiration also has a relatively simple equation.

$$C_6H_{12}O_6 + 6O_2 \rightarrow 6CO_2 + 6H_2O + 32\ C_{10}H_{16}N_5O_{13}P_3$$

The last compound on the end is more simply known as ATP (adenosine triphosphate) which is the energy molecule of all life and is used by the plant for nearly all of the biological processes needed for growth and survival. The resulting water is usually released through the stomata and the CO_2 used again for photosynthesis. All in all, it is an impressive way of living with very little waste through the entire process and both the photosynthesis and respiration equations above use very complex pathways. If one is interested in learning the chemical processes these can be explored in more detail by reading in depth about plant physiology.

Chapter 2

Vine varieties, clones, new varieties and vine production

Vine varieties

Individual grapevine cultivars (varieties) have been selected for various attributes since man realised their worth and started using them. Over the many centuries since then, those selected vines have been refined, cloned, cross-bred and hybridized and today, there are at least 1,500 known varieties used for wine production and undoubtedly many more to come. Following the arrival of *Phylloxera* in Europe and the controls placed upon the growing, grafting and distribution of vines, more importance has been placed upon variety and provenance. Since the arrival of wine *appellations*, which started in the 1930s, the variety or varieties that a wine was made from have assumed a much greater significance, especially in the latter half of the twentieth century when variety names started to make an appearance on labels, providing an easy shorthand way for consumers to recognise and engage with wine[7]. How varieties have developed and changed, and how new vines are produced, is the subject of this chapter.

Clones of grapevines

Individual varieties of vine are often further subdivided into clones, each of which, whilst conforming to the overall character of the variety, has different (sometimes very different) attributes. Clones are produced by selecting individual vines that show certain characteristics (such as better disease resistance, higher yield, early ripening, deep colour, small berries, etc), taking cuttings from those vines, planting them out and observing whether any of the cuttings have inherited the desired characteristic. By then selecting those cuttings that do have the desired characteristics and repeating the process over several generations, a new clone showing an exaggeration of the characteristics sought is produced. Although this may sound a simple operation, in reality it is very time-consuming and the outcome is never certain. A new clone will first have to grow to maturity and then prove itself over several vintages. Clonal trials are usually carried out by research institutes and universities and they will trial them on several sites and in different situations and only after extensive researches will they be approved by government authorities and released to commercial growers. Sometimes clones are selected by individual growers or from individual vineyards or *appellations*. Many growers in Italy for instance, treasure their regional clones of Sangiovese and almost every village seems to have its own clone of this widespread variety. For instance, Brunello di Montalcino, a clone of Sangiovese, is often considered to be a separate grape variety.

In varieties grown in many different climates and regions, there are large numbers of individual clones. Take Pinot Noir for instance. This variety is subdivided into

7 The first time the words 'Cabernet Sauvignon' appeared in French literature was 1850 and they were very seldom used until 1944. After that, their use picked up slowly, only really taking off in 1981. *Google Ngram Viewer for the words in French literature.*

clones suitable for different climates, some for warm regions, some for cool; into clones for different uses, dark skinned clones for red wine production or lighter skinned clones for (white) sparkling wine production; and some for different qualities of wine, higher yielding clones for basic red wine or lower yielding clones for better sites. In addition, there are clones that have an upright habit (*Pinot Droit*) and clones that have loose bunches (*Mariafeld* clones). ONIVINS (France's *Office National Interprofessionnel des Vins*) lists 45 Pinot Noir clones permitted to be planted in French vineyards. Another variety, Chardonnay, has clones to produce wines with high acidity and relatively little fruitiness (such as might be used in Chablis), whereas some growers in the New World prefer clones such as the Mendoza clone, which has both large and small grapes, and which has a marked tropical fruit character. ONIVINS lists 32 Chardonnay clones for use in France. Such is the importance of clones that in many *appellations*, not only is the variety of vines specified, but also the clones that may be used. The Champagne region is a prime example of this and the CIVC *(Comité Interprofessionnel du Vin de Champagne)* lists eighteen clones of Pinot noir, eleven of Chardonnay, and eleven of Meunier which may be grown.

The one major advantage that clones show over new cross-bred varieties (see later in this chapter) is that new clones retain the name of their parent variety. Thus, although a new clone may show marked differences in flavour and quality characteristics to other clones, from a marketing and *appellation* perspective it is considered to be the same variety, its varietal name is the same and therefore a new name on the bottle does not require explaining to the (sometimes easily confused) public.

8 Layering is method of filling in gaps in a vineyard by utilising shoots from a neighbouring vine. See later in this chapter for more detail.

Multi-clone Burgundy vineyard

Mass selection of clones – *sélection massale*

Not all growers like the concept of clones. To many, a vineyard planted with a single clone will have a uniformity of style and flavour that might be considered simple or one-dimensional and lack the complexity of a traditional multi-clone vineyard. Before *Phylloxera* made the planting of grafted vines a necessity, vineyards would seldom be grubbed up i.e. completely removed. Instead layering[8] might be used to replace vines that died or came to the end of their productive lives. The grower would take cuttings perhaps from the same vineyard, perhaps from that of a neighbour whose vines (of the same variety) had produced good fruit and simply root them *in situ*. In this way, a pre-*Phylloxera* vineyard would quite possibly consist of multiple, grower-selected clones coming from the best vines in that particular vineyard or region. Many old-world growers feel that their multi-clone vineyards are an important contributory factor to the *terroir* of their sites and help capture the history of their *appellation*.

Today, a grower who wishes to plant a

multi-clone vineyard will choose vines coming from a 'mass selection' (*sélection massale*) of source material. Grafting nurseries (*pépiniéristes*) will source scion wood from a vineyard with a known history of producing good wines, from which grafted vines can be produced. Growers can also source wood from their own or neighbour's vineyards and send it to a nursery for grafting. In this way, a newly planted vineyard will then consist of mixed clones of the parent vineyard which will continue the diversity of style and flavour found in that vineyard. In all cases, wood sourced like this would require testing for viruses. Mass selection is not confined to the old world. In areas of the new world with well-established vineyards, especially those where grafting is not necessary – Chile and parts of Australia for instance – and where anti-*Phylloxera* controls forbid the importation of plants or plant material, growers will routinely self-select wood from favoured vines for the production of new vines.

Natural mutations – Chimeras

Sometimes plants produce a shoot, a leaf-form, a flower or a fruit which is markedly dissimilar from the norm. This mutation is known as a chimera or more colloquially as a sport or bud sport. The best examples of these are a variegated form of a plant (a mottled white and green leaf for example), an abnormality such as a thornless blackberry or a differently coloured or shaped fruit or, in the case of grapes, grapes with both red skin and red flesh, known as *teinturier* varieties. What causes these differences can be one of many things and virus infection is often cited as a reason. In vines, the most common sport is a different form of grape – bigger, smaller, different shape, different colour – and if wood from the cane bearing the unusual bunch of grapes is taken, propagated and subjected to clonal selection, a whole new variety might be the result. White grapes from normally red grape-bearing vines or vice versa are actually quite common and there are many examples of varieties with both white and red versions: Gamay, Grenache, Muscat and Pinot to name just four. Sometimes the variation is in growth habit – more upright, more compact, shorter internodes, distorted shoots or leaves – and again, by selecting wood and propagating it, a different clone of a variety can sometimes be produced. These differences are occasionally sufficient for the sport to be considered a completely different variety: Kernling, a mutation of the variety Kerner, and Findling a mutation of Müller-Thurgau, are examples.

Producing new varieties by cross-breeding

Completely new varieties of vine are produced by crossing the male of one variety with the female of another. By taking pollen from the male parts (the anthers) of one variety and using it to pollinate the female part (the ovary) of another and then planting out the seeds that result, a completely new variety can be produced. The selection of the parent vines is the job of geneticists who attempt to determine whether the desired qualities of the parents will be transferred to the offspring. This is by no means a certain endeavour and whereas the father variety may have high yields, but poor-quality wine and the mother variety the opposite, there is no guarantee that a high yielding, high quality offspring will be the result. Sometimes it is the opposite. George Bernard Shaw a Nobel Prize winning author and Oscar winning playwright, but not someone noted for his matinee-idol looks, was approached by Mrs. Patrick-Campbell, the beautiful, but slightly empty-headed, leading lady of the time, who said: 'wouldn't it be wonderful Mr. Shaw if you and I had a child. It would have your brains and my beauty'. Shaw – ever ready with a *bon mot* – said: 'Well yes my dear, but think of the consequences should it turn out to

New varieties raised from seed planted out at Geisenheim Institiute for Grape Breeding

have my beauty and your brains!'

The actual mechanics of cross-breeding are relatively simple. Since almost all commercial grape varieties are hermaphrodites – that is to say they have both male and female parts on the same flower – the pollen-bearing anthers on one variety are removed with tweezers (emasculation) and pollen from a different male variety is then dusted onto the ovary. The pollen can be freshly harvested from a variety then at the right stage of development or can be saved from a variety with either earlier or later flowering characteristics and kept in cold storage. The artificially pollinated flower is then protected from the elements by placing a paper bag over it which stops airborne pollen from an unwanted variety reaching it. Once the flowers have set (been fertilised) the bag can be removed and the grapes allowed to develop normally. Once the grapes are ripe, the seeds are removed and planted out.

Each seed – and there will usually a hundred or more in one bunch of grapes – has the possibility of growing into a unique variety. In practice, many of the seeds will not germinate and of those that do, some will be weak and will be discarded. However, from those seedlings that do grow, the strongest and most disease resistant will be selected and grown on. In order to hasten the whole procedure, seeds will be grown indoors and forced to produce the maximum amount of growth in their first year. Once dormant (in their first winter) hardwood cuttings can be taken and a new plant produced from each bud on the cane. These plants are then planted out and within two years will be producing fruit which can be harvested, wine made and then evaluated. Only once fruiting has commenced and wine made can a proper assessment be made of the worth of the variety and this may take several years, especially with varieties whose wine takes some years to mature. In reality it will be decades –30 to 40 years is not uncommon – before a variety proves its worth (or more usually its lack of worth) for commercial wine production.

In earlier times, cross-breeding was not so organised and developed. In some instances, mainly female varieties (such as the table grape variety Madeleine Angevine) were grown in the proximity of other (pollen bearing) varieties and cross-pollination left to nature and to chance. Georg Scheu, a noted German vine breeder of the 1930s, bred several varieties in this way, known as 'freely pollinated'. Siegerrebe is one such variety.

Successful new varieties produced by cross-breeding are in general few and far between, although there are some notable exceptions. Müller-Thurgau – produced in 1882 at Geisenheim in Germany by Professor Dr Hermann Müller – is probably the most widespread of all cross-bred varieties and although now less common than previously, was once the most widely planted variety in Germany and still accounts for around 12 per cent of their total vineyard area (2017). It was also widely planted in New Zealand in the 1950s, '60s and '70s (before the introduction of Chardonnay, Pinot Noir and Sauvignon Blanc) and is still to be found in some of the more climatically challenged growing regions around the world. It was initially known as Riesling Sylvaner – as much due to its flavour profile as its possible parentage – and is also known as Rivaner in some regions. Geneticists have shown (now that the DNA of a vine can be analysed) that its true parentage is Riesling crossed with Madeleine Royale, a table grape developed in the Loire region. Another commercially successful cross-bred variety is Dornfelder, bred by August Herold in 1955 at the Weinsberg research station and which today (2016–17) occupies 7,648-ha (7.5 per cent of Germany's vine area) and is, after Riesling, Müller-Thurgau and Spätburgunder (Pinot Noir), their 4th most widely planted grape variety.

Other cross-bred varieties such as Scheurebe (Silvaner x Riesling), Bacchus (a three-way crossing of a Silvaner x Riesling cross interbred with Müller-Thurgau), Pinotage (Pinot Noir x Cinsaut) and Tarrango (Touriga x Sultana), have all achieved success, albeit in relatively limited amounts.

The main problems of producing new varieties by crossbreeding are the uncertainty of the outcome, the very long time taken to produce meaningful results and the difficulty of acceptance by the public of the names of new varieties. New varieties have to be named and under modern naming procedures (at least those in force in the EU), the chosen name cannot reflect the name of the parents. This is in order to stop confusion in the mind of the public when wines are labelled. Thus Ruby Cabernet (a 1949 Carignan x Cabernet Sauvignon cross whose wines bear little resemblance to Cabernet Sauvignon) would not be permitted this name today. New names are chosen that have as much marketing appeal as possible and the days of new varieties with difficult to pronounce names such as Reichensteiner and Huxelrebe are probably over, although some of the newer names – Johanniter, Hibernal, Solaris, and Staufer – still leave something to be desired.

By far-and-away the main reason for wishing to produce new cross-bred varieties today is disease and virus resistance. By using parent varieties that display natural resistance to the major diseases and viruses of vines (and these are often non-*vinifera* varieties), new cultivars are being produced that can be grown with less, and in many cases with no, recourse to chemical treatments during the growing season. Most of these new disease resistant hybrids are known as interspecific-crosses, that is to say they combine the genes from two species: *vinifera* and non-*vinifera*. These are dealt with in more detail in the section below on **Hybrid grape varieties**.

Although most of the world's wines are

produced from *Vitis vinifera* varieties, there are many varieties which are either wholly or partly members of other species. In North America, where *Phylloxera* prevented settlers making wine from the varieties they had taken with them from Europe, there were many hundreds of varieties developed from native American vines. Species such as *V. labrusca*, *V. rotundifolia* and *V. aestivalis* have been used to produce local varieties which, whilst not generally able to produce wine of equal quality to *Vitis vinifera* varieties, are able to cope with *Phylloxera* as well as some of the climatic limitations of the regions they are found in, such as hard winter frosts. Varieties such as Catawba, Clinton, Concord, Delaware, Niagara or Norton may not be well known but in certain parts of the USA they are widely grown and used for many purposes, including winemaking.

Hybrid grape varieties

American and other non-European vines have also been used as crossing partners with *viniferas* to produce what in the viticultural world are known as 'hybrids'[9]. These hybrid varieties were first developed in the latter half of the 19th century in a bid to develop varieties that could naturally withstand both diseases and *Phylloxera* damage. Crossings sometimes took many decades to produce, taking several generations to create the desired results and contained the DNA of perhaps more than 50 varieties. Their use in Europe is today very limited, in part due to an EU regulation that forbids wine from non-*vinifera* varieties being used to make Quality Wine (AC, DOC, DOCG etc)[10].

The reasons behind this regulation are steeped in viticultural history and have as much to do with the protection of (mainly French) *appellations* as for any good practical reason. Hybrids, usually being very disease resistant, are cheaper to grow and

in warm climates, highly productive. In the difficult decades that followed the introduction of grafted vines (1890-1910), when huge areas of newly planted vineyards swamped the markets with unwanted wine, it was felt that as hybrids generally produced a lower quality of wine they ought to be outlawed. They were therefore categorised as only capable of producing 'table wine' which is where they remain today. This regulation effectively stopped any further developments in hybrid crossbreeding and the area planted with them has declined ever since.

The late Professor Dr. Helmut Becker, renowned leader of the Geisenheim Vine Breeding Research Station, called this 'viticultural racism' and was convinced that one day the benefits of disease resistance through natural plant breeding would be recognised as a positive rather than a negative.

In recent decades, renewed interest in producing naturally resistant varieties that can be grown without chemical intervention has meant that several vine breeders, most notably the German state experimental viticultural station at Geilweilerhof, together with breeders in countries such as Austria and Switzerland, where organic wines are much in demand, have started to produce some interesting varieties which have very acceptable – even excellent – wine quality. Varieties such as Regent and Phoenix are both complex interspecific-crosses which can be grown without spraying and produce very good wines. Today there are well over 100 varieties of modern disease-resistant interspecific-crosses being grown around the world and growers interested in both organic and Biodynamic[11] viticulture are drawn to their natural disease resistance. They are generally known as PIWI varieties which stands for 'Pilzwiderstandsfähigen' or fungus-resistant. The most widely grown PIWI varieties are Bianca, Bronner, Chambourcin, Cabernet Blanc, Cabernet Jura, Johanniter, Muscaris, Phoenix, Regent, and Rondo. There are

9 Hybrids of other species – roses for instance – are not necessarily interspecies crossings (although they can be). Seeds of some vegetable varieties, known as F1 hybrids, are usually same-species crossing

10 Some red hybrids contain an anthocyanin called *malvidin diglucoside*, the presence of which can be used to detect whether a wine is 100 per cent vinifera or has been made using grapes from hybrid vines The EU imposes a limit of 15 mg/l on this substance in appellation wines.

11 The word 'Biodynamic' is a registered trademark of the Demeter organisation and should be written with a capital B.

however, many others and are often found in climatically challenged regions.

A further benefit is that many of these varieties – which definitely have non-*vinifera* blood in them – have been officially classed by the German authorities as *viniferas* in order to overcome their exclusion from Quality Wine production. The official state plant testing agency *(Bundessortenamt)* was asked to look at these new hybrids and determine if they differed in any way (apart from that of disease resistance) from pure *vinifera* varieties. Growth habits, grape type and wine quality were all assessed and compared. Having found no intrinsic difference, the agency decided that their similarity to pure *viniferas* was such that they WERE *viniferas!* (In such ways are EU regulations circumvented by some member states. It took the UK's agriculture ministry, DEFRA, five years to accept and adopt this ruling so that UK-grown wines produced from new interspecific-crosses such as Orion, Phoenix, Regent and Rondo could be made into English or Welsh Quality Wine). Although it would be an exaggeration to pretend that hybrids, modern or old, will ever replace pure *viniferas* in wine production, the idea that a natural alternative to a blanket of chemical protection in order to produce a commercial crop of grapes is available, is a welcome one.

DNA profiling

Now that plants can be taken apart genetically and profiled for their DNA, it is possible to determine the parentage of varieties where, through time or error, their ancestry had been lost. Thus has Zinfandel been exposed as *Primitivo* (if you are Italian) or *Crljenak* (if you are Croatian); the exact parentage of Müller-Thurgau explained (see above); and the parentage of Cabernet Sauvignon (Cabernet Franc x Sauvignon Blanc) brought into the open. This technique is also helping to explain how Pinot, for example, has not only several very distinct

forms – Pinot Auxerrois, Pinot Blanc, Pinot Gris, Pinot Noir and Meunier[12] – but within each variety, dozens (sometimes many dozens) of clones.

Genetically modified (GM) grapevines

The genetic modification of plants through natural means (hybridisation) is not new and has been happening since man became an agriculturalist rather than a hunter-gatherer and started to save seed and farm intensively. Since the discovery of DNA manipulation in the laboratory however, artificial genetic modification has become a reality. There are now several hundred million hectares of GM crops being grown worldwide, with alfalfa, apples, canola (rape-seed), cotton, maize, papaya, potatoes, soya, squash and sugar beet being the most widespread. Despite a ban on GM plants being grown in the EU, many Europeans will have come across them, or products made using them, via imports. In viticulture there are no instances of GM vines being used commercially, although many of the world's top viticulture research institutes and universities with viticultural sections, are developing and trialling GM vines. One of the major aims is to produce varieties that can be grown without recourse (or at least with less recourse) to chemicals, thus protecting several areas: the environment from their excessive use (it is often said that in Europe, vines occupy 8 per cent of agricultural land, but consume 80 per cent of its fungicides); the public, who do not like the thought of plant protection residues in wine; and growers, for whom chemicals, their purchase and application, are often a large part of the annual cost of growing vines. Other areas of research are resistance to diseases such as *Botrytis* and Pierce's Disease; resistance to viruses such as fan-leaf and leaf-roll; and drought resistance in rootstocks.

The International Grape Genomics Pro-

12 Often called Pinot Meunier (especially on back labels). In Champagne, where it accounts for over 30 per cent of plantings, it is known simply as Meunier.

gram (IGGP) is an organisation which brings together researchers from the world's major vineyard countries. The goal of the IGGP is:

> 'to understand the genetic and molecular basis of all biological processes in Vitis that are relevant to the crop. This understanding is fundamental to allow efficient exploitation of Vitis biological resources in the development of new cultivars with improved quality and reduced economic and environmental costs. This knowledge is also vital for the development of new vineyard and winery diagnostic tools. Traits considered of primary interest are pathogen and abiotic[13] stress resistance, quality traits for fruit and wine grapes and reproductive traits determining yield.'

If GM vines can be produced that require no spraying and can be properly tested so that their safety to both the environment and the consumer is guaranteed – or as guaranteed as much as anything can be – then it is likely that their introduction will eventually happen and the world's vineyards will use fewer pesticides[14]. There will be consumer resistance and the usual suspects will be out there talking about the end of the world being nigh. However, you very seldom hear anyone moaning about their underwear being genetically modified, despite 80 per cent of the world's cotton now coming from GM varieties; there are thousands of manufactured food products made using GM soya and no one worries much; GM rice is grown world-wide and I don't see Chinese restaurants being picketed; and many organic certifying bodies accept that a very small percentage of GM material is permissible in a so-called 'organic' product. In short, we already live with, use, wear and consume an increasing number of GM products and living longer with less of the world's population starving. Those really worried by the thought that wine from GM

vines will harm their health might perhaps also ponder on the 12–15 per cent of the wine in the bottle that is pure alcohol – a known killer!

Production of grapevines

Most vines are produced in specialist nurseries where industrial quantities of vines are grown annually. Many European nurseries have a world-wide trade in vines, storing them in a cold-store until they can be shipped to the southern hemisphere for their planting season. The websites of nurseries such as Guillaume, Mercier, and VCR are worth perusing for additional information on both varieties and rootstocks. Sundridge Nurseries and Novavine Nurseries in California and Yalumba Nurseries in Australia also have excellent websites.

There are essentially two types of vine which growers can plant: rooted cuttings and grafted vines.

Rooted cuttings

Rooted cuttings are produced by taking cuttings of about 250–300 mm from a parent vine which will then be placed in a cuttings bed where they will be allowed to grow and develop a root structure. This is usually after one summer's growth, although two is not unknown. The rooted cuttings are then lifted and sorted and can be planted out in the vineyard. Vines produced in this way are significantly cheaper than grafted vines and the process can be done by a vineyard owner taking wood from his own or a neighbour's vineyard. But there are risks in planting ungrafted cuttings (apart of course from *Phylloxera*). Diseases and viruses can be transported from one vineyard to another and growers using ungrafted cuttings must be sure of the health status of the vineyards they take wood from. On sites with favourable climatic and viticultural conditions (warm, well-drained soils, adequate water and weed-free), cuttings can

13 Abiotic factors are the non-living factors of the earth which affect the ability of living organisms to survive in an environment.

14 The term 'pesticide' in law means any product used in agriculture to control pests or diseases. This would include: fungicides, insecticides, acaricides (against mites), molluscides (against slugs and snails), and herbicides, plus any products used to deter animals, birds or other predators from damaging the crop. It would not include fertilisers and plant stimulants.

also be rooted *in situ* without the need to go through a cuttings bed. This latter technique is, however, rarely practiced as it does not give the certainty of planting an already-rooted cutting. In *Phylloxera* free regions, vineyards are usually planted with ungrafted cuttings, but produced by commercial vine nurseries where the provenance of the wood and hygiene during all stages of the production process can be assured. In Australia, their Vine Improvement Programmes (VIPs) control production of vines in *Phylloxera*-free areas.

Grafted grapevines

Grafted grapevines are produced by grafting a scion onto a rootstock. Scion wood is sourced from vineyards planted with vines which have been tested for varietal purity and absence of viruses. These special 'mother gardens' will be inspected throughout the growing season to identify vines showing abnormalities, diseases or viruses. Any vines that are found with these problems will be tagged so that when the scion wood is cut, the pruners will avoid them. At pruning time, canes of scion wood will be cut from the vines, taken back to the nursery and chopped into small pieces, each about 25 mm long, each piece bearing one fruit bud. These single-bud pieces of scion wood will then be soaked in disinfectant and placed into cold storage awaiting sale and/or grafting. Scion wood is often distributed worldwide and it is not uncommon to find wood from very well-known vineyards in France or Italy being grafted onto rootstocks in far-away countries.

Rootstock wood is sourced from rootstock vines grown by specialist growers, mostly in southern France and northern Italy. In many instances the vineyards for rootstock production are planted with genetic material supplied by the plant-breeding institutes that develop them (and who own the rights to the rootstock varieties and clones and earn royalties from them). Wood is harvested in the winter when the vines are dormant, taken back to the nursery where it is cut into 1.2 m lengths, disinfected and then placed into refrigerated storage until sold and distributed to nurseries producing grafted vines. Larger nurseries may well grow both their own scion and rootstock wood; others may buy in both types and concentrate on the grafting, rooting and growing processes.

For grafting to be successful, the two parts of the grafted vine have to be matched for size, so that the different layers of the cane match each other up and can join together. As was explained in Chapter 1, there are essentially four distinct layers of a cane: the outer layer (what the layman might call the bark) which is a protective layer; a second layer called the *phloem* which carries the sugars and starches produced by the leaves (through photosynthesis) which are transported to the storage areas of the vine, the canes, trunk and grapes; a third layer called the *cambium* which separates the second and fourth layers; and a fourth layer called the *xylem* which transports water, minerals and nutrients from the roots (which has extracted them from the soil) to the leaves so that the vine can grow and photosynthesise. To make sure that these different layers match up, the rootstocks and scion wood cuttings are separated into different sizes before grafting.

Originally vines were hand-grafted by teams of travelling workers (Hungarians were particularly adept at the job) who went from nursery to nursery plying their trade. Today, the grafting is almost always done by machine. The most commonly used machine is the Wagner[15] company's 'Omega 1–cut', so called because in one operation it joins the two halves of the vine – the single bud scion and the longer (300 mm) piece of rootstock wood – with an omega-shaped jigsaw type of joint which holds the scion and the rootstock tightly together. Immediately after grafting the head of the vine is

15 The Wagner company also make the most widely used planting machine and their website has videos of both grafting and planting machinery.

Bundle of 25 grafted vines

16 A callus is a collection of plant cells that form tissue around the graft and effectively seal the two halves of the grafted vine together.

the scion in view. These boxes are then placed into plastic greenhouses (polytunnels) where the vines can be irrigated and kept warm. They will stay there until the grafts have hardened, a callus[16] has started to form and roots have begun to develop on the end of the rootstock. Soil warming cables will often be installed beneath the soil for the boxes to sit on to speed up rooting. Once a callus has formed and roots have started to grow – it usually only takes a few weeks – the vines can be planted out in a nursery field for the remainder of the growing season. Some vine nurseries are using a product derived from a naturally occurring *Trichoderma* fungus in the battle to produce vines with less chance of developing trunk diseases in later life. See more in **Chapter 11– Diseases and viruses of grapevines, including trunk diseases.**

In order for the vines to develop a strong graft and a good root system, they will often be grown through a covering of black polythene laid over the soil which keeps out weeds, keeps in moisture and raises the soil temperature. Vines are normally grafted in March and April and will be out in their nursery beds by late May when the danger of spring frost has receded. During the growing season, the young vines will be sprayed against pests and diseases, trimmed to promote root growth and any weeds will be kept down to avoid competition. They are also usually irrigated to promote strong growth. Losses whilst the vines are in the nursery bed can be quite high, 40–50 per cent is not unusual and it can be as high as 90 per cent, caused by factors such as bad size-matching between scion and rootstock, weak callus development, diseases such as *Botrytis* infecting the graft and drought conditions immediately after they are planted out. Only vines with strong grafts and sturdy roots will be offered for sale.

Once the growing season is over and the vines have become dormant, they can be

dipped in a low-temperature paraffin wax that seals the graft and prevents the graft from drying out. The grafting-wax also contains a mild fungicide to keep out disease.

Hand-grafting of vines is still practiced in some nurseries and some growers prefer this method as they claim that in old vines – say over 40 years old – losses from graft failure of hand-grafted vines are lower than the loss of machine grafted vines. The usual hand grafting technique for vines is what in English is known as the 'whip and tongue' graft, a two-slice method of joining two pieces of wood together of the same diameter. In France this is known as *la greffe anglaise* and in German as the *Englische Kopulation mit Gegenzunge*. (Good to know that England is remembered for some innovation in viticulture!) Hand-grafted vines are usually around twice the price of machine grafted vines. A typical price for a machine grafted vine would be €1.25–€1.75 depending on variety, clone, rootstock and number ordered.

The freshly grafted vines are then placed upright into 75-litre callusing boxes and the lower three-quarters covered with moist sand and peat, leaving only the graft and lifted, inspected to make sure that the grafts are strong and the roots abundant, trimmed for ease of handling, and then disinfected, bundled into 25s and put into a cold-store where they are kept cool and moist and in the dark, so that they remain dormant. The new vines can be sold soon after lifting for early winter planting, but are more usually stored in the cold-store until the ground warms up the next spring when they are dispatched to growers for immediate planting. Vines can be stored for quite long periods of time if properly looked after and 6 months or more is not uncommon if, for example, European vines are destined for southern hemisphere vineyards. Vines unsold at the end of the planting season are often put back into nursery beds for another season.

In warm regions, grafted vines can also be produced by grafting single buds directly onto already-planted rootstocks, so called field grafting or chip budding. To do this, rootstock wood is first rooted in a cuttings bed (for a year or two) and then a rooted cutting is planted out into the vineyard in the correct position. Once established – which may take another year – the top of the growing vine is cut off and a single bud of the scion variety is chip-budded[17] onto the side of the already established rootstocks. This is then allowed to develop into a cropping plant. This method is usually only used in very warm climates where natural rainfall is not sufficient or irrigation not available and spring-planted grafted vines might struggle to establish themselves. It is also only practiced in regions where labour, trained in this technique, is available. In regions where frosts are common, the young vines grafted using this technique will usually be 'hilled up' (also called earthing up) with soil to protect them. This is also known as 'buttage' in French.

Top grafting

One further technique for changing varieties in a vineyard which should be men-tioned is that of top-grafting or top-working. This technique enables growers to take a mature cropping vine and, by graft-ing wood from another variety onto the top of the trunk, change the vine from one var-iety to another. Usually this is done in the spring as the vine is breaking into leaf. The existing trunk is cut off at about 500 mm from the ground, a split (or cleft) is then made in the top and into the split are in-serted two wedge-shaped pieces of wood of the new variety, each of which will bear one or two fruiting buds. The cleft is then bound up with plastic grafting tape, tightly bind-ing in the new pieces of wood, and pro-tected with a paint containing fungicide to seal the wound and exclude diseases. Given the right conditions and once the old trunk stops bleeding, the new grafts will

17 The piece of wood carrying the single bud is called a 'chip' and this is inserted into a cut made in the side of the root-stock and then bound in tightly with grafting tape.

Top-grafted vine. Note the irrigation dripper line attached to the fruiting wire

18 *Parral* is an overhead pergola
system. See Chapter 7 – Trellising, training and pruning

bond with the older wood and flourish. As long as suckers from the original variety are rubbed off as they grow and windy conditions do not damage the new shoots, this technique can be very successful. It is also much quicker and more cost-effective at changing from one variety to another than uprooting the old vineyard and replanting. One would only want to do this, however, with relatively young healthy vines (10–15 years old) which still had plenty of life left. The technique can be used on both grafted and ungrafted vines. A variation of this is to graft single buds into the side of the trunk, binding them into the side of the trunk in the same manner as the chip-budding described above.

Layering – *provignage*

There is one further way – not one that is to be universally recommended, but which certainly occurs – in which an individual vine can be replaced in a vineyard. This is known as layering (or *provignage* in French). If a single vine should die, through old age, disease or damage, it can be replaced by taking a suitably positioned cane from a neighbouring vine, laying it down onto the ground where the missing vine was, and burying it under the soil. Often the cane will be slightly cracked and a rock or stone placed on top of the buried cane to keep it in position. During the growing season, the cracked cane will throw out roots and eventually a shoot (or several) will emerge. This shoot can then be trained up a support and in due course the new vine can be separated from its neighbour and – *voila* – the empty space has been filled. This technique is routinely seen (even is some quite grand vineyards) and for the occasional gap, little

harm will have been done.

I recall seeing a *Parral*[18] system vineyard outside Mendoza in Argentina where about 50 per cent of the vines had been replaced through layering. The danger of this method in vineyards originally planted with grafted vines is that the layered vines will be on their own roots and therefore susceptible to *Phylloxera* (although in the instance above, this did not matter as the vineyard was flood irrigated, a technique of irrigation which kills the *Phylloxera* by drowning them). Layered vines will also inherit all the attributes – good and bad – of the parent vine, together with any viruses they may have. However, layering does allow the life of a vineyard to be indefinitely extended so that they may be said to be of great antiquity. It is though, rather like an old spade which may have had a new blade and several new handles in its lifetime and is therefore not quite as old as it appears to be!

Repiquage

The French have a unique term for replanting young vines in amongst existing older vines which is *repiquage*. However, as this lowers the average age of the vines in the vineyard it tends to be discontinued once the percentage of newer vines exceeds that of the original ones. At that point the time has arrived for the whole vineyard to be grubbed-up and replanted.

Chapter 3

Site selection

Site selection

Grapevines are planted on a huge variety of sites and to pretend that there is a formula for a perfect site would be wrong. The suitability of sites to grow vines will depend on a very large number of factors: climate, altitude, aspect, soil type, and drainage are just a few. All are important and any one may affect the choice of site. In the EU of course there are *appellation* rules regarding sites for vines. Most of the decisions about where to plant vines have already been taken and sites allocated and very few completely new sites for vines exist. However, there may still be a need to assess a site for its suitability to grow a certain variety or to assess whether a site is capable of producing a certain quality of wine. In those countries where vines can be planted without the *appellation* rules dictating, assessing sites is important and sites can be graded according to their overall quality, taking all pertinent parameters into account.

Climate – Macro–, Meso–, and Microclimate

Current thinking on climate divides the subject up into three separate climate levels: macro, meso, and microclimate. This construction was introduced by Dr Richard Smart in 1984 when he first started looking into canopy management.

Macroclimate describes the climate at regional level, a region being anything as large as say Bordeaux, where overall climate data can be determined by amalgamating results from a number of weather stations. A region might be anything from tens to hundreds of kilometres wide.

Mesoclimate describes the climate in a smaller region than a macroclimate region. This could be as small as an individual vineyard or estate or as large as a sub-region such as St. Estèphe or Pomerol. The climate at this level would be influenced by height above sea-level, shelter from prevailing winds, slope and aspect and presence of bodies of water. This area might be anything from a few tens of metres wide to perhaps a few kilometres.

Microclimate describes the climate that affects an individual vine and is the climate within the vine's canopy and its immediate surroundings. This is affected by a vine's relationship to its neighbouring vines, the row width and planting distances, trellising and training type, height of trellis and methods of canopy management.

Climatic influences

Grapevines respond to differences in climate and weather[19] perhaps more than any other fruit crop and the sugar level in the grapes at harvest is directly related to the quality of the site, all other things being equal. In many crops, sugar level is important,

19 It is important to understand the differences between climate and weather. Climate will set the general parameters of the basics such as average growing season temperatures, growing degree days, numbers of frost days, average rainfall – all of which will dictate which varieties can be grown. The weather on the other hand can vary hugely from one year to another and differences between one year and another can be quite wide, resulting in differences of both quality of wine and quantity of yields.

especially in crops which are eaten raw and where sugar is not normally added before consumption – apples and pears for instance – but in winemaking grapes it is especially important as it defines not only the level of potential alcohol, but also the general level of quality. Although there are many factors to consider in deciding when a crop of grapes is 'ripe', the sugar level in grapes is taken to be a very good indicator of ripeness. In addition, because the sugar level must be known for the winemaking process to take place, it is measured, charted and recorded in every vineyard, in every winery and by every grower. In many instances the financial value of the grapes will depend entirely on the sugar level at harvest. If sugars are too low, wines will be thin and unripe; if too high, they will be too alcoholic and wines will taste too 'warm' and may be unbalanced. Acid levels are also as important to winemakers as sugar levels and again, acids in grapes are measured and recorded in almost all wineries. If a climate is too cool, acids will be high and the wines acidic and aggressive; if the climate is too warm, wines will be flabby and short-lived. In red wines, you have the added dimension of tannins – ripe or unripe – and this aspect is also very climate-related.

The climate of any particular site – at least in the way in which it relates to growing grapes and the quality of the wine produced from them – is affected by many factors. The latitude, altitude and aspect (angle to the sun) of the land are of major significance. These are the most basic factors. Add on the length of the growing season, the number of sunshine hours, the diurnal temperature range[20] (which affects the speed of ripening and acid reduction), the site's relationship to the region's prevailing winds, the proximity of large bodies of water, the rainfall available to the vine, the humidity and the evapotranspiration rate and you start to get the picture. Follow these with the type and depth of soil, the

management of the vineyard floor (cultivated or grass between the rows), the layout of the vineyard (which direction the rows are running), the trellising and training system and a picture starts to form. Finish with the choice of rootstocks (or not), the type and clone of grape variety, the desired cropping level, the wine type and quality level to be produced and you have just about covered all the fixed bases. It then all depends on the way in which the vines are managed – pest and disease control, canopy management and irrigation regime all play their part – and you are then just left with the weather for the year in question. This last matter can probably have more effect on the quality and quantity of a particular vintage than any one of the above! (Someone once worked out that there are 3,000 separate decisions that are taken from site selection to bottle, any one of which could change the character and quality of the wine in question.)

Measurement of climate at macroclimate level

The measurement of climate is beset with difficulties and each method has its limitations. One of the first scientific attempts to assess sites for their quality was to measure their 'heat summation' – the so-called Growing Degree Days (GDD) or Heat Units system. In 1944, Amerine and Winkler, working at UC Davis, California, published their work on the subject. They took the mean temperature (the difference between the mean maximum and mean minimum temperatures) of a site on a daily basis during the seven month growing season (April to October in the northern hemisphere, October to April in the southern[21]), deducted 50°F (today 10°C) from the figure and added all the results up. Therefore, if on 1st April the mean temperature was 12°C, then two degree-days (12 minus 10) was recorded. If the average temperature on the 2nd April was 13°C, then three degree-days

20 The diurnal temperature range is the difference between daytime and night-time mean temperatures.

21 I have often seen southern hemisphere GDD totals taken over October-March, a 6-month period which of course makes comparison between northern and southern hemisphere growing conditions on the basis of GDD quite difficult.

were added and so on for every day during the seven months until a cumulative total was arrived at. (In practice, taking the monthly mean temperature, deducting 10°C and multiplying by the number of days in the month for the seven months arrives at an acceptable answer, although one that is slightly higher than taking individual daily temperatures.) Amerine and Winkler did this for representative sites throughout California and separated the whole state (for vinegrowing purposes) into five regions, running from Region I (the coolest) with less than 2,500° days F up to Region V (the hottest) with more than 4,000° days F. For each region a list of suitable grape varieties was drawn up which would give satisfactory results.

Whilst the Amerine and Winkler GDD system appears to work adequately in some regions (it is still recognised in California), in many other regions (especially in cooler, less continental regions[22]) it is felt to have shortcomings that make it unhelpful. Vineyards in regions cooler than Region I, of which there are many, ought not (according to the GDD system) to be able to make very acceptable wines. Tasmania and much of the southern island of New Zealand are cases in point. In order to counter this, a latitude temperature index (LTI) was developed by David Jackson and Danny Schuster (both working in New Zealand) in 1994. This system factors in the latitude of the region and therefore the length of day. This is an important consideration in more marginal and more maritime regions. It is calculated by taking the mean temperature of the warmest month (usually July in the northern hemisphere and January in the southern) and multiplying it by 60 minus the latitude. An example would be St. Émilion with a mean July temperature of 19.5°C and latitude of 44' 5'. The LTI in this case would be 19.5 x (60-44.5) = 302. The LTI is a more acceptable form of guide to climate in

Grapes damaged by too much exposure to the sun

22 A continental region is one with a large difference between the average mean temperatures of its warmest and coldest months. The opposite is a maritime climate where the difference is smaller. Thus Burgundy, situated hundreds of kilometres from the sea, would have a more continental climate than Bordeaux, situated near the sea.

cooler, less continental, more maritime regions.

Both GDD and the LTI suffer from the fact that they do not really take into account the continentality of the site, i.e. how influenced a site is by the land mass in which it sits and by any warming or cooling ocean currents. This measurement is arrived at simply by deducting the mean temperature of the coldest month (MTCM) from the mean temperature of the warmest month (MTWM). This throws up some interesting results. Take two towns: Bordeaux, France and Kentville in Nova Scotia, Canada. Both are at about the same latitude, both close to the sea, with similar MTWMs and LTIs, rainfall not too dissimilar, but very different winter temperatures and therefore very different continentality figures. Bordeaux's is 13.8 (19.5°C less 5.7°C); Kentville's 24.4 (19.2°C less −5.2°C). Whilst Bordeaux is able to support a viable grape-growing industry owing to its long growing season with around 200 days when the mean daily temperature is over 10°C, Kentville, with around 150 days over 10°C, whilst it does grow grapes, struggles to make good wines (but is better for apples which require less time from flowering to harvest). Likewise, Dijon: at 47' 20'N it is 2.7' (or 240 km) farther north than Bordeaux, with the same MTWM (19.5°C) but with much colder winters and a continentality index of 17.8. Dijon's number of days when the mean daily temperature is over 10°C is around 175, over 3 weeks less than Bordeaux's. This of course accounts for the fact that Bordeaux's principal grape varieties – Cabernet Sauvignon, Merlot, and Cabernet Franc – are not found in Burgundy, which is ideal for the lighter coloured, less tannic, Pinot Noir and of course Chardonnay.

On its own, the MTWM is a very useful guide and in Australia this simple measurement alone is used to assess sites with some accuracy. Richard Smart and Peter Dry first proposed this technique in 1980 and in many areas the MTWM and the GDD show a good correlation, although for cooler sites, MTWM is less useful as other factors, such as the length of the growing season and the influence of bodies of water, can compensate for lower summer temperatures.

Another factor which can give a quick guide to a site's quality – especially in cooler regions – is to add up the number of days in the growing season that are over a given temperature. 30°C is often used, although 29°C, 31°C or 32°C will also give similar results. Although this will vary widely from year to year, more so than GDD, if a ten-year average is taken, the results are strongly correlated with a site's ability to consistently grow and ripen certain varieties. This is because at these temperatures, the vine's reproductive instincts are stimulated, which results in many more viable flowers and therefore fruit. Take the UK as an example.

Up until 1988, the average number of days in the year when the temperature in the south of England rose to 29°C was around 1.5, the two warm years of 1975 and 1976 accounting for almost half of those days. The number of days in a year during the same period when it rose to 30°C or

more was less than 0.5. From 1989 to the present day (2018) the number of days of 29°C or more has risen to almost 5 per year, with the number of days of 30°C or more rising to just under 2 per year. On the face of it these might seem quite small changes, but they have been a very significant factor in what was once considered to be a marginal region for easy-to-ripen varieties such as Müller-Thurgau and Reichensteiner, to one which now has over 70 per cent of its production coming from Chardonnay and Pinot Noir (for sparkling wine) and is flirting with these two varieties, plus Pinot Blanc, Pinot Gris and Sauvignon Blanc for still wines.

The length of the growing season

The length of the growing season is also an important variable and many New World sites have much longer growing seasons than their European counterparts. The growing season in this sense is generally taken as the number of frost-free days i.e. the number of days between the last spring frost and the first winter frost. Obviously ten-year average dates must be taken as they are very variable on an annual basis. It is usually considered that at least 180 frost-free days are required (that would be from May 19th to November 11th, which would be a European norm) for successful grape production.

As well as the length of the growing season, the number of days between the start of flowering and the start of the harvest, can also be a useful indicator. Although often quoted as being 100 days, in Bordeaux it is more likely to be 110 (June 1st say to September 19th), whereas in many parts of Australia and New Zealand it is likely to be much longer: Tasmania 130 days, Central Otago up to 145. Exact times will of course, depend on grape variety and annual weather.

Summary on climate measurement

There are many factors that influence the quality of grapes produced on any individual site. To generalise one can say that the best sites are those to be found in regions with a relatively long, frost-free growing season (180+ days), with a summer rainfall of around 500 mm (or in drier regions the ability to irrigate), with an LTI of 200+, GDD of 1,000+ and on sites that are sheltered from cooling winds and that slope towards the sun. It goes without saying that sites nearer sea level will be warmer than those that are elevated, but in warm to very warm regions, a higher elevation above sea level may be a benefit[23]. Regions with high continentality will have low winter temperatures which may preclude growing *vinifera* varieties unless techniques against deep winter temperatures are taken (burying vines for instance).

But, being dogmatic about what will grow where and what type and quality of wine will come from a particular site can be dangerous. One can, by measuring as many parameters as possible, by making an educated guess at what varieties and clones to grow and how to trellis and train them, arrive at a considered decision about the suitability of a site for wine production. However, numbers rarely tell the whole story and, as has been seen time and time again in regions all over the world, until the fat lady sings (or makes the wine), you can never tell! Who would have confidently predicted the success of Pinot Noir in Central Otago, of Cabernet Sauvignon in Bolgheri or of Chardonnay on the chalk slopes of southern England, just by looking at the weather data?

Climate change and global warming

Much has been made in recent years of the influences on viticulture of climate change, most noticeably since the over-average warm years (in Europe) of 1995, 2003, 2006, 2014 and 2018. If one believes the worst-case-scenario climate-change pundits, the world's established vineyard areas are due for some fundamental changes in the next 50 years. Those grape-growing regions which are already hot had better start thinking about growing something else entirely and the warm regions had better switch to varieties more suited to Region IV. Some experts seem to think that most of the world's established winegrowing regions will enjoy – if enjoy is the right word – a rise in mean annual temperatures of between 1.5°C and 2.5°C. That may not seem that much, but it turns Bordeaux into the Barossa and the Barossa into somewhere that's too hot for winemaking!

Higher natural sugars, and therefore higher alcohols, are often cited as the fruits of global warming, but to my mind, the influences of improved plant material, better canopy management and much better (chemical and viticultural) *Botrytis* control which allows for a longer ripening period, are often underplayed, as is the role played by temperature control and more alcohol-productive yeast strains in the winery.

One of the negative effects of global warming and one not often mentioned, is the changes that are happening to the spectrum of pests and diseases that attack vines. As temperatures rise, pests and diseases associated with warmer regions will move northwards (in the northern hemisphere) and growers will have to adapt their growing and spraying techniques. An example of this is the Harlequin Ladybird *Harmonia axyridis*, (also known as the Multicoloured Asian Lady Beetle), a species native to Asia and introduced into the US for biological control of other pests. However, it has now found its way to Europe – once considered too cool for it – where it has already damaged wines. When disturbed, it exudes a substance called 'reflex blood' from its legs which has

23 There will always be exceptions to this generalisation. Some parts of the Napa Valley (those at the southern end, nearer San Francisco Bay) are cooled by sea fogs that roll in from the Pacific Ocean in the afternoon and sit on the valley floor, making it cooler than land higher up on the valley sides.

a foul odour and taste and can taint grapes and wine made from them. Since around 2000, a new variant of the common fruit fly, called Spotted Wing Drosophila (*Drosophila suzuki*), known colloquially as 'SWD' has been attacking all kinds of soft-fruit in Europe – apricots, cherries, blueberries, grapes, nectarines, pears, plums, peaches, raspberries, and strawberries – and causing immense damage. Unlike the common fruit-fly, the larvae of SWD hatch inside the fruits in question, feeding off the pulp, and only emerging when they are fairly well developed – not something consumers want to see as they eat the fresh fruit. When SWD attack wine grapes they cause increased levels of volatile acidity (VA) which is not something one wants in the winery and for growers selling grapes under contract, might well render their crops unsaleable. Pierce's disease, caused by the bacterium *Xylella fastidiosa* and transmitted by sap-sucking insects (such as the blue-green and glassy-winged sharpshooters in California) was once confined to warmer parts of the Americas. In 2013 it was discovered in olive trees in Puglia in southern Italy and has since worked its way northwards, affecting olive trees in Spain (as far north as Madrid) and in Corsica and southern France. A wide range of species are potentially in danger, including vines.

The world has warmed, is warming and despite what most governments are doing to reduce greenhouse gas emissions and to prevent further warming, most climate change scientists think that there is still a way to go before the juggernaut of higher temperatures and more unpredictable weather can be stopped. Viticulturalists, who plant vineyards with a view to getting at least 30–40 crops out of them, and in many cases far more, will at some stage, have to take on board that the variety they are planting today, may well not be right in two- or three-decades time. Where *appellation* rules allow (or do not exist), growers will have to make changes to the varieties they grow which will naturally impact upon wine styles. In addition to varietal change, winemakers in regions that are currently temperate will need to learn about acidification, about alcohol reduction and about the other tools in the warm/hot winemaker's locker. From certain perspectives however, it is not all doom and gloom. For centuries, the northern hemisphere's northerly limit for vineyards has been taken to be around the 50th parallel which is Germany's Rheingau (as well as Falmouth on the Lizard in Cornwall). Today however, it is creeping ever northwards. Holland, Belgium and Denmark now have hundreds of hectares of vineyards each, and they are starting to appear in larger numbers in almost all of the Scandinavian countries. In the UK, the area under vine in the UK has gone from 0.40-ha (1-acre) in 1952, via 761-ha (1,880-acres) in 2004 to an estimated total of around 3,250-ha 8,030-acres) in 2019. Likewise, sugar levels, surely the most direct and potent measure of global warming, have risen. In the UK, in the 1950s to 1980s, Chardonnay was not grown and could not be ripened, and the cool-climate varieties we did grow achieved 5–7 per cent natural alcohol. Anything in double figures was a winemaker's sweet dream. Since the 1990s and onwards to today, what were once considered impossible varieties to grow and ripen, Chardonnay, Pinot Blanc, Pinot Gris, Pinot Noir and even Sauvignon Blanc are all being grown and achieving natural alcohol levels of 10 per cent and more. In 2018, a year which surpassed everyone's expectations in both quantity and quality, Chardonnay achieved 12 to 13 per cent, a sure sign of the sun's influence on UK viticulture, and of course, of global warming.

Site selection at the mesoclimate level

Location: The reasons for choosing the right site for growing vines are the obvious ones: to select a site that will grow grapes of the right quality and at least-cost for the type, style and quality level of wine that is to be produced from them. There may be more emphasis upon yield and cost of production if the grower is principally a grower and seller of grapes, as opposed to a grower-winemaker who may be able to offset additional costs in producing higher quality grapes – perhaps at the expense of quantity – because of the added-value achieved by selling the grapes as wine. There will also be other considerations. The cost of the land will be important, as may be the proximity of the site to markets, to a winery or to personnel. The exact location of land suitable for growing vines will depend on many different factors and grape variety and wine style must be borne in mind (or at least adapted) if the best wine is to be produced from any particular site. Considerations such as water availability (in climates with dry summers), shelter from prevailing winds, proximity to bodies of water and/or away from enclosed pockets of land if spring or autumn frosts are likely to pose a hazard, may all be more important than – say – the ideal soil, the optimum altitude or the best aspect.

Altitude: As you rise above sea-level, the annual mean temperature falls by around 0.5–0.6°C per 100 m rise and, invariably, sites become more exposed to prevailing winds. The effect of this is that the growing season will be shorter and ripening will occur later, taking the harvest further into the autumn where the weather is likely to be less clement with the dangers of frosts and disease more of a problem. In cool regions, most suitable sites for grape growing will be below 300 m above sea level. In warmer regions this may rise to 1,000 m and in hot to very hot regions, where it would be far too hot for wine grapes at sea level, vineyards may be planted at 1,000 m or more. In the Southern Tyrol vineyards are planted up to 1,200 m, in Cyprus and near Granada (Spain) to 1,400 m and in Mexico, Bolivia, Ecuador and Argentina, vines are planted at between 2,000 m and 2,600 m.

The highest vineyards in the world, as confirmed by Guinness World Records (2018), are at 3,563-metres (11,690-feet) at the 'Pure Land & Super-high Altitude Vineyard' in Lhasa, Tibet where there are 68-ha (168-acres) of vines. What the wine from the 'Vidal, Muscat and an indigenous icewine variety named Bei Bing Hong' actually tastes like is not reported. At these heights above sea level, grapes may well have difficulty in ripening in some years and may have to be blended with riper fruit from lower altitude vineyards.[24]

Aspect: Sites that slope towards the sun (to the south in the northern hemisphere and the north in the southern) are usually preferred over flat sites or sites facing away from the sun. The amount of incoming solar radiation – known as insolation – is greater the more the site is angled to the sun. This is true up to about a slope of 40° (and much steeper than that and the site would be impossible to farm). The effect is not so marked at midsummer, but will be more significant at the end of the growing season when the sun's heat is weaker. George Ordish, in his book *Vineyards in England and Wales* (Faber & Faber 1977 p.175) states that: *the difference between a level site and a slope of 30° in a southerly direction is only 8 per cent in midsummer, but in mid-October the difference is 70 per cent.* The warmth of the soil and the ease with which grapes will ripen are directly related to each other and although there are other factors such as soil type, soil covering (or lack of it) and soil moisture levels which play a part, aspect (after altitude) is the most important factor.

24 Planting vineyards at higher and higher altitudes is one thing. Planting them at altitudes where the vineyard can produce grapes which can be turned into wine worth drinking is quite another.

Snow starting to melt on south-facing slopes in Baden, Germany

This is known as a 'thermal zone'. Hills or mountains that project above the valleys that surround them (such as the hill in Corton or the Kaiserstuhl in Baden) have large thermal zones and are thus warmer than other sites in the same area. Cool air travelling down vineyard slopes will, at certain times of the year, be so cold as to freeze and will settle in 'frost pockets', land from which there is no escape route for freezing air. Vines planted in these pockets will suffer frost damage unless protective measures are taken.

Slopes also tend to have thinner – and therefore less vigorous – topsoils which will be better for vines. In regions with high rainfall, sloping sites may suffer from soil erosion especially where tractors and other machinery have cut tracks into the rows between the vines down which water can flow. On these sites it is important to stabilise the site with vegetation, otherwise one of the annual tasks will be the collection of washed-down soil from the bottom of the slopes and carting it back to the top for spreading. This quite often happens on the slate and stone covered sites on the Rhine and Mosel. Sloping sites usually, but not always, have better natural drainage than flat sites and therefore dry out more easily and warm up more quickly, all of which are to a vine's advantage.

Sites that have a south-south-east or south-east aspect (in the northern hemisphere) will catch the morning sun, therefore warming up more quickly at a time when night temperatures will have cooled the site. They may also be more sheltered from prevailing winds. In cooler European regions, it is traditionally held that sites that face in this direction are the best. South-south-westerly or south-westerly facing sites (again, in the northern hemisphere) will warm up in the mornings more slowly, but this will be compensated by staying warmer into the evening. Soils that retain heat – dark soils or stone rich soils – may well benefit from this. However, in many regions the prevailing wind comes from this direction and this may well cool the site. In warm regions, this may be a beneficial aspect, lowering the extreme heat of the middle of the day. In the southern hemisphere, slopes that face east tend to be favoured over those that face west.

Apart from the advantage of being angled towards the sun, sites that slope – as opposed to those that are flat – have the benefit that air, as it is cooled by the land (which starts to lose heat once the sun has ceased warming it) travels down the slope to be replaced by warmer air from above.

Proximity to bodies of water

The fact that good vineyard sites are often close to bodies of water, be they man-made irrigation lagoons, natural lakes and rivers, estuaries, bays and even seas and oceans, is well known. Water is able to store heat more effectively than land and in the winter, when the air temperature falls, is able to release that heat. This effect is important on the macro-scale. The north-west coast of Europe is warmed in the winter by the Gulf Stream which brings warmer waters from the Gulf of Mexico. It is estimated that it warms the land it touches by 9°C above that for the latitude. This makes the west coasts of Scotland and Ireland a haven for tender Mediterranean plants, whereas land at similar latitudes on the opposite site of the Atlantic are very cold in the winter. On a mesoclimate scale, examples of vineyard regions which benefit from proximity to bodies of water are many: Bordeaux and the Gironde, the Rhine and Mosel Valleys in Germany, Austria's Burgenland and the Neusiedler See, Lake Balaton in Hungary and the Hunter Valley in Australia are all examples. Other regions with very cold winters – the Finger Lakes in New York State and the vineyards of the Niagara Peninsula in Canada – are examples where proximity to large bodies of water prevents winter frost damage and makes the growing of *vinifera* varieties possible.

In the summer, warm air from the land rises in the afternoons to be replaced by cooler air from the water, thus equalising the daytime temperatures and humidity levels. Sometimes, very large regions can be affected in this way. The southern parts of the Napa and Sonoma Valleys are prime examples of this. Here, high afternoon temperatures on the valley floor, where until relatively recently most vineyards were planted, are lowered by cool air and sea fog coming in from the cool Pacific via San Francisco Bay and the Petaluma Gap. This makes it possible to grow cool climate varieties such as Chardonnay and Pinot Noir in what is unarguably a warm climate, yet still retain good acidity.

Diurnal temperature variation

Traditionally, regions with a small diurnal temperature variation i.e. those where night-time temperatures remain relatively high, were held to be preferable to those with a large diurnal variation i.e. where night-time temperatures were relatively cool (below 15°C). The reason being that regions which remained warmer during the

night, heated up more quickly in the day, thus advancing maturity of the grapes, helping the sugar building process, dropping acidity more quickly and speeding up the change in the balance of acids in the grape from a high percentage of malic acidity to a high percentage of tartaric acid[25]. This effect has been noticeable in the UK over the past twenty years where night-time temperatures have risen, meaning that the vine's leaves warm up earlier in the mornings, allowing the vine to start photosynthesising sooner. This gives the vine more time in the day to produce sugars and starches, accounting in part for the changes in varieties and the increases in both natural sugar levels and wine quality.

In recent decades and in some new world regions (mainly warmer ones attempting to grow fruity high-acid white varieties such as Riesling and Sauvignon Blanc), growers have challenged this old-world view and claim that a wide diurnal temperature

Terraced vineyards on the Mosel in Germany

25 Malic acid, the most common acid found in apples (fruits of the Malus family), tastes harsher on the palate than tartaric acid and is responsible for some of the unripe characters in wines. Grapes are one of only two fruits in which tartaric acid is found (the other being tamarind) and is a much more taste-friendly acid than malic. As grapes ripen, malic acids change to tartaric acids and the relative proportions of the two acids are one of the guides to the grape's ripeness. In general terms, the higher the proportion of tartaric, the riper the grapes.

range, with warm days and cool nights, aids the retention of acids in the grapes which preserves the crisp fruit flavours in their wines. Austria's Wachau region, most of Chile's winegrowing areas and California's Santa Cruz Mountain region all enjoy a wide diurnal temperature variation.

Conclusion to site selection

The location, altitude and aspect of a site – all other things being equal – will ultimately determine the quality and quantity of wine produced and therefore the financial success of a vineyard. These factors are unchangeable and are the reason why the best sites are valued so highly.

Craggy Range Te Muna vineyard

Chapter 4
Grape-growing regions of the world

Table 1: Top twenty grape-growing countries of the world (2018)

No.	Country	'000 Ha
1	Spain	969
2	China	875
3	France	793
4	Italy	705
5	Turkey	448
6	U.S.A.	439
7	Argentina	218
8	Chile	212
9	Portugal	192
10	Romania	191
11	Iran	153
12	India	151
13	Moldova	147
14	Australia	146
15	South Africa	126
16	Uzbekistan	111
17	Greece	106
18	Germany	103
19	Afganistan	94
20	Russia	92

Note: Lists of world vineyard areas and most planted varieties are notorious for their inaccuracy. Many varieties have several different purposes and their actual use may vary between one or more purposes according to the vintage, economic conditions and, in the case of EU countries, the prevailing demand by the authorities for wine for distillation (a market stabilisation technique). In addition, information provided by growers on vineyards grubbed up and not replaced and on completely new ones planted may well take several years to filter through to those who have interest in analysing such data, assuming returns are made in the first place. The data over the next few pages has been taken from the OIV (Organisation Internationale de la vigne et du vin) 2019 report 'State of the World VitiVinicultural Market'.

As can be seen from Table 1, the grapevine is planted throughout the temperate and warm regions of the world. Only in regions where summer temperatures are too low for grapes to ripen, too hot (and usually too dry) for vines to survive the heat or where winter temperatures are too severe, are vines not grown. They are the classic Mediterranean plant. The grape is also one of the few agricultural crops that can be converted into a product that ages (wine and brandy) and, as it ages, increases in value and over which there are numerous social and religious conventions. In short, it is one of the world's most rewarding crops.

Grapes are grown for many different purposes:

- Making into still and sparkling wines, flavoured wines (vermouth etc), dessert wines and fortified wines.
- Wine for distillation into brandy for consumption.
- Wine for distillation into spirit for fortifying other wines.
- For grape juice and grape concentrate for use in both winemaking and in food production.
- Consumption as table grapes.
- To dry and turn into raisins, sultanas and currants for eating, cooking in the home and food manufacturing.

The world area under vines for all purposes has fallen from a high of 10.2 m. ha in 1980 to 7.8 m. ha in 2001, and to 7.6 m. ha in 2017. As might be expected, Europe leads the world in wine production, with around 58 per cent of the total, down from around twenty years ago when it was nearer 75 per cent. Italy has the most vineyards with 17 per cent, France next with 15 per cent and Spain 13 per cent. The USA now produces 9 per cent of the world's wine, Australia and Argentina 5 per cent each and China and South Africa 4 per cent each. Despite the slight decline in the area under vine since

26 Enrichment is the correct term for what is often called Chaptalisation.

27 Rectified Concentrated Grape Must (RCGM or – in French – MCR) is a colourless, odourless and tasteless liquid sugar made from grapes. It is the EU's answer to overproduction in the Club-Med countries. It can be used for enrichment, although it is more expensive than sucrose, but is widely used for secondary fermentation of sparkling wines and for making up *liqueur de dosage* in both Champagne and other sparkling wines. They don't put that on the back label!

2001, world wine production averages around 270 m. hl, with highs of almost 300 m. hl in 2004, to lows of 250 m. hl in 2017 (when many European vineyards were frost affected). World wine consumption has averaged around 245 m. hl, leaving a surplus of around 25 m. hl, much of which is distilled into industrial alcohol or converted to grape concentrate and grape sugar.

Average yields across the world in 2017 were 33 hl-ha, with the highest average yields being found in Australia, 92.6 hl-ha, South Africa 86.4 hl-ha and Germany 75.5 hl-ha showing what modern, well-managed, often irrigated vineyards can produce. Italy managed 61.1 hl-ha, but France only 46.6 hl-ha, the result of the spring frosts. Portugal and Spain managed 34 hl-ha and 33.2 hl-ha respectively, the result of the large number of low-yielding, dry-farmed vines. At the bottom of the charts are Greece, 24.5 hl-ha, Romania 22.51 hl-ha and China 12.4 hl-ha.

Climatic differences

The vine is grown as far north in the northern hemisphere as the UK, Finland, Sweden and Norway (albeit in very limited amounts in those last three) and as far south in the southern hemisphere as Alexandria in the south of New Zealand's South Island and BioBio in the south of Chile. In these cooler regions, varieties are selected that are able to produce ripe fruit at lower temperatures and often enrichment[26] (the practice of adding sugar or another sweetening agent such as concentrated grape must or rectified concentrated grape must[27] to juice prior to fermentation) will be used to raise alcohol levels in the bottle. Grape juice can also be concentrated to raise sugar levels and increase alcohols either naturally by freezing or drying, or mechanically with various devices such as reverse osmosis filters and refrigeration systems, although these are today less commonly seen as in many regions natural alcohol levels are too high.

Excess acidity can also be removed either chemically by precipitation with calcium carbonate ($CaCO_3$) or via a malolactic fermentation[28]. In cooler regions, sparkling wines (Champagne), wines aged *sur lie* (Muscadet) and wines with residual sugar (German Riesling, Loire Chenin Blanc) are often found. All of these types of wine are made in part to soften or change the usually high acidity levels. Red wines are less common and when they are found, tend to be lighter in colour (red Sancerre, German and Alsatian Pinots) with lower alcohol levels and higher acidities than red wines from warmer regions.

The grapevine is also grown in parts of the world where winters are very severe; in Quebec, Canada, parts of the Russian Confederation and in Ningxia, China, where earthing up in winter to protect the grafts against winter frost may be necessary, or even, in extreme conditions, burying the vine completely. The grapevine is also found where summers are very hot. Australia's Barossa Valley, California's Central Valley and the hotter South African vineyards are examples. Here natural alcohols will be high, even excessive, and acids will be low. Alcohol reduction (by blending or by removal) may be practiced and acid will be added as a matter of course. Varieties will be grown that tolerate hot climates and vineyards will be irrigated not out of choice, but for survival. In very hot climates, where wine production is not possible, table grapes and grapes for drying will be grown.

Climate and location

Grape varieties differ widely in their adaptability to different climates, although this has as much to do with the style and type of wine produced as with other factors. There are also local reasons, such as *appellation* regulations and marketing reasons, why some grape varieties are confined to fairly small geographical regions. In general terms, white varieties require less heat than reds and are therefore found in cooler areas, but it is not just a matter of temperature.

White grape varieties

Chardonnay is as an example of a variety with a very wide geographical spread. It is grown in the coolest winegrowing regions such as the UK where its high acidity and clean, crisp flavours make it ideal for bottle-fermented sparkling wines. It finds a good home in Champagne, for sparkling wines, and Chablis and the Côte d'Or where it produces high quality dry white wines with enough acidity to cope with barrel fermentation and malolactic fermentation. In warmer regions, even into some of the very warm wine growing areas – the Barossa Valley, California's Central Valley and many South African vineyards – it can still make solid, sometimes buttery wines, often with oak as an added dimension. Natural alcohol levels across all regions will range from as low as 7–8 per cent in which case pre-fermentation enrichment and possibly chemical de-acidification will be needed to bring about wines with the correct balance for the desired wine style, and up to 15 per cent and

28 A malolactic fermentation (MLF), more correctly called a 'malolactic conversion' is where malic acid is changed to lactic acid through the activity of a bacteria, *Leuconostoc oenos*. These bacteria are often present in wineries and given the right conditions, will multiply and carry out the MLF spontaneously after the alcoholic fermentation. In other wineries it can be added either with, or after the alcoholic fermentation. In wines where the MLF is not wanted, the addition of SO2 will prevent it.

Table 2: Most widespread white wine grape varieties (2018)

No	Grape Variety	World Ha	Largest area of variety found in
1	Airén	218,031	Spain
2	Chardonnay	212,213	USA
3	Sauvignon blanc	129,116	France
4	Ugni Blanc/Trebbiano Toscano	111,349	France
5	Rkatsiteli	75,317	Georgia
6	Riesling	63,936	Germany
7	Pinot gris	54,441	Italy
8	Viura/Macabeo	48,244	Spain
9	Aligoté	35,073	Moldova
10	Muscat of Alexandria	33,850	Spain

High-density Chardonnay vineyard near Epernay, Champagne

even 16 per cent in the warmer regions where acid addition will almost always be required and even alcohol reduction in some cases. Natural acid levels will range from a high of 18 g/l (as tartaric) down to as low as 4 g/l. In all cases however, good, even great wines can be produced which will differ in style and type, as well as yield and quality, even though they should all have a recognisable Chardonnay signature.

Other white varieties such as Chenin Blanc find a home in both coolish regions –

the Loire where dry, sweet and sparkling wines are made from it – and the hottest regions of South Africa where it is the mainstay of both their table wine and distilling industries. Riesling again finds a home in both cool regions (Germany) and warm regions (Barossa Valley), plus it also performs well in climates in-between these two: Austria and Australia's Clare Valley. Some white varieties, even though they are important in terms of hectarage planted, are very local. Take Airén as an example. This is the most widely planted white variety in the world, more widespread than Chardonnay, yet is almost totally confined to La Mancha in Spain. And Rkatsiteli – the fourth most widely planted white grape variety – is found mainly in Georgia, Moldova and the southern regions of the Russian Republic.

Red grape varieties

In general, red varieties (and ignoring red varieties such as Pinot Noir and Gamay used for white sparkling base wines) have less of a climatic/geographical spread mainly because that for red wines, not only should the juice have the correct balance of sugar and acid, but so also should the skins and the pulp of the grapes. This is because these almost always remain with the juice throughout the complete fermentation process in order to aid colour and tannin extraction. Unripe red grapes will produce too much astringency and bitterness. Having said that, some varieties, Pinot Noir is an example, do have a fairly wide geographical distribution being found in moderately cool regions such as the UK, the Loire (Sancerre) as well as in the cooler parts of warm regions such as the Carneros region of the Napa and Sonoma Valleys. In cooler regions, Pinot Noir has a dual-purpose role, being good for red wines in warm years when skins and pulp are ripe, and reserved for still rosé or sparkling wine production in cooler vintages. Cabernet Franc,

No	Grape Variety	World Ha	Largest area of variety found in
Table 3: Most widespread red wine grape varieties (2018)			
1	Cabernet Sauvignon	336,705	China
2	Merlot	268,193	France
3	Tempranillo	230,986	Spain
4	Syrah	188,890	France
5	Grenache	160,845	France
6	Pinot noir	118,202	France
7	Bobal	62,874	Spain
8	Sangiovese	60,031	Italy
9	Malbec/Cot	56,410	Argentina
10	Monastrell/Mourvèdre	56,252	Spain

another variety found along the Loire where crisp red wines (sometimes served chilled) are produced, is also found in warmer regions, although often (but by no means always) in a blend.

Red varieties such as Cabernet Sauvignon, Merlot and Syrah/Shiraz are seldom found in very cool regions, but dominate in Mediterranean climates and the hotter regions. These three varieties, being strongly associated with high quality wine producing regions such as Bordeaux and the Rhône Valley, have been successfully transplanted for good commercial reasons into all other warm quality growing regions throughout the world. Varieties like Grenache and Zinfandel are much more climate specific and need considerable heat to ripen and make good wine. As with white varieties, some of the most heavily planted reds are confined to small geographical regions. Most of the world's Sangiovese is found in Italy; the world's Carignan in southern France; and the world's Bobal and Monastrel in Spain. These four are all in the top ten of the most planted red varieties, yet social, commercial (and maybe even quality) reasons have kept them localised.

With all varieties, however, there is considerable blurring at the edges. Styles of wine can help overcome climatic limitations. The sweetness in many German wines is there to balance what some might see as excessive acidity, not solely because the Germans like sweeter wines! The Champenois discovered centuries ago that by double fermenting their wines (thus reducing the acidity even more than with just a single fermentation), allowing their wines to sit on the lees (in the bottle) to gain flavour and character, and by adding a

Grapes being picked from a pergola at Quinta do Noval in the Douro Valley

sugar-syrup *dosage* just before sale, even some of the world's thinnest, leanest and most acidic Chardonnay and Pinot could be magically transformed into what are unarguably truly great wines.

Global warming, and the riper grapes it brings, is making it possible for varieties to extend their geographical spread. Chardonnay is now to be found in many German wine regions previously dominated by Riesling, along the Loire where previously only Muscadet (from the variety Melon de Bourgogne) was produced and even as far north as the UK where it is mainly used for sparkling wines, although in warm vintages, excellent still wines are also made. Even quite cool growing regions now produce red wines, often using varieties such as hybrids and PIWI varieties bred to cope with lower temperatures. Of course, there are also social, marketing and legal reasons for the spread of these varieties, so it is not just down to climate change.

Chapter 5
Soils for vineyards

Soils for vineyards

The soil in a vineyard is one of the most stable of factors in the complex mix that goes into determining the quality of the grapes that come from that vineyard. Although some ancient vineyards sites have been considerably altered by man over the centuries (and even in some cases, the millennia) that vines have been grown on them – one thinks of the man-made terraces on the great European wine rivers such as the Mosel, Rhine, Rhône and Douro and others – most sites contain the same soils and have the same structures as they did when they were first cultivated. For certain they have been improved, drained, had manures and fertiliser added, and been managed for sustainability, but deep in their lower reaches, where vine roots can still penetrate, the soil remains essentially unchanged. The European model of soil assessment, based as it is upon its relatively old soils and from the centuries of experience gained on these soils, sometimes looks with suspicion on the much more recent soils found in many of the New World regions and on the considerably shorter length of time that vines have been grown in these areas. In the old world, the notion of *terroir* as an immutable, unchangeable, forever-certain concept, is still widely held to be valid, enshrining as it does an element of uniqueness that is unquestionable: Chablis is Chablis, St. Émilion is St. Émilion, Chianti is Chianti,

because they are where they are and nothing can change that. However, this concept is not universally accepted.

Despite what adherents of the concept of *terroir* might have one believe, vines will grow (or perhaps one should say that they can be persuaded to grow), and good wine can be made from the grapes they bear, in almost any type of soil. The essential requirements for grapevines are the same as any other perennial plant: the soil should provide a sufficient anchor for the plant and sufficient (but not too many) nutrients and water for it to crop successfully and to survive until the next growing season. Whether soils have a high sand content, a high clay content, are loamy, are rich in chalk or stones, rich in iron or some other mineral, is not what ultimately affects the flavour and quality of wines. Winemakers and wine-tasters often describe high-acid, crisp, lean wines as being *flinty* or of having *minerality*, implying – and these terms are especially used when the wine in question is known to come from a region or vineyard having flint-rich or mineral-rich soils – that the wine has in some way been *flavoured* by elements imbibed by the vine in the course of the summer. Scientifically this is not provable[29]. If minerals could somehow leach out of the soil and infuse grapes with flavours, what's to stop a grower sprinkling the minerals supposedly causing this effect on to his or her vineyards and artificially inducing the vines to suck these up? I was

29 If you think this an invalid argument, question whether you have ever described a wine as 'steely'. If so, does it mean that you believed it contained or had been flavoured by steel? I doubt it. Jamie Goode in Wine Science (p.126 of 2005 edition) believes 'minerality' might be a fermentation-derived quality and one associated with sulphur compounds and reductive winemaking techniques, not a terroir characteristic at all.

present at a memorable Circle of Wine Writers tasting in London where Randall Grahm (from the Bonny Doon Winery) gave us several flights of wines which had been 'rocked' by having different types of rock and stone immersed in them. I cannot say any were successful (and I later learnt that they might have been positively harmful as unwanted trace elements had leached out of some of the stones!). The concept of 'minerality' in wine as being soil-derived also seems illogical when wines growing on lean, low-fertility, stony soils which by the nature have low levels of minerals, are said to have 'minerality', when wines growing on fertile, higher-vigour soils which are rich in minerals are said to lack 'minerality' The question of 'minerality' in wine is one therefore that is more in the taster's mind, than in any chemical changes brought about by the wine having been grown in a certain type of soil.

Potassium uptake by the vine is worth mentioning at this point as there is good evidence that a high potassium level in wines is associated with low pH levels in the wine i.e. high acidity wines. Growers in warm regions therefore, where natural acid levels tend towards the lower end of the spectrum, will do what they can to increase the uptake of potassium by their vines. Some rootstocks are said to take up potassium than others (Ramsey and Schwarzmann for instance), although there is research to suggest that it is certain varieties that take up more potassium, regardless of rootstock.

However, what different soil types will do is cause a vine to grow in a specific way, mainly because different soil types hold water in different ways and different soil types cause a vine to grow more or less vigorously. This in turn will affect the way that the vine bears and ripens its crop, upon crop level, upon sugar and acid levels in the grapes and upon the quality of the wine produced from them. But that is not the

New terraces on the Douro ready for re-planting

same as saying that a certain soil type is responsible for the quality and character of the wine or has in any way flavoured it. Two widely differing soil types may well have similar effects on the pattern of vine growth and therefore the wines from these two soils may well be very similar.

The most important and defining elements of a soil are its structure and its texture. A soil's structure and texture are defined in part by the percentages of sand, silt, loam or clay in the soil; whether there is gravel, stone or rock present; and what the organic matter content of the soil is. Other factors such as the depths of the different layers and the way in which the soil has been managed and treated will all play a part in defining a particular soil. A soil with the correct structure and texture – open, freely draining, not too rich, with adequate levels of organic matter and good water and nutrient holding capacities – will allow vines to root deeply, to be less influenced by excessively wet or dry conditions, not to be overly vigorous and to carry a balanced crop of grapes. Vines growing on soils with different textures will differ in their ability to root and this in turn will affect the way in which they grow, bear fruit and ripen a crop. It is these differences that account for the differences in wines, not the

30 Soil scientists call these layers *horizons* and generally differentiate at least five if not eight in most soils. For farmers and growers, three is quite enough.

31 Protozoa are microscopic single-celled organisms that live in the soil. They are vital to the break-down of plant matter in the soil.

actual chemical content of the soil. Good vineyard soils, despite their differences in soil type, do however share some common elements.

The best vineyard soils are usually those that have an equal balance of sand, loam and clay, good natural drainage, yet are able to store sufficient moisture to keep the vine supplied with water throughout the growing season and sufficient oxygen for roots to breathe and grow. The presence of stone, flints or gravel will aid drainage to the lower levels, where moisture will be conserved for the plant, and be less likely to erode in times of heavy rainfall. These soils may also reflect heat and light up into the fruiting zone in daylight hours and also trap heat during the day, releasing it in the early evening. Soils should also be sufficiently deep in both their upper and secondary layers for extensive rooting to take place. Vines with extensive root systems can overcome quite extreme variations in water and nutrient supply.

However, even with soils which have good natural drainage, there may be a requirement to provide artificial drainage to take away water at critical times of the year. In the early part of the season, when bud-

Three soil layers showing clearly in New Zealand's Gimblett Gravels district

burst occurs and the microscopic root-hairs start to grow from the roots in order to take up moisture and nutrients to feed the growing leaves, it is crucial that the roots should not be deprived of oxygen, something which happens to them in waterlogged soils. Roots also need to get rid of the carbon dioxide they produce and this must be able to escape.

The soil of a vineyard is also the factory floor and the soil must be able to carry farm traffic, even after recent rain, and ideally not be liable to rutting or erosion. In the autumn, when rainfall can be expected even in the driest of regions, heavy, wet soils will make harvesting difficult and they will become more easily compacted by heavy equipment. The depth of soil is also very relevant. Soils have several layers and each will be important, depending on what plants are being grown. For vines, which are very deep-rooted, long-lived, perennial plants, there are really three layers[30] that should be considered – topsoil, subsoil and *subsolum*.

Topsoil: The first layer, commonly known as the topsoil, is important since it provides the interface between the grower and the plant. This is the (usually) friable i.e. easily crumbled, soil that will immediately absorb any rainfall or irrigation water falling on to it, will contain the majority of the organic matter in the soil and most importantly, will contain the soil organisms – yeasts, moulds, fungi, mycorrhizae, bacteria, protozoa[31], algae and worms – that are crucial in a healthy soil. The worm population of a soil is a very good indicator of its overall health and there can be as many as 4 million worms per ha which together would weigh over 1,000 tonnes. Each worm will produce around 4.5 kg of casts – earth, grit and vegetable matter – per year which will help improve the soil. Worms will be active in many soils down to 2 m and will provide channels for water to drain into the soil and for carbon dioxide to escape.

Topsoils can be shallow (150 mm or less)

in which case their water-holding and nutrient capacity will probably be limited and vines may be hard to establish (and may need irrigating in the first few years). Some shallow topsoils however, especially those over chalk, may well be very satisfactory for vines as a vine's roots will be able to penetrate into the chalk which is both friable and water retentive. Shallow topsoils over impervious material, such as clay or even rock, will not be so suitable.

Deeper topsoils (up to 1m) may well provide an ideal environment for vines to root, but may be so fertile as to be too vigorous leading to excess lush growth at the expense of fruiting. Vines will root in the topsoil, but it is better if they are encouraged to root in the deeper levels. This is so that they are less affected by rainfall and/or irrigation, fertilisers and any nitrogen released by the breakdown of organic matter (leaves, prunings, mulches and any applied manures) or fixed by vegetation planted between the rows such as clover and other leguminous plants. Deeper rooting can be encouraged by ploughing the surface of the vineyard to discourage shallow rooting and in extreme circumstances, by root-pruning[32]. A low-vigour rootstock may also help overcome the problems associated with vigorous soils.

The topsoil will also: provide the surface for tractors, sprayers, harvesters and other machinery to run on; will grow the grasses or green crops that carpet the alleyways between the vines; and will either be cultivated or be sprayed with herbicides beneath the vines themselves. The topsoil is also the surface that the sun warms and which will promote the growth of the vine at bud-burst. The quicker a soil warms to 10°C, the quicker bud-burst will occur and the longer will be the growing season. Darker soils, high in organic matter, will warm faster and retain more heat. Soils that are wet and that dry out slowly will be slower to warm. Cold and damp soils will also not favour the formation of the cytokinin hormones, pro-duced in the tips of the roots, which affect cell multiplication and the growth and development of both shoots and flowers. Vines low in these hormones will be slower to come into leaf, produce less fruit and ripen it more slowly.

Subsoil: The second layer is generally known as the subsoil and it is here that the vine will (hopefully) place the majority of its roots. Soils in this layer will be less friable than in the topsoil, will contain less organic matter, but should still contain sufficient flora and fauna, albeit less at lower levels than at upper, to provide aeration and drainage. The depth of the subsoil will be very variable and it is impossible to generalise. However, it is not uncommon for vines to root to at least 3 m in depth, with instances of them rooting much more deeply. For vines to root properly, the soil at this level must be friable enough for the roots to penetrate and be open enough for the root hairs to grow in the early summer. Soils that are rich in stones and gravel will usually be very suitable for vines as whilst they may be lower in organic matter, they will encourage deeper rooting. Vines with deep root structures will be less affected by periods of high or low rainfall and will generally be less vigorous than shallower rooted vines.

Subsolum: The third layer, called the subsolum, is the soil below the subsoil. In some cases this may provide a rooting area for the vine. In others it may be so impervious as to form a barrier to root growth. Usually, this layer is at least 3 m below the surface and generally only a few roots will penetrate here. However, even with little root activity, it is important that water should be able to drain away and not cause waterlogging. In extreme circumstances, this third layer will consist of hard compacted soil (especially clays), or, worse still, of more-or-less solid rock. Depending on how deep this layer is, a soil with an impervious layer may prove less suitable for vines. Great vineyard sites

32 Root-pruning is carried out using a tractor-mounted implement fitted with cutting blades (tines) that slice through the soil at around 300 mm and cut some of the roots. This makes the vine send out fresh roots into the lower soil levels.

almost always have very deep water-tables, allowing roots to penetrate deeply, even in winter, without encountering waterlogged soil. In many parts of the Medoc for instance, the water table in the winter is at least 5 m below soil level and 6 m in the summer. This factor alone goes some way to explain the unique nature and quality of this region.

To investigate a vineyard's soil properly, it is always wise to excavate trial holes (with a mechanical digger) before vines are planted. Usually holes of at least 1m deep (but often deeper) are dug with vertical sides, which allow one to see how deep each soil profile is. These holes will also (usually) reveal the presence or absence of a plough-pan[33] which will need breaking up; whether there are stones, rocks or chalk in the soil; and even where the water table is. They will also give a good idea of how well or otherwise the soil is drained and whether artificial drainage is needed. The number of holes per hectare will depend very much on the uniformity of the soil throughout the site, something that can be largely determined by taking numerous soil samples with a hand-held soil auger, prior to digging the larger trial holes.

Soil pH

34 See Chapter 14 – Nutritional
disorders and other viticultural
problems for more on iron
chlorosis

35 Green manuring is the planting of specific green crops in
the vineyard to provide
material for humus production.
See Chapter 6 – Vineyard
Establishment for more details.

The measure of the acidity or the alkalinity of a substance is known as its pH. Soil is said to be neutral when it has a pH of 7.0, below that it is said to be acidic, above that alkaline. It is said that vines prefer a soil with a pH of around 6.5 i.e. slightly acidic, although with the right rootstock, vines will grow well in soils with lower and higher pH levels. Soils with a pH of less than 5.0 are usually unsuitable for growing vines (or indeed many other fruit crops) as the high levels of chemicals in these soils – such as manganese and aluminium – will damage roots. Soils that are acidic (low pH) can be corrected by the addition of an alkali com-

pound (lime or chalk) in order to bring the soil up towards 6.5 pH. Alkaline soils – typically those with a high active calcium carbonate content of 30 per cent or more and with pHs of up to 8.5 – will support grapes although iron chlorosis[34] will often be a problem unless a suitable lime-tolerant rootstock is used. It is often easier to live with a very alkaline soil than to attempt to correct it. The alkalinity of a soil can be reduced slightly by the incorporation of organic matter. Over many years of green manuring[35] and/or the addition of farmyard manure, very alkaline soils can be improved, but it is usually a struggle. The relevance of the pH of a soil must always be viewed in the light of soil type. Lean sandy soils of say pH 6.5 will contain fewer nutrients than a loamy soil of the same pH level. Soils that are at the extremities of acceptability, whether they be acidic or alkali, must always be treated with more care and with greater attention to the type of fertilisers used than those nearer the ideal pH 6.5 level. It should always be borne in mind that what matters to the plant is not what the mineral content of the soil actually is, but how those minerals are made available to the plant. The availability of minerals is very often dependent on soil pH. For instance, soils at either end of the pH spectrum, whether highly acidic or highly alkaline, tend to lock up nutrients which the vine's roots then cannot assimilate. See chart on right. Conversely, soils in the ideal mid-range of pH 6.0 to 7.0, will readily give up the minerals contained in them. There are also however, relationships between individual minerals: soils high in calcium tend to lock up boron, iron and magnesium; soils rich in potassium tend to be magnesium deficient; soils well supplied with phosphorous tend to be zinc deficient. What can also play a part is both the choice of rootstocks and scion variety. Some rootstocks are better at dealing with certain excesses or deficiencies and some varieties produce better wine on certain types of soil. Other factors such as water stress, temperature levels and crop loads will all play their part in a vine's health and its reaction to one mineral or the other.

Humus in soils

Humus is an important constituent in the soil and acts in many different ways upon the plants growing in that soil. Humus is made from any plant material – leaves and canes – deposited on the vineyard floor during and after the growing season; any plant material grown in the rows such as weeds, grasses and green manures; any mulches used under the vines to suppress weed growth and/or to conserve moisture; and any manures having a straw or compost base. It is formed as the organic matter breaks down and is what is left after anything else has been used up. It is usually dark in colour (often black) and warms up more quickly and absorbs more heat than lighter soils. Soils with a high humus content tend to be more fertile than soils with a low humus content as minerals necessary for plant growth are held by the humus. Humus is usually confined to the topsoil layer and although worms and other soil organisms will take it down to lower levels, it is in the surface layer that it is most useful.

Humus benefits the soil in many different ways: it acts as a buffer between the vineyard floor and the roots, absorbing moisture falling on the vineyard (dew, rain and irrigation) and allowing it to be released slowly; it also acts as a binder in soils, helping keep fragile soils together, preventing erosion and soil loss; it prevents soil compaction which might be caused by tractors and machinery; it opens up the soil, allowing air to penetrate to lower levels and carbon dioxide produced by the roots to escape; it helps soil trap nutrients – both those applied to correct deficiencies and those produced by the breakdown of or-

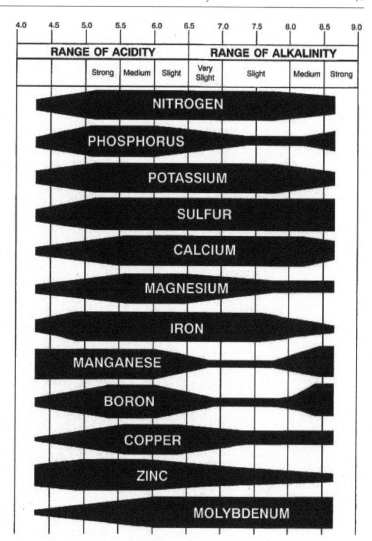

ganic matter (mainly nitrogen) – and allows those to be released slowly to the roots. In short, its importance cannot be overstressed. It brings life and health to a soil and maintains the structure of that soil for the many decades over which continuous cropping will take place. Where once many farms and estates had animals whose manure mixed with straw would be spread on the fields in the spring, today this is the exception and alternative sources of humus have to be sought.

Availability of elements to plants at different pH levels

Availability of water

In the old world, and in pre-global warming times, the availability of water for irrigating a vineyard was not often a consideration. In almost all *appellations* irrigation was not allowed and, in any event, even if it was, where would the water come from? Now, with higher average temperatures and a less-predictable pattern of rainfall (and often less annual rainfall), irrigation in traditionally dry-farmed European wine regions is becoming more common. Water availability is still an issue and in many traditional regions, even if a water source is available, is there land to build lagoons? However, in the dryer parts of the new world, the availability of water for irrigation may well be THE deciding factor of a site's suitability for profitable grape growing. Water is usually available from one of a number of sources: water courses (rivers and streams) from which it can be pumped; natural bodies of water which act as reservoirs; man-made reservoirs which can be filled in the winter from suitable water sources; and underground aquifers which can either be used to fill up reservoirs or which have sufficient flow to feed irrigation systems either directly or via a small buffer reservoir – in either case a pump will usually be needed to bring the water to the surface.

Whatever the source, enough water must be available even in drought years and reservoirs may need to hold enough water to supply a vine's needs even though winter rains have been lacking. The amount of water a vine needs depends on several factors: the soil type; how much natural precipitation there is during the growing season; how large the crop is; the type of grapes being grown; and, most importantly, how the water is applied. Application techniques vary widely in the efficiency with which they supply the vine with water. More in **Chapter 9 – Irrigation**.

Terroir – 'A concept not easily grasped'

As has been hinted at the beginning of this chapter, my understanding of the concept of *terroir* is not one with which I suspect many vineyard owners in Bordeaux or Burgundy would agree! The idea that the <u>site alone</u> is responsible for determining a wine's intrinsic style and quality cannot be taken – at least not by me – as a wholly plausible one. This is not to deny that certain sites will usually – even perhaps always – produce wines of a certain style, typicity and quality. That much is obvious when you compare wines from any of Burgundy's famous villages or the Mosel's much-fragmented vineyards. Some sites have the edge which others lack, some sites are in balance with their vines and surroundings and manage by a combination of human intervention and nature to produce magical wines year-in and year-out.

But to suggest that *site alone* is responsible for quality ignores such major influences as plant density, variety, clone and rootstock variations, trellising and training systems, yield levels, canopy management and a whole host of other vineyard practices. Add on to these the influences of picking date, fruit selection and all the many character-changing processes that a wine goes through in the winery and cellar – to say nothing of the complexities of ageing – before it gets into a consumer's glass and – at least to my mind – *terroir* starts to look much more like a marketing concept than anything else. Regional, sub-regional or even vineyard *typicité* is just as much a product of winemaking school as it is of *terroir*. After all, if many of the winegrowers in an area are using the same clones and rootstocks (as specified in the AC regulations), adhere to the same *appellation* yield levels, pick at much the same time, use similar techniques in their wineries and age their wines in barrels made from French oak, their wines are likely to taste similar – especially if they are attempting to produce wines which conform to their customer's expectations. Do wine-lovers expect Volnay to taste 'elegant, with a certain delicacy' (Michael Broadbent's description from his *Pocket Guide to Winetasting*)? If so, perhaps (some) winemakers make them to taste like that? Gevrey-Chambertin on the other hand should be 'full-bodied, firm, yet velvety' (another MB quote). Do winemakers have these descriptions in their minds as they plan the vintage? After all, you must have some differentiation between wines from two different *terroirs!*

The origins of *terroir* lie surely in the aspirations of growers in established regions to protect their livelihoods and that is where it should stay. No one could pretend that Chablis is today any worse in general than it was 50 years ago when the *appellation* area was around 500 ha compared with today's 5,592 ha[36] (in fact it is undoubtedly a lot better owing to better plant protection measures, stainless steel tanks and refrigeration). The planting of thousands of hectares of additional land – and by no means all of it on the *vrai* Kimmeridgian chalky-marl that is traditionally meant to define Chablis vineyards – in order to satisfy the demands of the world's restaurant lists and wine-shop shelves was done for good commercial reasons, and the protection of the name Chablis was done in the name of sustainability of the grower's businesses and for no other. Some of the finest estates in Bordeaux – Ch. Lafite Rothschild for instance – occupy much bigger tracts of land than they did when classified in 1855. Has their magical *terroir* been able to jump a few

fences? The fact that New World growers – for long advocates of a *terroir*-free wine world – have now woken up to the need to define and fight over exactly whose wines can bear the names Napa or Coonawarra is some indication that *terroir* is, at its root, a marketing-led concept.

James E. Wilson in his magisterial book on the subject Terroir states that: *'the true concept is not easily grasped but includes physical elements in the vineyard habitat – the vine, subsoil, siting, drainage, and microclimate'*, and, as if that was not quite enough, goes on to say that: *'beyond the measurable ecosystem, there is an additional dimension – the spiritual aspect that recognises the joys, the heartbreaks, the pride, the sweat, and the frustration of its history'.* As Wilson says – the true concept is not easily grasped!!

Alex Maltman in his scholarly study of the subject *Vineyards, Rocks and Soils* takes a more professorial look at the subject and whilst he easily dismisses the possibility of a straight-line relationship between soil geology and wine flavour, he admits that there are 'multifarious other aspects of nature' that come together to affect the flavour of wine, many of which we do not fully understand and some of which we have not even started to investigate. I fear it's probably a case of known unknowns, and even unknown unknowns.

36 2017: 3,690-ha AC Chablis, 839-ha Premier Cru, 56-ha Grand Cru, 1,007-ha Petit Chablis.

The photograph was taken in Lanzarote and shows a vineyard planted with Malvasia. Each vine is protected by a dry-stone wall, made of the local black volcanic rock, and set in a man-made depression which is covered by a layer of small pebbles of the same volcanic rock. These are called 'zocos' and, as far as I am aware, are unique in the world of viticulture. There being no natural ground-water and precious little rainfall, the vine is kept watered by dew which is attracted to the black pebbles at night and which then drains down to the vine's roots. All the vines on the island are planted in this (or a similar) way.

Chapter 6
Vineyard establishment

Vineyard establishment

The establishment of a vineyard requires a considerable outlay of capital and it is not usually feasible (or financially practical) to change the basic layout of a vineyard once planted. Mistakes made in variety, clone and rootstock selection, planting densities, row widths and trellising designs cannot easily be rectified afterwards and many of the pre-planting operations – sub-soiling[37], rock and stone removal and drainage – can only be carried out before planting and must be done properly. In other words, you need to get much of the basic detail right first time if the investment is to be a sound one.

Precision viticulture

Precision viticulture (PV) has been defined as 'using knowledge of spatial variation to make better decisions'. This has been brought about by the advent of Global Positioning Satellites (GPS) which have revolutionised almost every aspect of life, including agriculture. The use of GPS monitoring systems, satellite imaging, field-mapping using electromagnetic sensors and earth radar, is bringing advances to farming that only a few decades ago were impossible to imagine. Tractors and other powered machinery are steered in straight lines using GPS, and their seed drills, fertiliser spreaders, sprayers and harvesters can be programmed to respond in different ways when their GPS systems tell them where they are in the field. Both arable and horticultural farmers now have digital maps of their land and have harvesters that record yields in real-time as they travel across the fields, allowing them to plant at higher seed rates and spread greater amounts of fertilisers on productive areas to maximise yields. Likewise, irrigation systems can be fine-tuned to provide water to those areas of land that can respond to higher rates of water and deliver higher yields and precious water is not wasted. Drones are also starting to make an appearance in agriculture (including viticulture) for a variety of reasons, vigour mapping and disease monitoring being the most common in vines.

Although by no means common in viticulture, the use of PV is becoming more common and will, in time, become much more widespread. One of the first uses of infra-red imaging (initially by taking pictures from a light aircraft) was to track the advances of *Phylloxera* in the Napa Valley. The Normalised Difference Vegetation Index (NDVI) of a vineyard gives a very good indication of the vigour of the vines. Low-vigour patches of vines (those most likely to be damaged by the insect) show up as red and higher vigour areas as green. On-site inspections can confirm the suspicions and over the course of a few years, the pest's progress can be charted. The NDVI will also give a good picture of the Leaf Area Index

37 Sub-soiling involves the use of implements to disturb the soil at the level below the topsoil to break up compacted layers not reachable with a conventional plough.

(LAI) of the vine, the ratio of leaf area to soil surface area: the higher the figure, the greater the leaf area and therefore the greater the vigour of the vine.

Site surveys using electromagnetic sensing and earth (or ground) radar, coupled with physical soil sampling and testing, enable growers to map their fields in advance of any preparation work, and sub-divide them into areas of soil type (usually into areas where vine vigour is the determining factor) that may require different physical treatments: fertiliser requirements, irrigation systems, rootstocks, varieties and clones. In this way the right vines can be planted for the soil they are growing in and better, more cost-effective, crops will be harvested. Vine growth stages and vigour mapping is a base for PV in vineyards and then all treatments to the growing vines – pruning loads, canopy density, canopy management techniques, pest and disease control, irrigation and finally time of harvesting – can be fine-tuned to improve crop quality and optimum quantity. In time, as more and more sites are surveyed, planted and subsequently monitored using these techniques, their use will become more routine in large-scale modern vineyards. GPS controlled self-driving sprayers, or tractors pulling sprayers, that once have been shown a route for spraying will automatically follow that same route spray-round after spray-round, allowing one operative to operate two sprayers, are becoming more widely seen in top and soft-fruit orchards, plantations and vineyards. Self-driving mowers are also making appearances in vineyards and orchards. GPS vine planting machines are the norm now, making for very accurate row widths and intervine distances.

Site preparation

Many sites will need some re-grading before they can be planted. This might be a little as filling in a few odd depressions and removing a few humps and bumps or (as I have seen at Gallo's Frey Ranch in Sonoma) complete reforming of a north facing slope to a south facing slope by the removal of all of the topsoil, then the removal of substantial amounts of the subsoil (used in this instance to cover their new 100,000 barrel barrel-hall with 3 m of insulating soil), then re-grading the slope and replacing the topsoil back onto the site. This type of extreme gardening is, however, rare. (It was described to me later as 'the way the Good Lord would have wanted it had he had the money'!)

The transformation of many of the old river-facing terraces on the Rhine and Mosel (and the other vineyard rivers in Germany) through what is known as *Flurbereinigung* or 'parcel cleaning' has dramatically altered both the look and the economic viability of grape growing in these areas. Prior to this reorganisation, a typical grower might own many relatively small parcels of vines – often only a few rows with perhaps as few as 10 vines per row – spread out over several kilometres, all of them difficult (or very often impossible) to mechanise, each served by its own narrow walkway up which all labour and materials would have to travel and down which all grapes would have to be hauled. In short, these vineyards were very labour-intensive and uneconomic except where high wine prices prevailed. The *Flurbereinigung* commission gets growers together, agrees on a scheme to remove the old terraces, builds tall walls and wide roads, lay a mains water supply for spraying water and generally re-grades and realigns the land. Growers are then given back their vineyards in larger individual parcels (although a smaller area overall as some land is inevitably lost to the new roads and turning areas), spread out as equitably as possible over the whole area. The result is that growers have vineyards which can be driven to, vineyards that can be mechanised either through the use of

Crawler tractor and sprayer working in the Scharzhofberg vineyard in the Saar Valley

38 Fallowing means leaving a field 'fallow', i.e. without a crop, to rest the soil.

39 A tilth is a fine, friable layer of topsoil than can be easily worked.

crawler tractors or with winches on the sides of tractors, and vineyards whose grapes can be loaded onto transport right by the vineyard and taken directly back to their wineries. This has made these sites much more economical to farm and has preserved wine production on these unique riverbank sites.

Many sites will require both draining and sub-soiling before planting. Draining will usually be carried out before sub-soiling, in which case the sub-soiling tines must be set so that they do not disturb the drains. However, where there are known to be areas of compacted soil or there are known to be rocky areas, this may well take place in advance of draining. In this instance, any exposed rocks or very large stones will have to be removed from the site before further work can continue. If the site is to be irrigated, then it may well be at this stage that the basic framework of a water supply – mains and header pipes – is installed so that the soil is not disturbed at a later stage. This matter will be more fully covered in **Chapter 9 Irrigation.** If old vines have to be removed before new ones can be planted, then it is important to make sure that as many of the old roots as possible are removed and burnt or taken off the site and the site thoroughly ripped to disturb roots that cannot be pulled up. These sites may require a period of fallowing[38] – sometimes

planting with a green manure crop (see below) that can be ploughed back into the soil – which will help clean up the site and put some humus and fertility back into the soil. Even with sites that have not been previously planted with vines and where time allows, a season of fallowing during which time weeds can germinate and be sprayed off with weedkiller, followed by a green manure crop, is often a good idea and a way of getting a cleaner and healthier site before vines are planted. Sites with pernicious perennial weeds may well be sprayed before planting with hormone weedkillers (such as those containing 2,4–D) whose use in established vines would be either illegal, unwise, or both. If these particularly effective weedkillers are used, care must be taken that they do not drift onto and damage neighbouring vineyards. Growers farming organically and biodynamically, who cannot use weedkillers, may well go through two seasons of planting cover-crops and ploughing in to clean up their sites before planting.

After all of the above operations have taken place, sites will need cultivating in order to produce a smooth tilth[39] so that planting can take place. If farmyard manure, compost or fertilisers are needed, these are often applied before the site is ploughed so that they end up nearer to the rooting zone once ploughing has taken place (which turns the surface layer over and buries it).

Ploughpan

In some sites an impervious ploughpan, a layer of compacted soil, may have been formed by ploughing land at the same depth over several years. Where this occurs, crawler tractors with several deep ripping tines (usually between 500 mm and 900 mm long) mounted on the back will be used to rip through the soil from one side of the site to the other and then again at right angles, so that any hard compacted soil (or even sub-surface rock) is dislodged. Following this fairly brutal operation it may be necessary to remove any large pieces of rock before ploughing at a more conventional depth (200 mm–300 mm), after which normal cultivations can take place.

Drainage

As has already been mentioned, in some soils and in regions where there is ample spring and summer rainfall or where vines are to be irrigated, it may be necessary to drain the sites artificially. In soils with a high clay content and where the slope of the site and the planting orientation allows, a site may be drained with a mole drain – a torpedo shaped device which when dragged through the soil creates a self-supporting drain – even after vines have been established. Depending on the soil type, mole drains may last for several years but will eventually require renewing. However, in most soils that require drainage, a network of perforated plastic pipes will be installed below soil level in advance of planting. (Prior to the 1980s porous clay pipes, often called 'tile drains' were used.) The actual design of the drainage system – the depth of and the distance between the runs of pipes – will depend on many factors, soil type and annual rainfall being the most important. Typically though, pipes will be laid at 0.80–1.00 m depth and with 10 m between the lines of drains. A laser-guided drainage machine will be used to ensure that all pipes are laid so that they fall from high to low and that any drainage water drains away into a suitable watercourse.

Drainage is not a cheap option and can normally only be done before the site is planted. It is therefore wiser to drain a site before planting than to regret it afterwards. One of the reasons why the top estates on the left bank of the Gironde were for many years more successful than the right bank is that their natural drainage is better.

Drainage machine laying drains before planting

However, following the 1855 Bordeaux Classification (which only covered left bank properties), the fortunes of the top châteaux improved and their higher wine prices allowed them to install drainage in their vineyards. It is only in recent decades (in reality since the end of the 1939–45 war) that top right bank properties (Petrus, Lafleur, Cheval Blanc, Ausone etc) have been able to drain their vineyards to improve their growing conditions and with them their fortunes.

Green manures

Green manures (sometimes also called cover-crops) are crops specifically planted to clean up the soil by suppressing weeds and to provide organic matter which can be ploughed in, thus increasing the organic matter content and over time, raise the humus status. The exact type of cover-crop

Green manure helping improve soil structure and organic matter content

Crawler tractor with deep ripping tines for subsoiling

Young windbreak of Italian Alders

planted will differ for a wide variety of reasons, but might include mixed cereals such as wheat, barley, oats and rye, legumes such as mustard, peas, beans, vetches and clovers, root vegetables such as turnips or fodder radishes which root deeply and help break up the soil or maybe just fast-growing grasses. If sown well before planting, they will usually be left to grow to their maximum height before being ploughed in. (This technique can also be used in established vineyards, but care must be taken that they do not deprive the vine of moisture and nutrients.) Some plants such as brassicas (mustard, rape seed and oilseed radishes) can act as biofumigants, reducing the numbers of nematodes[40] which are virus vectors[41].

40 See more on nematodes in Chapter 12 – Pests of grapevine

41 Vectors are insects or other organisms (nematodes for instance) which may do little damage themselves, but act as carriers of diseases and viruses from one plant to another.

Windbreaks

Many vineyards suffer from wind exposure which cools the vines, reduces rates of growth and delays ripening. The vine is a sugar-producing plant and when its leaves are moving, its rate of photosynthesis is reduced. The stiller the leaves, the better the photosynthesis and therefore the better the ripening. Pre-planting tasks may well therefore include the establishment of a living (as opposed to an artificial) windbreak. By the time the vines start cropping, the windbreaks will be big enough to provide some shelter, getting better as the windbreaks grow and mature. Sometimes windbreaks are planted a year or two before the vines

are planted so that by the time the vines come into cropping, the windbreaks will have put on some growth and will be providing a good level of protection. Suitable types of tree for windbreaks will depend upon climate and locality. The basic rule is that the trees should be in leaf before the vines flower and remain in leaf until after harvesting. They should also not have too pervasive a root system (i.e. one that might deprive neighbouring vines of water and/or sustenance), they should be compact and upright, be capable of being lopped once they reach the correct height and have a root system deep and strong enough to prevent them being blown over in high winds once they get mature. An effective windbreak should filter the wind rather than stop it, the reason why impervious evergreen conifers with year-round foliage are not usually satisfactory. Evergreens will also be more likely than deciduous trees to harbour birds and their nests. A general rule of thumb is that a windbreak will provide protection over a distance of ten times its height i.e. a 10 m high windbreak of suitable trees will shelter a 100 m wide vineyard. Living windbreaks may require drip irrigation in dry regions, at least until they are established, will usually need protecting from rabbits, hares, deer etc and will require as much weed control (and indeed care and attention) as the vines they are intended to protect. Once established, a well-managed windbreak will be a useful tool in helping to improve the microclimate of the vines.

Alternatives to living windbreaks exist in the shape of synthetic netting and plastic strips of various types which can be erected along the windward side of the vineyard, but these will require a strong system of posts, wires and anchors if they are to remain intact when confronted by a winter gale. Larger vineyards, which cannot be protected with just one windbreak along the windward perimeter, may well require internal windbreaks, thus dividing the vines up into separate blocks. As long as the windbreaks are not too high and do not shade the vines to one side of them, this can be a very effective way of improving the microclimate. Natural hedges however, are usually the easiest (and visually the most attractive) option. Some vineyards have experimented with netting the vineyard completely – all sides and overhead – in an attempt to shelter the vines and exclude the birds. All-over netting has been shown to increase substantially the heat summation in wind-exposed vineyards, making for riper grapes and better wines. The netting used overhead must be chosen so that it does not block too much light and has a mesh sufficiently large enough to allow snow (if that is a possibility) to fall through it, rather than settling on top (which would bring the whole structure down).

Hail netting

Although relatively rare on vines (its use in soft fruit, stone fruit and citrus is much more widespread), netting against hail is found in regions where this problem is anticipated. North Italy and Mendoza in Argentina are examples. Netting is erected on a system of posts and wires that are (usually) independent of the vine's posts and wires, thus not impeding the annual vineyard work. The netting is almost always left up all year round as the expense and time taken to put it up and take it down would be prodigious and in addition, hail, although more common in midsummer, does not always stick to a convenient timetable. Netting needs to be strong enough to take the shock of what can be the considerable force of a hail storm, to be able to stop even quite small hailstones (a hailstone of 10 mm can easily damage a bunch of grapes), and yet allow enough light through so that the vine's growth is not impeded. In cooler climates, a light reduction of five per cent may be excessive; in warm/hot regions, fifteen per cent may be acceptable. The netting is usually arranged on a 'plough and furrow' system (in other words a series of Vs) with the bottom of the V in the middle of the row between the vines with a slight gap in-between the join. Thus, the hail hits the peak of the inverted V (which is directly above the row of vines) and slides down the sides into the furrow (which is directly over the centre line of the alleyway between the vines), through the gap and onto the vineyard floor. This gets rid of the hail and stops it settling on the net which would undoubtedly either break the net, strain the support system to destruction, or both. If the weave of the net is too tight and the region is one that can experience snow, then a heavy snowfall can also destroy the netting and its supports. There are other advantages in installing hail netting. In very hot regions it can provide a degree of shade;

Juice cartons keeping rabbits and weeds at bay

Rabbit fencing

that the upkeep of the netting is too time-consuming and if they lose a few vines to predators it's a price worth paying. However, on sites where rabbits, hares, rodents, badgers, deer, wild boar and any other land-based predators are known to be a problem, and where it is practical to do so, it is often more cost-effective (and undoubtedly more effective) to net the perimeter of the whole site. Netting against rabbits and hares needs to be at least 900 mm above ground with another 300 mm buried in the soil – 150 mm vertically and 150 mm angled out away from the vineyard. This will prevent rabbits digging their way in. Deer netting needs to be of a suitable height to keep out the type of deer in the area and a wire-mesh fence of between 1.75 m and 2.40 m in height will usually be required. Protection of sites against more robust predators – wild boar and badgers are examples – who view a fence as more of a challenge than a barrier, may well prove impossible with netting and local culling (where legal) the only option. Where perimeter netting is used, and the proposal is to use herbicides for weed control, then each vine will ideally also be protected with a 500 mm high spray-guard until the trunk of the vine is robust enough to take a herbicide spray, typically after two year's growth.

Where perimeter netting is not used against rabbits, hares and other small pests, it will usually be necessary to protect each vine with an individual guard. These are often made of netting (of a synthetic material or of metal chicken-wire mesh) or are solid-sided (some have ventilation holes in them) and made of plastic of some sort. There are many different designs: some merely slip over the top of the vines, others have an openable side panel, some are round, others square or triangular. In some countries, sleeves made from waxed card-board (they often seem to be misprinted milk or juice cartons) are popular. Whichever type is used, they all act like a mini-

in windy regions it will provide excellent growing conditions for the vines and improve ripeness levels; in all regions, the birds will be deterred, although additional side and end nets will usually be needed during the last 6–8 weeks of the growing season.

Protection against predators

In many situations perimeter netting is impractical or impossible owing to a wide variety of reasons. Many growers take the view

Vines in Quebec covered against the frost prior to the winter snows

Tender shoots damaged by frost

greenhouse which – depending on the weather conditions – will promote the growth of the young vines (or sometimes fry them). The atmosphere inside these guards can also get very humid and lead to fungal problems although the type with ventilation holes help overcome this. Most guards are very fiddly to use, require tying to a stake or cane and make the job of shoot selection and side-shooting much more difficult and costly. My preference is always for the perimeter netting solution, although for it to be effective over the long-term, needs looking after and patrolling regularly. Growers who do use individual plastic guards however will have the benefit of protection from weedkillers in the first two years should they choose this method of weed control and once the vines are established (say by year 3) the guards can be removed and assuming they haven't started to disintegrate from UV exposure, can be reused in another new vineyard.

Frost protection

Winter frost: Against extreme winter frosts i.e. frosts that occur in mid-winter usually between December and February in the northern hemisphere and where temperatures fall to below –20°C to –25°C, there is little protection that is practical. As has

been explained before, grafts can be earthed up for protection (*buttage*) but this offers none against the trunk and canes of a vine. When temperatures fall to these levels and the vine has some moisture in its woody parts (which naturally freezes), very substantial damage will result. Extreme years such as 1956 in Bordeaux saw huge areas completely destroyed by winter frost and replanting was at many properties the only remedy. Even prolonged periods of relatively mild winter frost will increase the incidence of problems such as Crown Gall (caused by the bacteria *Agrobacterium tumefaciens*) and *Eutypa lata*[42]. When temperatures fall to below –25°C, unprotected vines will often be killed. As has already been mentioned, in some parts of the world, vines will be laid on the ground and covered with soil or a protective fabric prior to snow arriving so that they are insulated against very deep winter temperatures.

Spring frost: Spring frosts, frosts that occur in April and May and even very occasionally in June (in the northern hemisphere) and where temperatures fall to between –1°C and –6°C, come in two types: advection and radiation frosts. An advection frost occurs when very cold, frost-carrying, air blows into a vineyard region (sometimes from a considerable distance away) and displaces warmer air. This type

42 See Chapter 11 – Diseases and viruses of grapevines, including trunk diseases for more on these and other diseases.

Early morning in a vineyard using irrigation for frost protection

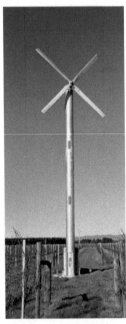

Frost windmill

there are several protective measures that can be taken.

Techniques of frost protection include various methods of heating the vineyard such as individual 5 litre paraffin wax candles (called *bougies* in France), burners powered by gas, or burners which use oil of one type or another. Burners using a mixture of waste sump-oil and paraffin (known as smudge pots) were once popular, but now seldom seen, owing to air pollution issues. In addition, there are always reports of growers resorting to burning hay and straw bales soaked with old oil and even lighting old car and lorry tyres if things get desperate. Whatever type of burner is used, they should be strategically placed throughout the vineyard and progressively lit as temperatures fall. There are also tractor mounted air-blast fans that blow hot air, heated by oil or gas, into the vineyard; tractor-powered fans that collect the cold air and blast it upwards into the warm air layer creating air circulation; and even electric heating cables strung along each row. Other techniques include large windmills that mix up the hot and cold air layers and in New Zealand, helicopters are used to hover over the vines and perform the same task as the windmills. Very often a vineyard owner will use two or more of the above – oil burners plus a frost-mill – depending on the severity of the problem.

Another technique, widely used in citrus and other soft fruits, involves spraying the vines with a fine mist of water as soon as the temperature falls to freezing. This water then freezes on the canes and buds and protects them from damage. Unlikely a technique as this might sound, where enough water is available, it is a fail-safe method. As water freezes, it releases a small amount of heat (known in scientific circles as the latent heat of freezing) and this heat, coupled with the igloo-effect of the layers of ice that form around the canes and buds, protects them from any damage. Once the

of frost is unusual in the spring and is more associated with winter conditions. The only technique to counter an advection frost is to avoid planting in a frost pocket.

The second type, a radiation frost, (also known as inversion frost) usually occurs on a clear, still, dry night when long-wave radiation from the ground to the air is not impeded by cloud cover or high concentrations of water vapour in the air, and rapid cooling of the air immediately around the vines takes place. This layer of cold air is then trapped beneath a layer of warmer air (hence the term inversion) and cannot escape. Typically, this cold, damaging layer will start almost at ground level and rise to between 15 m and 30 m above the vineyard floor. This type of frost is the one most likely to damage vines and is the one that can be more easily, although expensively, controlled.

The best protection against any type of spring frost is to select a site that is out of an area likely to be frosted or, if frost is a possibility, to plant the vineyard so that cold air can drain downhill towards an unplanted area where natural ventilation will allow the frost to be blown away from the vines. Where this is not possible, however,

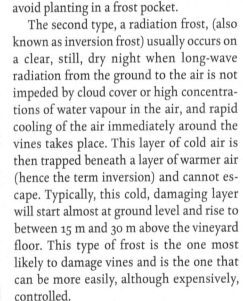

temperature has risen to above freezing, the water sprays can be turned off and the ice slowly melts as the day warms up. This technique – known as the aspersion technique – uses prodigious amounts of water (up to 25 mm–30 mm per night) and, if stored water is used (as opposed to water drawn from a river or canal), it is important that enough water is available to keep the sprays running for the maximum number of days and the maximum depth of frost that is likely to occur. It is no good running out of water in the last few hours of a 6-day frost period. It is also essential to make sure that the soil does not become waterlogged and poorly drained soils may well suffer in this respect. Given the amount of water this technique uses, it is not popular in regions where water is scarce and will be needed in the summer.

All of the above techniques might be termed active methods of frost protection which involve on-the-spot expenditure of manpower and materials at the time of the frost. Constant monitoring during likely frost periods is necessary and individual vineyards, which may well be some distance from habitation, will have to be visited and temperature readings taken throughout the night when a frost is anticipated, although remote monitoring systems which send texts and emails can at least warn one of impending frosts. There are however, a number of passive measures that can be taken to reduce, but perhaps not completely eliminate, frost damage.

The state of the vineyard alleyways is important in relation to frost danger. Clean, clear, bare earth will hold onto heat during the day – even more so if the earth is slightly damp – when compared to a vineyard covered with grass or other vegetation. This heat is then released to the atmosphere during the evening and night and helps ward off frost. An un-mown, long, grass sward which holds moisture is the worst state and likely to exacerbate frost

damage. Many growers with frost-prone vineyards will burn off all vegetation on the vineyard floor with a contact weedkiller in the early Spring, allowing it to grow back after the frost-dangerous weeks are over. Having vines trained to a high-wire system such as GDC, *Sylvoz* or Blondin[43] will help as the lowest temperatures are always nearest the soil. The temperature can be up to 1°C higher at 1.50 m above ground level than at 0.75 m. Vines that are pruned later in the spring will have a delayed bud-burst and frost damage may well be reduced, so pruning frost-prone areas last may help. Some growers will leave additional canes on their vines, so-called 'sacrifice canes', leaving them to carry a crop if frost-damage has occurred; removing them if there has been no frost damage. Planting varieties that are naturally late in breaking out of dormancy (such as Meunier) may also be advantageous. Some varieties also show a marked tendency to produce viable secondary flowers after the primary ones have been frosted (Pinot Noir and Chardonnay for instance) and growing these in frost-prone areas might be considered. Other aids include sprays based upon liquid acrylic polymer (Anti-Stress, Frost Protect, Frost Shield and widely used in citrus plantations) that can be sprayed on the vines and protects them from a low level of frost. Overhead covers and nets (perhaps used against hail and/or birds) will also offer substantial protection from frost. In some regions, insurance against frost can also be taken out (as it can against hail) but this tends to be an expensive option.

Vineyard layout

Deciding exactly how to lay out the vineyard – which ways the rows should run, how long the rows should be and where access roads are – will depend on several different factors and no two sites are the same. However, there is usually one outstanding feature (such as the site is bounded by neighbouring

43 See Chapter 7 – Training, trellising, and pruning for descriptions of these training systems.

Snow-covered wide terraces in a German vineyard with two rows per terrace

vineyards that have their rows running in one direction or the site has one strategically positioned boundary that makes a certain row orientation obvious) that makes the decision a simple one.

In general terms, rows should be planted so that they run up and down a slope (at least where it is at an angle greater than about 10 degrees) as otherwise tractors and machinery will tend to slip sideways. Rows should ideally run north-south unless there are local reasons why a more easterly or westerly-facing vineyard is favoured. In the northern hemisphere, some growers prefer to plant their rows aligned to a more south-westerly direction to catch more afternoon sun, the theory being that by then the vineyard will have warmed up and will stay warm into the early evening. Others prefer a more south-easterly orientation on the grounds that the rows will warm up more quickly, drying out the night-time dew. In other situations, rows orientated at 90 degrees to the prevailing wind may well provide for better growing conditions as cooling winds are stopped by the first few rows of vines they encounter. For vineyards in the southern hemisphere, these row orientations are reversed.

On a purely practical and financial basis,

the best ways to align the rows is parallel to the longest site boundary or to an existing feature such as a roadway, hedge or neighbouring property. This will ensure that the rows are as long as they can be (within reason) and the number of row ends, each of which will require a straining post and anchor, is minimised. This will also minimise the number of short rows which require lots of extra turns when mowing or spraying. The layout of almost every vineyard is a compromise between what is the absolute best for the vines and practical considerations such as the way the site naturally slopes or an existing boundary. It is better to plant straight up and down a slope even though the rows may face almost west, rather than plant them facing due south and have problems with machinery slipping across the slope for the rest of the lifetime of the vineyard.

Steep sloping sites can be terraced in a variety of different ways. Many narrow terraces, where access is only possible on foot, can still be seen all over the (mainly old) world and often produce great wines. However, the cost of working these sites is high and, unless the value of the grapes is also high, makes them relatively uneconomic. The design of terraces that can be accessed by machinery – width, turning spaces etc – will depend on local site factors and mechanical requirements. A well-terraced sloping site on which wheeled or crawler (caterpillar) tractors can be used, is preferable from an access and economics point-of-view, to a very steep slope where only winch-drawn implements or hand-work can be used, even though as the rows may run at right-angles to the slope and therefore possibly also to the sun, some slight diminution of quality may be experienced. On some extremely steep sites (especially in Germany, Austria and Switzerland) all kinds of ingenious aerial ropeways and monorail installations can be seen which facilitate access to the vines for looking after them during the growing season and at harvest time for the removal of the crop to the winery.

Sites on slopes, with dips and hollows in the ground, with bends and curves in them or with a generally irregular shape, will require careful planning if the optimum arrangement of rows is to be achieved. Posts in hollows will be dragged out of the ground by the tension of the wires if the hollow is too deep and they may require additional ground anchors to stop this happening. Rows that are not absolutely straight will tend to be pulled over to one side and in time, the posts may lean and eventually collapse.

The question of the length of individual rows, whether to break them up into blocks, whether to provide internal walkways for personnel, areas for loading grapes at harvest time and sheds for equipment storage, are all matters that individual circumstances will dictate. Vineyards farmed using large (standard width) tractors which can trail large-capacity sprayers and other farm machinery and where harvesting machines are the norm, will naturally need wide headlands (the space between the ends of the rows and the vineyard boundary) in which to turn around. In these instances, land lost to cropping will be paid for by increased efficiencies in working the site. On sites with very expensive land, where every possible square metre must be given over to cropping, narrow tractors, sometimes articulated in the middle, or crawler tractors, both of which can more-or-less turn in their own length, will be preferred. In many French vineyards, straddle tractors – *enjambeur* – that are high enough to straddle one or two rows at a time, will be used so that row widths can be kept to a minimum and planting densities to a maximum. Straddle tractors allow for rows as narrow as 800 mm and plant densities as high as 15,000 vines-ha.

Very long rows – much over 200 m – are best avoided as there are limits to the distance over which wire can be strained tight

Straddle tractor – enjambeur

and rows this length will need very firm end-posts (anchor-posts) and anchors. If long rows are chosen, decreasing the distance between intermediate posts from say 6 m to 5 m will help keep wires tight (as there will be less sag when subjected to a heavy crop), although of course this increases the number of posts in the vineyard and therefore the cost of establishment. Long rows are not liked by vineyard personnel purely for access reasons. When you have to walk to the middle of a 400 m row in order to start pruning or retrieve your jacket (or your lunch) which you left on a post, you soon learn to appreciate shorter rows. This situation can be helped by the provision of walkways running across the vineyard, although straining posts then have to be provided in the middle of the rows. Very long rows can also be difficult for harvesters which, given a heavy crop, may well fill up before the end of the row is reached, necessitating an unprofitable trip to the end of the row to disgorge the harvest. It is best to work out the optimum row length for the site, divide the site up into workable-sized blocks and keep to one variety/clone/rootstock combination per block. This will make it easier to treat each block as a separate unit as different variety/clone/

rootstock may require different spray and fertiliser treatments or harvesting at different times.

Although most vines in modern vineyards are planted in rows and trained to posts and wire, there are of course some systems of planting where each vine is supported by an individual stake without interconnecting wires. Whilst this system is less frequently found today, there are some regions where it is commonly practiced. Many very steep sites (the Mosel is a prime example) have vines planted to single poles and each vine is an individual entity. Having worked on very steep vineyards with vines trained on wires, the attractions of a single-pole system are compelling. As most of the work in these vineyards is manual (tractors cannot be used on such steep slopes) all operations in a site with posts and wires require one to work downhill from top to bottom, (working uphill is virtually impossible), then to climb back up to the top in order to start all over again. On sites without wires, workers can start at the top and traverse the site from side to side, eventually ending up at the bottom. There is then only one climb to the top before going home! Other planting systems *Gobelet* for instance, where vines are grown as individual bushes with only a short post used to support the trunk, will also commonly be found on steep hillside sites and on sites where mechanical access is not possible.

Dormant vines in cold storage awaiting planting

Planting vines

The timing of planting will depend on the site and the climate of the region. In warm areas, where winter and spring frosts are unlikely to be a problem, vines can be planted at any time from early winter to late spring. Vines are usually stored by nurserymen in cold-stores until distributed and should arrive at the vineyard site in a dormant state. They can be kept unplanted in cool, moist conditions a week or two until required for planting, but are best planted soon after they arrive. If spring frosts are likely to be a problem, planting is best delayed until this danger is past. Vines planted as late as May or even June (in the northern hemisphere) will usually catch up with vines planted in March or April of the same year, provided that there is enough moisture in the soil.

Planting vines is actually a relatively simple operation that belies the amount of work required once planting has taken place. Vines usually require preparing before they are planted (although many supplying nurseries will do this for the grower). Each vine needs to have its top-growth cut back to one bud and in the case of some of the planting systems outlined below, the roots trimmed quite severely so that they do not fold back as they are placed into the ground. The top quarter of the vine has usually been re-waxed by the nursery using soft grafting wax to seal in the moisture, protect the vine from fungal attack and from drying out. Trimming the roots very short (shorter than 50 mm) always seems to make the vines slower to get off the mark after planting and most growers prefer to use a planting system that allows the roots

GPS guided Wagner vine planting machine

to be left at around 100 mm long. Vines must be kept moist and out of direct sunshine whilst waiting to be planted and, in warm regions, may well require watering after planting. Sometimes peat, and occasionally fertiliser, is placed into the planting hole before planting. The use of planting dips containing mycorrhizal fungi is also becoming more widespread, the aim being to get the vine's roots interacting with the soil as quickly as possible. Some planting machines will deliver water and/or fertiliser into the planting hole as the vine is planted.

Where the vines are to be hand planted, it will be necessary to mark out every position of every vine prior to planting if accuracy and orderliness is required. Sometimes only the positions of the ends of the rows are marked and then the distance between each vine is gauged by stretching a wire fitted with markers at the position where a vine is to be planted between the end posts. Some growers merely use a tape measure and mark each vine position with a planting cane. Whichever system is adopted, it is more efficient and makes life much easier (and looks much tidier), if vines follow an exact grid pattern.

There are a number of different ways of

actually putting the vines into the ground: a spade can be used to dig a good sized hole for well-rooted vines; a large dibber[44] can be employed to make a hole for each vine; a water-lance which digs a hole with water pressure is a very quick method where soil conditions are right. Vines can also be machine planted with a laser-guided or GPS guided planting machine which can plant at very accurate row widths and intervine distances and which also require little or no pre-planting marking out – a considerable cost and time-saving benefit. Whichever system is used, and the actual method will depend on the scale of the operation, the state of the site and the condition of the soil, each vine needs (ideally) to be firmly placed into the ground with as little airspace as possible around the roots and with the roots nicely spread out and not pointing upwards. With machine planted vines this is not always possible (much will depend on how the site has been prepared and the type and moisture state of the soil), but the advantages of rapid, cost-effective and accurate planting without the need to mark the site out, more than compensate for a planting machine's heavy-handedness. Vines are fairly robust plants and unless mistreated

44 For non-gardeners, the term 'dibber' may be unknown. A dibber is merely a piece of wood (often an old spade or fork handle) with a pointed end or a purpose-made metal implement that can be used to make a hole of a suitable size for planting.

Care of vines after planting

Once planted, vines will lay dormant for a while, maybe a week or two, but will then, depending on the temperature, start to show signs of life. Buds will start to push and small green shoots appear. At this stage, their training can start.

There are several techniques for training young vines and each individual grower will take a different view on the best way to do this. Growers in dry regions, who do not mind their vines establishing slowly (and who do not wish to install expensive trellis-work in the first year), will often leave the vine almost completely alone for the summer after planting allowing them to de-velop multiple shoots which can be trimmed back in their first winter. The only care they would give the vine is to keep the weeds away from the vine, to cultivate the rows, tie the new shoots up if they are in danger of falling onto the soil and if necessary, protect the vines from pests and diseases.

Other growers will take the view that the vines need training (up something) as soon as possible. In this case, bamboo canes, wooden or metal stakes or strings tied from the vine itself up to a wire are options. Whatever support system is used, the aim is the same: to start the task of growing a single sturdy shoot which will eventually become the trunk and from which will come the first fruiting cane or canes. The young vine will often produce a number of small shoots to start with and all of these, except for one, need to be removed by rubbing or cutting off. The shoot selected should be the one that is the best positioned (and is often not the most strongly growing shoot) which will grow straight up from the rootstock and eventually turn into the trunk. Once se-lected (all other buds/shoots having been rubbed off), this single shoot is encouraged to grow straight and true by removing the side-shoots, thus concentrating all the vine's energy into it. This work will con-

prior to planting (left to dry out or exposed to too much light or too high temperatures) will almost always survive and grow into mature plants, given enough water and care and attention in their first few years.

Grafted vines should always be planted at the correct depth and ideally the graft should be about 50 mm above the level of the soil. The danger of planting a vine with the graft too near to the ground is that soil might build up against the graft (vines often settle deeper in their planting holes after they have been planted) and some-times unwanted (and very vigorous) shoots will grow from the rootstock variety and/or roots will grow from the scion variety at the point of the graft. These roots, coming from the *vinifera* scion, will of course not be resis-tant to *Phylloxera*. The actual height of the graft above the soil level will also need to take account of the method of weed control, and growers using mechanical weed hoes often prefer their vines to be a little bit higher out of the ground, than growers using herbicides. This is because many mechanical hoes create a mound (or hill) of earth around the vine which can lead to scion roots as outlined above.

tinue until the autumn, by which time the new vine may well have grown to a considerable height. 1.5–2 m of new growth in vineyards without a water shortage is quite usual.

The cane, as it grows, needs tying to whatever stake is chosen for it to grow up. There are many different types of tie ranging from simple paper-covered metal twist-ties, to sophisticated clipping and fastening devices designed to speed up the task. Whatever type of tie is used, it should be able to stretch and expand as the cane turns into the stem, and the stem turns into the trunk. If individual rabbit guards have been used, these will have to be raised (or undone – it depends on the exact design of the guard) and then replaced. This extra work is one of the reasons against using this type of rabbit protection in favour of the whole-vineyard perimeter netting approach.

At the end of the first growing season, before the vine sheds its leaves, and especially if the leaves are wet and there is a strong wind, the strain will be too much and – if unsupported – the vine and the stake are likely to end up on the ground. Installing the whole trellis system within the first few weeks after the vines are planted is the ideal solution, in which case the individual vine stakes can be permanently tied to the first wire and become part of the overall trellis. The training of the vine in its first season should continue for as long as the vine needs it. Subsequent training will depend upon the training and trellising system used and will be dealt with in **Chapter 7 – Trellising, training and pruning**.

There is no doubt that time and energy and inevitably money spent on vine training in the first year of a vine's life is seldom wasted and pays dividends in years to come. Vines that grow up twisted and untrained, with shoots emerging from the grafts at odd angles, often cause problems in future years, especially if mechanical hoes and swing-arm mowers for weed control are to be used.

Weed control in vines

Keeping weeds under control is undoubtedly one of the most important tasks when looking after newly planted vines. Weeds will use up water and nutrients to the detriment of the young vine's needs and in addition, will physically crowd out, and sometimes even smother, the vine. This will often give rise to increased disease problems as damp weed foliage impacts upon the tender vine. The exact method used to keep newly planted vineyards free of weeds will depend on several factors and will often (but not always) be the same as those used in a grower's established vineyards. There are mechanical means such as hoeing or strimming by hand; cultivating with a hoe or rotary cultivator, both of which would be mounted onto a tractor; or even burning off with a gas-powered flame-thrower. One can also use mulches, both natural and synthetic. Herbicides are another, widely used and very effective, option. Alternatively a permanent grass strip can be left under the vine which can be kept mown, although this latter method will normally only be used when the vines are established and have a guaranteed water supply. All of the above options are also those available to growers once the vineyard is established and starts cropping and therefore the two phases really need to be considered together before a weed control system is adopted.

Hand-hoeing is both time consuming (and therefore expensive) and a misdirected hoe easily damages a young vine. A wound to the side of the young trunk, whilst not perhaps causing the vine an immediate problem, often gives rise to a lesion that in years to come may well prove fatal if something like Crown Gall infects the wound. Wounds from hoeing and strimming can also lead to an increased incidence of trunk diseases. Young grafts are quite tender and again, a sharp knock with a hoe will often destroy the vine. Strimming is usually a

*Mechanical undervine
weeder*

solution only where the number of vines to be weeded is small and is, again, time consuming and very likely to damage the tender first year's growth. With both of these methods, there is also the fact that they are usually used *after* the weeds have grown, by which time some of the water and/or nutrients will have been taken from the vine. Burning weeds with a gas-powered flame thrower is a little-used technique (although it appears to be popular with organic growers) and cannot be used on young vines with tender stems. In established vines it is effective, although needs to be carried out regularly if the whole vineyard is not to be set on fire!

Tractor mounted under-vine cultivators and mowers – of which there are many different types – work by having a blade, rotating cultivator or mower which swings out and away from the vine when a sensor activates a hydraulic or spring-loaded arm to which the implement is fitted. This method of weed control requires each vine to be attached securely to a fairly stout support otherwise, over time and with a poorly tensioned swing-arm, the vine will be rocked and loosened in the ground. In addition, the swing arm's sensor tends to strike the vine itself as often as it strikes the vine's support stake which can result in bruising and lesions which can give rise to problems in later years. The number of times a tractor will need to pass through the vineyard to keep it weed-free using a mechanical hoe will depend on several factors, climate being the most obvious. In regions with summer rainfall, where weeds will not immediately wilt and die upon being uprooted, it might be necessary to pass through the vineyard between six and eight times a season. In hotter climates, this might be reduced to three to four passes. If the tractor is equipped with a mid-mounted hoe and rear-mounted mower or cultivator, then at least two tasks can be undertaken at the same time.

Mulches, be they natural such as chipped tree bark, peat, chopped straw or other organic matter; or inert such as stone or crushed shells; or synthetic, such as polyethylene film or plastic woven material laid in a continuous strip, have their advantages. In the case of loose natural mulches, these will rot down in time and increase the soil's humus levels, although may lead to nutrient imbalances which will require addressing. However, they will not give 100 per cent cover and many weeds will grow through and emerge above the mulch and additional mulching to smother them (or manual weed removal) will be often be needed during the growing season. However, they will conserve moisture, are natural and can be visually and aesthetically attractive. In some hot regions a technique known as 'mow and throw' (or 'slash and throw') is adopted (more usually in older cropping vines, rather than in young ones) where whatever grows in the middle of the rows (grasses and weeds) is cut by a mower which then throws the material beneath the vines.

Continuous plastic or fabric mulches, laid in strips of around 800 mm wide with the edges buried into the soil (leaving around 400 mm visible) can be laid before the vines are planted and, using a water lance or dibber type of planting system, the vines can be planted through it. This type of mulch provides almost perfect weed control, retains almost all the available moisture and is, after installing, a labour-free option. It is however, unsuitable in soils with high stone contents (as the plastic mulch will get torn) and can be damaged by rodents and birds, both seeking sustenance beneath it. It is also a relatively expensive option. Depending on the type of material selected, it will eventually start to break down and fragment and unless ripped up and removed from the site, will start to blow about and collect in unsightly heaps in field corners and up against hedges and fences. Removing it is at least a one-off job, even though a time-consuming and costly one. After removal, some other sort of weed control system will then be needed.

The final option – that of chemical weed control – is one used in many different types of crop and brings both benefits and risks. The benefits are simplicity and economy. If carried out at the right time and using the right product(s) for the anticipated weed spectrum, a single tank-mix spray containing a residual weedkiller (which stays in the soil and stops weed seedlings from germinating) and a contact or systemic weedkiller (the two are not necessarily the same) which either burns off (the contact type) or kills off by penetrating the plant's root system (the systemic type) will keep the soil clean of weeds – at least as clean as it needs to be which may not be 100 per cent devoid of weed growth – throughout the growing season. In rich soils and in cooler (and therefore moister) regions, especially where there may have been previous crops where weed control was not a high priority (pasture for instance), a second spray in mid-summer – a week or two after flowering is usually a good time – may be needed. Often a winter clean-up spray will be applied to burn off any weeds that have escaped so that the soil is clean throughout the dormant season. Weed-killers are very cost-effective as their application is usually quick and they use less tractor and man-hours than mechanical means. Although the materials look expensive when compared to other systems, using chemicals is in fact a cheaper option – hence the reason that their use is worldwide and widespread. Growers who use impervious plastic planting sleeves or tubes around each vine can use chemical weedkillers in the first two years with much less worry about damage, as each vine is protected.

The disadvantage of using chemicals for weed control is that if used incorrectly they can easily damage and/or kill the vine (especially in the first year or so). Often growers will use a very light approach in the year of planting (perhaps just a residual and a mild contact weedkiller, both at half-strength) coupled with some hand weeding/strimming before continuing with a full programme of weedkillers in year two and later. In some soils, mainly those with low levels of organic matter, residual weedkillers may be less successful. Over time, the continued use of chemical weedkillers may result in lower levels of humus in the soil, although this can be addressed by occasional mulching. Another disadvantage of herbicides is that they are not always considered to be the most environmentally friendly of products. Therefore, for reasons of being seen to be 'sustainable', non-chemical methods of weed control are sometimes to be preferred. Champagne, for example, is hoping to end the use of all her-bicides in the vineyard by 2025.

Chapter 7
Trellising, training and pruning

Gobelet pruned vines in the Eden Valley, Australia

Trellising, training and pruning

Almost all vines are trellised and trained to a greater or lesser extent. Some vineyards – a very few and usually only for promotional or historic reasons – are planted without a fixed row width or equal vine spacings which is known as *en foule*[45] training. However, although this might once have been traditional in some regions, it is far from practical today where tractors have almost entirely replaced horses and mules. Most grapevines today are grown in rows and many are trained onto wires so that they can be: accessed by both labour and machinery; treated against pests and diseases; and harvested cleanly and easily. How they are trained and trellised will depend, as does so much with vines, on the usual suspects: climate, site, soil type, wine type/quality, mechanisation, economics, *appellation* rules and – of course – personal preference.

Training and trellising are required for a vine in a modern vineyard for the following reasons:

- To provide a physical support for the vine so that machines such as sprayers and harvesters can work efficiently and without damaging the vine.
- To provide the best environment (microclimate) for the health of the vine and the crop.
- To make access for hand operations possible.
- To produce grapes of the right quality and right quantity and at the correct cost.
- To make sure the vineyard keeps cropping for several decades.

At its most basic, a training and trellising system can consist of nothing more than a single short stake to which the vine is tied. The advantages of this are simplicity and cheapness; the disadvantages are that the vine's annual canes and fruit will be near (or more probably on) the ground, spraying against pests and diseases will be more difficult, and harvesting slower. There are, however, plenty of vineyards planted like this with vines trained to a simple *Gobelet* system and whilst this system may limit the degree to which vineyard operations can be

45 *En foule* means 'in a crowd' and is a system of random planting where any dead vines are replaced by layering. This can result in a vineyard with up to 25,000 vines per hectare.

Scott Henry pruned vines in New Zealand. Rows 2.30 m wide and 1.20 m between vines

High-wire Sylvoz trained vine with both spurs and hanging canes

mechanised, it is no limit to the quality or quantity of wine produced.

At their most extensive (and expensive), training and trellising systems such as the overhead pergola systems – *Parral* and *Tendone,* and Geneva Double Curtain (GDC) and Lyre systems – require very strong end supports and anchors, an intermediate post every 4 m to 6 m and up to 10 wires per row. In addition, there may be cross bars, T bars, Y bars and supports and assemblies of all shapes and sizes. In short, the cost of training and trellising a hectare of vines can range from a few hundred dollars to over $40,000. What then, determines the choice of a trellising, training and pruning system?

Pruning – an overview

Except where vines are minimally pruned (of which more later) grapevines are pruned annually during dormancy (winter pruning) in order to remove the old fruiting wood and replace it with freshly grown wood for the coming season. This allows growers to assess each vine individually and to leave the correct amount of fruiting wood for the anticipated yield and so that the vine will be balanced in its efforts to grow canes and produce fruit. A vine that is carrying too little fruiting wood will tend to grow too vigorously with the result that both crop and canopy will be shaded; a vine that is carrying too much fruiting wood will be less likely to ripen that crop and may not be able to provide itself with enough reserves for its long-term health. The concept of the balanced vine is one that sounds good in theory. In practice it is an elusive quarry and sometimes difficult to capture.

The fruiting ability of a vine is very variable and cropping levels are notoriously difficult to predict. In cooler regions where weather conditions tend to be more changeable and summer rainfall unpredictable, differences in yields between vintages are often as much as 50 per cent, even though the vines have been left with exactly the same amount of fruiting wood after pruning. In warmer regions, and where irrigation is not available, very hot years and lack of water will also have the effect of reducing the crop. Frost in the spring will also of course have a detrimental effect upon cropping levels.

The grape vine is very responsive to

weather. In terms of yield, it is influenced by the conditions in both the year of the harvest AND the year preceding it when the fruiting buds are being formed. Warm, dry weather in the previous year, with good wood ripening weather in the autumn, will result in the buds being well charged with flower potential for the coming year. An early harvest (the result of an early spring and a warm summer) will allow the vine to build up good levels of reserves (starches and sugars) in its woody parts[46] which will improve its chances of starting off the next year in good heart. In the year of cropping, a warm spring will start the annual cycle early and by flowering, the vine will be in the best possible condition to pollinate the maximum number of flowers. In addition, bunches will be able to expand and bunch weights will be at the top end of expectations. In these circumstances, the vine is likely to produce a maximum crop. The opposite conditions, with poor weather during the previous year (especially when there may have been a heavy crop), followed by a hard winter, will leave a vine with a much lower cropping potential for the coming season. A cold, late spring and poor flowering conditions will result in the vines suffering from *coulure* or *miller-andage*[47] and yields will be much reduced. In many instances the grower, having left

what was judged at the time to be the correct level of fruiting wood for the yield required, is often caught out by weather conditions beyond his or her control. Whilst crop thinning can help reduce a potentially heavy yield, there is nothing that can be done to compensate for a light crop.

Canopy management

During the growing season, the task of the grower is to manage the vine from winter pruning, through flowering and fruit-set and throughout the summer until harvest. All this can be summarised under the term canopy management. The science of canopy management has achieved prominence in viticultural circles since the publication in 1991 of *Sunlight into Wine*, the seminal work on the subject by Richard Smart and Mike Robinson. The subject was of course not new in 1991. Smart and Robinson, in the forward to the book, acknowledge the University of California's Centennial Symposium in 1980 as a starting point for their researches and the book is really a summary of their work, firstly in New Zealand (working for NZ's Ministry of Agriculture) and latterly around the world. Prior to 1980, Professor Nelson Shaulis (under whom Smart studied for his PhD), working at Cornell University's New York State Agricultural experimental station in Geneva NY, worked on canopy design for the production of Concord grapes, inventing the GDC training system in the process, and is considered to be the founding-father of canopy management. Professor Dr Alain Carbonneau who was first at Bordeaux University and then Montpelier University and who devised the Lyre training system, was also a major influence on modern canopy management practices.

To summarise such an essential aspect of modern viticulture in a few paragraphs is well-nigh impossible and what follows is but a flavour of the subject. Much of Smart

46 Roots, trunk, spurs and/or canes.

47 The terms *coulure* and *miller-andage* are more fully explained in Chapter 14 – Nutritional disorders and other viticultural problems.

Two arm spur-pruned vines at the start of the growing season

and Robinson's work is still controversial, especially in traditional regions where low-vigour, balanced vineyards are a fact of everyday viticultural life, and Smart's missionary zeal to change traditional practices is not universally admired!

Sunlight Into Wine is concerned with the *'indirect relationship between sunlight and wine – that is, the effect of exposure of grape clusters (bunches) and leaves on wine quality'* and attempts to answer the following question: *'does a vine need to be struggling or low-yielding to make high quality wine, or, perhaps is it necessary for the leaves and clusters to be well exposed to the sun?'*

The management of the grapevine canopy (as set out in *Sunlight into Wine*) covers the following activities:

Winter pruning which determines the number of buds left on the vine for future cropping.

Shoot thinning (or de-suckering) which alters the number of shoots which grow into maturity.

Summer pruning (hedging) which shortens the annual growth of canes, but may cause laterals to grow.

Shoot devigoration which aims to reduce shoot length and leaf area.

Leaf removal which opens up the canopy in the grape zone.

Trellis system changes which are designed to increase or decrease the canopy surface area and adjust the canopy density for light exposure.

The four rules of canopy management are:

1. Measurement of canopy quality.
2. Pruning the vine in relation to the weight of wood produced by the vine.
3. Trellis design.
4. Annual canopy management.

1. Measurement of canopy quality

The quality of the canopy can be assessed by measuring the following parameters: the canopy gaps, size and colour of leaves, canopy density, fruit exposure, shoot length, lateral growth and the growing tips. By scoring the canopy for each of the above, an overall assessment can be reached and the question *'is enough light reaching the grapes and canes'* can be answered. The vineyard can then be categorised as having low, medium or high vigour.

2. Pruning the vine in relation to the weight of wood produced by the vine

The weight of wood produced by a vine during the year is a good indicator of the vigour of the vine. By weighing all the wood produced by say 10 average sized vines and then relating it to the weight of grapes produced by the same number of vines, a ratio of yield of grapes to weight of wood produced can be found. This is known as the Ravaz Index[48]. For each category of vineyard – low, moderate or high vigour – a Ravaz Index level can be set and the vines pruned accordingly. As a very rough guide (and much more detailed discussion can be found in *Sunlight Into Wine*), the crop should weigh between 5 and 10 times the weight of the prunings (Ravaz Index of 5–10). If the crop weighs more than 12 times the weight of the prunings, the vines are very low in vigour i.e. they have not produced enough wood (or they have been over-cropped); and if the crop weighs less than 3 times the weight of the prunings, the vines are over-vigorous, having produced too much wood and not enough fruit.

3. Trellis design

The design of the trellis is central to achieving a balanced vine. In low vigour vineyards, trellis design may be extremely simple. In moderate and high vigour vineyards, trel-

48 Louis Ravaz was a noted French viticulturalist of the 19th and early 20th centuries who wrote several important books on viticulture.

lises such as the multi-cane Vertically Shoot Positioned (VSP), Scott Henry, Te Kauwhata Two Tier (TK2T), GDL, Lyre and *Sylvoz* systems may be needed[49].

4. Annual canopy management

During the growing season (after winter pruning), operations such as shoot removal prior to flowering, topping (hedging) of the vines to increase yield and remove excess growth (summer pruning), removal of bunches to reduce crop load (green harvesting or crop thinning) and leaf removal to open up the canopy and improve light penetration can all be practiced to improve grape quality.

High vigour vineyards

In high vigour vineyards, additional techniques may be employed to bring the vines back into balance:

• Restriction of water supply to reduce shoot growth (only achievable in dry regions where vines are irrigated).
• Cover-crops can be grown in the vineyard alleyways to reduce the amount of water and nutrients available to the vines and thereby reduce vigour.
• The density of vines can be increased to create greater competition for water and nutrients.
• Root pruning to reduce root area so that water and nutrient uptake is reduced.

High-density or low-density vineyards?

The density of vines in a vineyard can vary widely: some have over 15,000 vines-ha, others less than 800 vines-ha. Why? What effect does this have upon quality and quantity and what are the practical and financial considerations?

Subject to certain upper yield limits, for any given site, soil, variety/clone/rootstock combination and nutritional state and taking one vintage and its weather in isolation, the crop from a hectare of land depends not on the density of vines, but on the number of fruiting buds spread over that hectare, *however those buds are trained and trellised.* Each bud has within it the same potential to fruit and each of the several inflorescences within the winter bud has the same potential to be pollinated and produce the same number of bunches of grapes. In theory then, it matters not whether those buds are carried by a smaller number of vines or a larger number. In other words, for a given yield, a vine, properly pruned and bearing the correct number of buds for the space it occupies will provide that yield. The 'charge' of buds, as it is often called, is usually expressed in the number of retained buds per square metre of space that the vine occupies.

In practice of course, this is not entirely true. Somewhat perversely, a vineyard with a low vine density (smaller number of vines per hectare) might well be bearing a larger crop than one with a high-density (higher number of vines per hectare), owing to the prevailing climate, the variety being grown, and the rainfall or irrigation situation. This is because a vine's capacity for production in vigorous soils and in warm conditions (where low-density planting is common) and where vines are well supplied with water and nutrients is *higher.* In cooler conditions with leaner, less well-fed soils, especially in dry regions where irrigation is not allowed and where high-density planting is more common, a vine's capacity for production is *lower.*

Climate – and all the factors that stem from differences in climate – will probably be the most important factor in a grower's decision on vine density. In general terms, as has been explained before, high-density plantings are preferred in cooler climates, as individual vines will be placed under less strain, will ripen less fruit per vine more easily (even though cropping levels *per hectare* might be the same) and will be more likely to produce and ripen fruit even in poor seasons. The root system of a vine occupying say 2.60 m² (2 m wide rows x 1.30 m between vines = 3,846 vines-ha)[50] will probably occupy all the space available to it and be in competition with the roots from its neighbouring vines, thus helping keep vigour under control. A vine that is less strained will have more reserves of starches and sugars per kilogramme of crop, will be able to put more into producing fruiting ability for the coming season, and will produce better pollen and fertilise its flowers more easily. Also in cooler climates, where more square area of leaf is required to ripen a kilogramme of grapes than in warm/hot climates, canopy management is easier if cane-pruned VSP systems (Guyot, Pendlebogen, Scott Henry, Smart-Dyson etc) are used as the leaf-wall will be narrower (or thinner), the fruit will be nearer to the (weaker) sun and protective sprays will get onto the grapes more easily. In cool climates, where summer rainfall is common and irrigation is not normally needed (or provided), it is worth remembering that the amount of water falling is the same whatever the number of vines per hectare are planted. Therefore, vines in high-density vineyards will receive less water per vine than in low-density ones and their roots will be in competition for resources thus helping with vigour control.

In warmer climates, where less square area of leaf is required to ripen a kilogramme of grapes, the soil warms up more quickly and vines will be less likely to suffer from cold spells at budburst and flowering. This puts less strain on the vine and allows incoming starches and sugars to be put to use supporting a higher crop level per vine, rather than having to replace reserves in the structure of the vine. As the sunshine is stronger and the incoming heat and light greater, the vine's canopy can be denser and

the grapes nearer to the centre of the row more shaded, yet still obtaining enough heat and light. Vines in warm/hot climates are also more likely to be irrigated which enables an individual vine to be more easily fed with water and nutrients, despite not having a root system the same size as the square area it occupies. An irrigated vine occupying 10 m² (4 m x 2.50 m) will not need all of this area for its root system.

Discounting any *appellation* regulations, one of the most important considerations a grower needs to take into account is their individual economic situation and how quickly a yield is required from a newly planted vineyard. A vineyard with a high vine density will come into full cropping sooner than a low vine density as there is much less permanent wood to grow and train before fruiting can begin. What this means in reality is that a 2 m x 1.30 m VSP trained vineyard (3,846 vines-ha @ 2.60 m² per vine) might provide a 35 per cent crop in year two, a 75 per cent crop in year three and a 100 per cent crop in year four and all subsequent years. The converse of this is say a 4 m x 2.50 m GDC trained vineyard (1,000 vines-ha @ 10 m² per vine) which might not produce any crop for three years and a full crop not before year six. Against this must be set the capital investment in the vineyard and the amount of work (labour and machinery hours) required to get to the stage of full cropping. This is likely to be much higher for the quicker yielding high-density vineyard because of the higher number of vines to buy and look after and the many more posts and wires to buy and install.

Of course, by year six, both vineyards will be fully cropping producing – in theory – the same yield as each other (given the same level of buds per m² left after pruning) and the establishment costs purely a balance sheet issue. The total cropping level of the two examples above, taken over the complete life of the vines, the posts and the wirework, could well be exactly the same

50 When stating planting distances in this format, the width of the row will come first, and the distance between the vines within the row, second.

Single pole trained vines
1.00 m x 1.00 m on the
Mosel

sity vineyard has 5,000 metres run of row per hectare, whereas the low-density one only 2,500. In other words, a tractor and its driver and the sprayer or mower towed behind it will cover twice as much vineyard in the day in the low-density, wide-rowed vineyard for the same expense of capital, labour and fuel. A grape harvester will also be more productive on wider rows, again because it will cover more area for any given row distance, and in addition, a larger harvester will carry a bigger tonnage of grapes before it has to stop and empty. Other operations such as pruning and canopy management, whilst perhaps not showing quite the saving as the examples above (as each vine needs some individual treatment) will still be cheaper *per hectare* in low-density vineyards. Sprayers can have larger tanks, thus needing less stoppage time for filling up with water and materials (if the water supply is far away, or a slow supply, filling up can take longer than emptying the contents over the vines) and with the lower run of row length per hectare, will show very considerable cost savings.

and an additional two or three years onto the life of a vineyard that is expected to last 40 or 50 years is neither here nor there. However, expensive vineyard land needs to be financed and a return may therefore be required as soon as possible. In these situations, a high-density, earlier yielding system may well be preferred. There is also the added human factor which growers planting vineyards for the first time will meet. When the decision has been made to buy land and establish a vineyard, would you rather have your crop in three years or six? The answer is often the former which means adopting a high-density, close-planted system.

Another factor that has an economic basis is the degree of mechanisation of the vineyard work. In general terms, wider rows allow for standard-width tractors and machinery to be used. These are produced in much larger quantities and are therefore often cheaper to buy and run than their cut-down narrow versions. Added to this is the fact that the number of running metres of vineyard is pro-rata the row width, thus favouring low-density, wide-rowed vineyards. In the two examples above, the high-den-

Other considerations for vine density and training system might include the requirements of the climate and/or site – terraces, steeply sloping sites, a requirement for shade, and the demands of a particular harvesting machine – all of which could possibly dictate row width and training style. On sites with potential frost problems it might be prudent to have the vines trained higher off the ground to minimise damage. Growers who need to use bird netting may well find that a VSP system provides better support for the nets. Many New Zealand vineyards have adopted the Lyre system (which is in effect a double VSP system) of training precisely for this reason as the nets can rest on top of the canopy and be self-supporting.

Row width

One of the first decisions a vineyard owner will have to take is: 'what row width should I adopt?' Whilst this decision may sound easy, upon it hangs a whole variety of long-lasting consequences. In many instances, row width is determined by machinery requirements: existing tractors are suited to a 2 m row width; the grower wishes to be able to drive down every row in the farm's truck (or 'ute' as I soon learnt to call them in New Zealand), thus dictating a 2.80 m to 3 m row width; or the picking contractor requires a 3.50 m row width for the harvester.

Effectively, the row width is determined by the width of the largest piece of machinery which is required to fit down the row: too narrow and vines will be damaged; too wide and fruiting potential will be lost and land will be wasted. In cooler regions, where vines are often cane-pruned and trained to VSP systems, narrow vineyard tractors, (which can be wheeled or crawler/caterpillar tractors), will be used which can fit down rows as narrow as 1.00 m. In some vineyard regions, straddle tractors (*enjambeur*) which are raised over the rows of vines (versions are available that fit over one or two rows at once) allow for planting widths as narrow as 800 m with planting densities as high as 15,000 vines-ha. Narrow vineyard versions of standard tractors are very common in most mainstream European growing regions, but less-commonly found in the new world (although this is changing). Here they will almost certainly not be manufactured and demand may be so small so as to make clearance of the safety requirements for an individual country uneconomic for manufacturers and/or importers. These very narrow tractors are usually around 800 mm – 1.00 m wide thus allowing for row widths of around 1.50 m – 1.75 m.

The next type of vineyard tractors are

How wide is your tractor?

those of around 1.25 m –1.50 m wide, usually standard farm tractors which have had narrow axles (and sometimes slimmer tyres) fitted to reduce their width, which will work in row widths of between 2 m and 2.50 m (the actual width will depend very much on the trellising/training system, of which more later). Standard tractors will range in width from around 1.75 m to 2.50 m requiring even wider row widths (and therefore lower planting densities). The actual width of a tractor is also determined by the settings of the wheels upon the axles (on most tractors the wheels can be moved inwards or outwards to suit row-crop work[51]) and on the type of tyres used (some soil-types may need wider tyres in order to spread the load out over a greater surface area). Whatever tractor is used, all other machinery, whether trailed behind the tractor, such as sprayers, mowers, cultivators etc, or self-propelled such as harvesters, must also be taken into account when determining row width. One thing is certain, too narrow a row width for the tractor or machinery will result in damage to the vines.

Having determined the width of the widest piece of machinery and/or equipment that will be used down the row, the actual row width will depend upon the

51 Row-crops, such as vegetables or fruits, are grown in rows with gaps left at exact intervals down which a tractor's wheels may pass without damaging the crop.

VSP trained vines 2.30 m row width and 1.30 m in the row at Hush Heath, Kent, UK.

52 The 'crown' of a vine is, on cane-pruned vines, where the trunk ends and the annual fruiting canes emerge. It is generally just below the lowest (i.e. the fruiting) wire.

training system used. Cane or spur-pruned VSP systems will have a canopy that extends either side of the centre line of the row by around 350 mm, which when added to say a 1.30 m wide tractor, would give you a practical row width of 2 m (1.30 m + 2 x 350 mm). A pruning system such as a high-trained spur-pruned single-wire system with a downward hanging canopy which extended by say 700 mm on each side of the centre line of the row, would result in a row width of nearer to 2.70 m (1.3 m + 2 x 700 mm). A Lyre or GDC system might extend 1.00 m each side of the centre line of the row which would result in a row width of nearer 3.30 m (1.30 m + 2 x 1.00 m), although in this instance, a wider tractor would probably be used (which would result in a wider row). These are the simple calculations that need to be made to allow sufficient access for machinery without damaging the vine and the canopy, yet not having too wide a row which simply wastes space and lowers the potential cropping ability of the vineyard.

Intervine distance and vine densities

For any given row width, the intervine dis-

tance sets the vine density. The closer together the vines are planted, the higher the density; the farther apart, the lower the density. Apart from *en foule* vineyards already mentioned, where random planting can produce vine densities of up to 25,000 vines-ha, the shortest intervine distance would be around 0.80 m which, with a 0.80 m row width, would produce a vine density of 15,625 vines-ha. At the other end of the spectrum, the planting distance within the row is determined by the natural limits of the vine itself. The intervine distance for *cane-pruned* vines is determined by the length of ripe cane that the vine can grow and then, at pruning, can be laid down on the fruiting wires. With a height to the crown[52] of the plant of around 0.75 m and an overall leaf-wall height of 1.50 m, canes will seldom be more than 0.75 m long and therefore, when laid down on either side of the vine, occupy a distance greater than 1.50 m. Any longer than this and there is the danger that the buds at the extremities (having been the last to be produced and therefore the youngest) will not be fully ripe and the buds may not be very fruitful. A more usual planting distance for cane-pruned vines would be 1.20 m – 1.40 m. With a row width of say 2 m, this gives rise to a density of between 4,167 and 3,571 vines-ha. This is fairly typical vineyard density for double-Guyot VSP trained vines.

With *spur-pruned* vines planted on extensive systems such as Lyre, GDC or overhead pergolas, vines can be spaced as far apart in the row as 3 m with row widths of up to 4 m. These very extreme (but not unheard-of) spacings would give rise to a planting density of 833 vines-ha, almost nineteen times less vines per hectare than in a traditional Burgundy vineyard. One might well ask: why such a disparity?

The main reason why vines are closely spaced is that *in very general terms* if an individual vine is carrying a smaller crop, it will find it easier to ripen its fruit. Therefore, for a yield of say 10 tonnes-ha (approx. 70 hl-ha) each vine in a vineyard with 10,000 vines-ha (1 m x 1 m) would be bearing 1 kg of fruit; in a vineyard with say 4,000 vines-ha (2 m x 1.25 m) each vine would be bearing 2.50 kg of grapes; and in a vineyard with only 1,000 vines-ha (4 m x 2.50 m), each vine would be carrying 10 kg of fruit. This variation of fruit per individual vine ought not to have a bearing upon fruit quality, but in practice it often does, especially in marginal climates where the weather in the final weeks of ripening can be unpredictable.

A vine's capacity to ripen a given level of fruit depends on many factors, but quality of site (quality of light and heat levels) is the most important. Therefore, in cooler regions, where good weather in the ripening weeks cannot always be guaranteed and light and heat levels may vary widely from vintage to vintage, vineyards with higher vine densities are favoured. Conversely, in hot regions, where light and heat levels are (a) higher (b) more guaranteed and (c) where vines are irrigated, then extensive, low-density systems will be favoured. In addition, vines in warmer, irrigated regions will be able to carry a much greater crop per vine than in cooler regions and wide spaced spur-pruned systems are capable of bearing much higher crop levels. In hot regions where vines are dry-farmed, then wide spacing may still be preferred in order to be able to use the same equipment, even though each vine may be carrying a relatively small crop. Other reasons why low-density systems with wide rows are preferred are that where land is cheaper, there is no need to make use of every last square metre and wide tractors, large capacity sprayers, wide mowers and big harvesters are more economical to use and grapes can be produced at a much lower cost per tonne. Wide rows also make for a lower cost vineyard as the number of posts, end assemblies, anchors, vines, vine stakes and vine guards are lower, as is the amount of labour needed to look

3 m wide rows and spur-pruned vines in an irrigated, warm climate Australian vineyard

after the vines in their first few years. Then throughout the life of the vineyard, wide rows are cheaper to farm – the run of row per hectare is directly related to the row width – and by using large, efficient equipment, the cost of production per tonne of grapes is significantly lower.

There is also the quality argument that says that if each vine produces less fruit, the quality of that fruit – and therefore the wine made from it – will be better. This view is very much a traditional old-world view and of course good – even very good wines – can come from wide spaced vines, each of which individually is bearing a much greater crop. The question of wine quality has much more to do with overall levels of crop for any given site and season, rather than yield per vine. As low-density, wide-rowed vineyards (a) cost less per hectare to establish, (b) cost less per hectare to farm and (c) in the right climate can produce higher yields, they tend to be favoured by growers trying to produce grapes/wines at least possible cost. Therefore, whilst it is true to say that the wine from wide-rowed vineyards might be in general be lower in quality than wine from narrow-rowed vineyards it is NOT because the rows are wide. It is because for economic reasons, low-cost producers favour wide

High capacity grape harvester in one row, discharging into a gondola in the adjacent row

rows and low-density vineyards.

Trellis height

The overall height of the trellis work – and therefore by inference the length of the canes – will depend to a certain extent upon the requirements of the vine itself. In cooler climates, grapes need around 12–15 leaves per cane in order to ripen their crop. In warmer regions (because the sun is more powerful) they need fewer. On VSP systems used in cooler climates, it is sensible to train the vines at least some way off the ground so that the grapes are not splashed by earth when it rains as *Phytophthora* rot, caused by mud getting onto the skin of the grape, is often found on fruit close to the ground. Having a good gap beneath the vines also allows for good air-drainage which will help dry out both fruit and foliage, making for healthier conditions and less *Botrytis* at harvest time.

Many traditionalists hold the view that fruit ripens more easily the nearer it is (within reason) to the ground as heat stored during the day in the top-soil will be released to the atmosphere once the sun goes down. How scientific this is, is open to question and there are probably more con-siderations that go against having the fruit very near to the ground than for having it at a more human-convenient height. Most manual operations – pruning, side shoot-ing, leaf work, canopy management and last (but by no means least), harvesting – are much easier if the lowest wire (commonly known as the fruiting wire) is higher rather than lower. Having said that, on *vignes basses* (low vines) in traditional regions such as Burgundy, overall trellis heights of 1.20 m with fruiting wires at 300 mm are not uncommon, making for a very back-break-ing harvest. This height would, however, allow compact and space saving straddle tractors to be used and would also allow for very narrow rows and therefore high vine densities.

The overall height of the trellis should also show some consideration towards the width of the rows and it is generally not ad-visable to have the top of the leaf-wall higher than the rows are wide. Some would advise that the height of the vines is no more than 80–85 per cent of the row width. If this ratio is exceeded, then some shading of the lower portions of the trelliswork will result. How damaging this is depends on orientation of the vineyard, the size of the crop, the height of the fruiting wire off the ground and the overall quality of the site and climate. In very warm, well-sheltered sites, with the vines carrying what might be termed a mid-range crop of say 10 tonnes-ha (about 70 hl-ha), little harm will be done if the overall trellis height exceeds the row width by up to 25 per cent. In vineyards with wider rows, overall heights can be greater. Typical *vignes hautes* (high vines) – although rarer in France than in most other European countries – would usually have an overall height of 1.60 m, with the fruiting wire at 600 mm (giving a leaf-wall height of around 1 m) and therefore a row width of around 1.50 m – 2 m. These examples are again for VSP systems, either cane-pruned or spur-pruned. Slightly wider rows say up to 2.50 m wide, might well have an overall height of 2 m, a fruiting wire at 1 m and a leaf-wall of 1 m high.

On wider rows (2.50 m and greater) the question of vine height is less important as the leaf area is not provided in a single-plane leaf-wall but spread over several planes (such as is found with Lyre and GDC) or by allowing the vine to sprawl and grow multiple shoots. Overall heights on wide-rowed vines are seldom over 2 m, except where the vines are trained overhead (*Parral, Tendone, Pergola* etc). Much higher and no machine or person would be able to pick the grapes (although picking with tall ladders from tree-trained vines in Italy and Portugal is still a common sight).

Height of fruiting wood

This aspect is really covered above, except to say that most machine harvesters require the fruit to be no lower than 400 mm from the ground and will have a problem picking it if it is above 1.75 m from the ground. Obviously if the grapes are hand-harvested, the constraints on fruit levels are those of the patience and/or backs of your pickers at the lower end and the height of the ladders you buy them at the upper!

Downward trained vines

With several training systems, the vines are encouraged to grow, in part or in whole, in a downward direction, rather than in the upward (vertical) direction of VSP systems. Grapevines prefer sending their shoots upwards – the vine is after all by nature a climbing plant – and there is plenty of evidence to show that although upward growing shoots are more vigorous, the number of potential flowers created within buds on canes growing upwards is greater. In some situations, this fact might be of relevance and a good reason to train vines vertically. However, vine shoots that can be persuaded

Cane-pruned vine just after bud-burst.

to grow downwards – as can be found on systems such as GDC, *Sylvoz* and (the lower canes or spurs of) Scott Henry – will have shorter internodes, smaller leaves, be less vigorous and have a lower number of potential flowers within their buds. However, the shorter internodes and lower vigour will make the leaf-wall less dense and therefore allow more light onto the fruit and potential fruiting wood, thus compensating for the lower fruiting potential of the buds. The grower has to decide: is excess vigour likely to be more of a problem than low yield or vice versa?

Types of pruning

There are in essence two types of pruning: cane pruning and spur pruning. The thorny question of whether vines are to be pruned using cane or spur pruning is – yet again – one that cannot be settled simply and where the philosophy of the grower or the grower's economic circumstances may well be the deciding factor.

Cane pruning

Cane pruning is generally known as Guyot pruning after Frenchman Dr Jules Guyot (1807–1872) who, in 1860, wrote *Culture de*

Two cane 'Pendlebogen' pruned vine

53 Apical dominance is the tendency of buds most distant from the trunk of the vine to break first and be stronger than those nearer the trunk. Some varieties are more prone to this, which is why some respond better to spur, rather than cane pruning – or vice versa.

la vigne et vinification in which were set out (apparently for the first time), the principles behind pruning. The essential point about cane pruning, also known as replacement cane pruning, is that the fruiting buds for the coming season are all positioned on a cane (as opposed to being on spurs). A cane (sometimes also known as a rod) is a length of fruiting wood which bears a number of fruiting buds. The exact number of buds on a cane might be as few as 4 or as many as 12. This will depend on inter-vine distances, variety of vine, internode distances and – above all – the crop level aimed for. As well as leaving the canes on the vine, one (or sometimes two) short two-bud stubs are left (called thumbs) to provide a starting point for the replacement canes for the following year. The number of canes per vine is also variable and there are single-cane, double-cane and even four-cane Guyot systems.

The cane(s) selected will have grown in the season prior to the one in which it is retained for fruiting and will be selected primarily for position on the vine, but length, diameter, number of buds and overall condition will also be considerations. The length of any one cane (and therefore the maximum number of buds that that cane can possibly bear) is dictated by the

height of the leaf-wall and the length to which canes have been trimmed during summer pruning in the previous growing season. Its position of attachment to the 'parent' part of the vine is important for the long-term maintenance of the vine. Ideally the cane or canes should come from around the crown of the plant: not too near the ground (although in desperation a very low shoot can be selected) and – more importantly – not too high. The selection of a cane that emerges from too far above the crown only makes matters worse in the future and reduces the yielding potential of that vine.

The advantages of cane pruning are: that all the buds for the current year's cropping are borne on one-year old canes with the buds well away from older, more disease-prone, wood; the buds are all evenly spaced at about the right distance apart so that annual shoots are not too crowded; and the flexibility of the cane means that it can be bent in an arch (if the training system allows), thus interrupting the sap flow and counteracting the natural proclivity of some varieties towards apical dominance[53]. Cane pruning also spreads the fruiting buds along the cane, which overcomes the problem of varieties which have blind (or less fruitful) buds near to the point at which the cane emerges from the previous year's wood. One disadvantage of cane pruning is that the number of retained fruiting buds along a given metre of row length is restricted to the number of buds on any given length of cane, multiplied by the number of canes retained and there is no opportunity to increase this number. (Leaving multiple canes is not a solution to this as they would then be too near to one another and the annual shoots too crowded together.) Another disadvantage is that it is a time-consuming pruning system, requiring knowledgeable pruners who can see not only the vine's needs for the immediate fruiting season, but also for the next year and even the year after that. Not only is the actual pruning i.e.

the selecting and cutting of the canes time-consuming, but the after-pruning actions – cleaning up the cane, cutting out last year's wood and disposing of it and bending and/or tying down the cane(s) – are also time consuming. Apart from the use of powered secateurs[54], it is very difficult to mechanise cane pruning. Canes are also more prone to frost damage, the buds not being near a body of older wood which can partially protect them. As a counter to this, growers in frost-prone regions will sometimes leave one or two more canes (sacrifice canes) than they actually need and then cut them off once the danger of spring frost is over if no frost damage has been suffered.

Growers in regions where yield restrictions are in force or where lower yields are required may sometimes remove every other bud on a cane by trimming them off as they prune, thus halving the fruiting potential of the vine, but spacing out the canes so that each will get more exposure to light and air. This is known as *ébourgeonnage* in France and is commonly seen in good Bordeaux vineyards where yields are restricted.

Cane pruning – conclusions

In cooler winegrowing regions, where high-density vineyards trained to VSP systems are common, cane pruning is considered the norm. Yields can be controlled by shortening canes or by removing every other bud along a given length of cane. The leaf-wall with VSP cane-pruned systems is usually quite thin, meaning that fruit, shoot and bud exposure is good and fungicides and insecticides can easily reach the interior of the canopy. Vine densities may well be high – even very high – and this means a considerable investment in vines and trelliswork. However, earlier yields and better fruit quality go a long way to offset these additional costs.

Cane-pruned vine with every other bud removed at Vieux Château Certan.

Spur pruning

Spur pruning differs from cane pruning in that the fruiting buds for the coming year are borne on spurs, not canes. A spur is a short stub of wood usually holding a number of very short pieces of cane, each bearing one or more fruit buds. A spur on a mature vine may be carrying a minimum of 2 buds and perhaps a maximum of 10 – this latter number would be extreme. The exact number will be the grower's decision and will depend on the desired yield. Spurs are carried on older wood known as a cordon which is in effect an extension of the vine's trunk which has usually been trained horizontally.

The advantages of spur pruning are: that for any given metre of row length, the number of retained fruiting buds is (almost always) higher – sometimes very much higher – than the number retained on a cane pruning system; the number of buds can also be increased or decreased at every annual pruning depending on the yield required; the larger yield per metre of row length permits row widths to be greater for any given yield when compared to cane pruning, thus allowing the use of wider (and therefore more efficient) machinery; and the larger number of buds per vine –

54 Secateurs can be electric (powered by a battery pack), pneumatic (powered by a tractor-mounted compressor) or hydraulic (powered by tractor-mounted oil pump).

Inverted L-shaped spur-pruned, cordon-trained vines, planted at 2.80 m x 2.50 m in the Napa Valley

Established spurs on a cordon-trained vine

and therefore the larger number of shoots and bunches – tends to depress the overall vigour of the vine, useful in irrigated high-vigour vineyards.

Other important advantages are economic: many spur pruning systems can be partially mechanised and pre-pruning machines can greatly reduce the man-hours required for pruning; the spurs can be trimmed and cleaned up very easily; unwanted wood can be left to fall to the ground; there is no bending or tying-down of canes; spur-pruned systems can be pruned with less-experienced staff than cane pruning; and fruiting buds left on spurs are also better protected against frost

damage, being nearer a body of older wood. With such a list of advantages, one might be left wondering why anyone did anything else but spur-pruning!

The disadvantages of spur pruning are: that on varieties prone to having blind buds on the first few buds away from the older wood, yields will be lower (this can, however, be counteracted by leaving a greater number of spurs or spurs carrying an extra bud or two); buds near the older wood will also be more prone to fungal diseases as the older wood becomes a repository for diseases; unless some shoot-selection is carried out early in the season, shoots, canes and fruit will be too crowded and the canopy too dense; and the final, and probably the most important disadvantage, the cropping potential will be too high for vines in regions with the possibility of adverse weather during the ripening period.

Spur pruning – conclusions

In warmer regions, where sunshine is more abundant and more consistent and irrigation is very often available, spur pruning is the norm. The reasons are that the ability to expand and contract the potential yield at each pruning is valuable and the job of pruning can often be partially mechanised. Spur-pruned systems are also in essence easier systems to learn how to prune and quicker to carry out, both of which have positive financial implications. There are some notable exceptions to this general rule such as the *Cordon de Royat* system used in Champagne. Here, local tradition, a desire for relatively high yields, coupled with the ability of spur pruning to safeguard against spring frosts (owing to the greater body of permanent wood left) means it is a practical choice.

Minimal pruning

Having written at length about different

pruning systems, it may come as a surprise to some to know that there is a pruning system which requires virtually no (or at least very little) pruning at all. This is known as minimal or zero pruning. Left to its own devices, a vine will climb whatever structure is nearest (be it a tree or a trellis) expanding by dividing each year, fruiting on the new wood and carrying on until such time as it reaches its own physical limit of expansion. At that point, the vine's annual extension growth on each cane is very small and fruiting is confined to a large number of very short canes. This is how vines grew in their natural state for the millennia before man tamed them for his use. One might think that a grapevine left to its own devices would eventually get so large that it would exceed its own powers and die. In fact, the opposite is true. Pruning actually harms a vine and tends to weaken rather than strengthen it. Unpruned vines are in fact quite happy left to their own devices.

The commercial use of minimal pruning was developed in Australia for growing Sultana (Thompson Seedless) grapes for dried fruit production. Vines were trained to a simple single high-wire system and trained into long cordons and left to grow, develop side-shoots and expand at will. Only when they touched the ground were they mechanically trimmed at the bottom or when the alleyways between the vines became impassable. It was found that a good crop – often comparable and sometimes exceeding that on trained vines – was produced. Bunches were smaller, as were the individual berries, than on conventionally pruned vines and ripening could be up to two weeks later. However, in warm climates, where the weather is still hot at harvest time, this delay was of little concern. Acid levels in some vine varieties were higher and this was found to be a positive advantage in some instances (Merlot for example which in warm climates is often low in acidity). Minimally pruned vines can be machine harvested

Two-armed spur-pruned vine with well spaced shoots. Evidence of shoot removal shortly after budburst.

and, apart from the summer trimming, there was almost no annual canopy work. The main advantage of this system is fairly obvious: cost.

The disadvantages are: that the vines occupy slightly more space for a given yield; are more prone to powdery mildew (which likes shaded canopies) and other fungal diseases; and some insect problems (mealy bug for instance) are more prevalent. There can also be problems of shaded canopies and shaded fruit if there is too much water which promotes excessive growth. In very dry regions, where most of the summer water is supplied via an irrigation system, this problem is less likely as growth can be managed by keeping the vine short of water. It is generally therefore, not a system for cooler, wetter regions where fungal diseases are typical (although I have seen it in use in Marlborough, New Zealand).

To pretend that this system of growing grapes is widespread would be wrong (although every time I read about its multiple advantages I wonder why not). However, it will be encountered all over the world and it is a system that some growers find useful. I have seen successful minimally pruned vineyards growing Merlot at Swanson Vineyards in Rutherford, California and on Sauvignon Blanc in Montana's Brancot vineyard in Marlborough, New Zealand – two very climatically different regions.

Different trellising, training and pruning systems

The list of trellising, training and pruning systems below is very general and not at all exhaustive. Many regions will have their own local versions of standard systems which differ slightly and individual growers will also adapt systems to suit their own machinery and sites. There are also many experimental systems – Lincoln Canopy, Te Kauwhata Two Tier (TKTT), Ruakura Twin Two Tier Trellis etc – which are rarely found in commercial viticulture (or even outside New Zealand). For a fuller description of most of the systems below, plus a few more, consult both The Oxford Companion to Wine (under Training Systems) and Sunlight into Wine. See bibliography for details.

Trellising, training and pruning systems – summary

The best trellising, training and pruning system for any particular vineyard will be the one that satisfies several criteria: climate and site must be taken into account; the question of investment and return will be important, as will anticipated yield and wine quality; local *appellation* regulations may also play a part in some regions; and tractor and machinery sizes may be a deciding factor on row width. Growers will often keep to the same row width and pruning system for simplicity and economy of operation (to have some vineyards on one row width and system and others on another can be very inefficient) and often the simplest systems are the best. What simple systems lack in fine tuning and complexity and inability to respond to every nuance of the weather conditions, they make up in ease (and therefore cost) of installation and of working. In cooler regions, narrow VSP systems will suit high-quality wine production. In warm/hot irrigated regions where high

---

Ballerina: A spur-pruned system, similar to Smart-Dyson (see below), but with about 1/3rd of the canopy growing vertically and 2/3rds growing downwards.

Basket: Describes cane-pruned vines where no wires are used and annual canes are secured back to a single pole forming a general basket shape. Much the same as single-pole training.

Blondin: High-wire spur-pruned single curtain system used in the UK and similar to one half of a GDC system. Named after the first person to cross the Niagara Falls on a (single-wire) tightrope.

Bush: Free-standing spur-pruned system without support wires. Similar to Gobelet.

Chablis: French cane-pruned system used with Chardonnay in Champagne, usually consisting of four or five short, bud-bearing, canes.

Cordon: General term to describe a length of spur-carrying older wood. Also name for spur-pruned system used in Champagne on Pinot Noir.

Cordon de Royat: French spur-pruned system found in Champagne and Burgundy: It is usually a one-sided cordon (in an inverted L shape) carrying between 4 and 8 spurs depending on appellation rules. Two-sided cordons are not unknown.

Dopplebogen: The term means double-bow in German and is the same as single-pole.

Espalier: General term to describe multi-layer spur-pruned systems. Not usually found in vineyards, but often seen on walls and fences in gardens and with apples and pears.

Éventail: French for fan and describes a system using four or five short canes (perhaps 5-6 buds each). Seen in Burgundy.

Flachbogen: German term for flat single-cane or two-cane cane pruning.

GDC: Geneva Double Curtain. Spur-pruned divided canopy system originally developed at Geneva in New York State for the variety Concord. Foliage hangs down in two curtains. Can be machine harvested.

Gobelet: French term for bush trained spur-pruned vines. So-called because of the goblet shape made by the fruiting arms.

Guyot: The overall name for many different types of cane-pruned vines.

Guyot Double: French term for two-cane cane pruning.

Guyot Simple: French term for single-cane cane pruning.

Halb-bogen: German term for semi-arched single-cane or double-cane cane pruning.

Head trained: Head trained vines are grown without wires and are in effect high-trained bush or Gobelet vines. Trained onto single posts with annual canes hanging down towards (and often touching) the ground. Many of the old dry farmed vineyards in California are head trained where the system is known as California Sprawl.

Kniffin: General term to describe wide-spaced cane-pruned systems. There are 2-cane, 4-cane and even 6-cane versions. Canes are trained downwards and annual shoots more-or-less find their own space. Popular in Canadian vineyards. Also known as umbrella systems.

Lenz-Moser: High-trained, wide spaced cane-pruned system used in Austria and Germany (and named after the grower of the same name).

Lyre: Cane or spur-pruned system with two VSP leaf-walls coming off one vine. Looks like a lyre (a musical instrument if you were not quite sure) if viewed end-on. Can be retrofitted onto standard VSP vines if rows wide enough and machinery narrow enough.

Minimal: Also known as zero pruning. System where vines are left unpruned and fruit on short canes. Vines only trimmed back when they get out of hand.

Pergola: General term given to any overhead pruning system. Usually (but not necessarily) spur-pruned. Also known as an arbour (or arbor) system.

Parral: South American overhead spur-pruned system. Similar to Tendone.

Pendlebogen: German term for steeply arched (pendulum arched) double-cane cane pruning.

Single-pole: From the German Einzel-pfahl. Cane-pruned vines trained to a single pole (or stake) without connecting wires. Canes often trained in a heart-shape. Common on steep hillside sites.

Scott Henry: Cane or spur-pruned system with four canes or four cordons where the annual growth from the top wood is trained vertically and from the bottom wood downwards. Popular in New Zealand. Named after grower from Oregon.

Smart-Dyson: Similar to Scott Henry except that annual wood comes from two opposed cordons rather than four, with both upward and downward facing spurs. Named after viticulturalist Richard Smart and grape grower John Dyson who first used it in his vineyards in Gilroy, California.

Sylvoz: High-trained combination cane and spur trained system where several short canes (6-10 bud) hang down from the cordon and are tied to a wire. There is also a variant (the Casara system) where the hanging canes hang free.

Tendone: Italian overhead system. Usually (but not always) spur-pruned. Similar to Parral system used in Argentina. Also used in northern Portugal. Useful if you want to grow another crop beneath (winter vegetables or early spring greens).

Te Kauwhata 2 Tier: This strange sounding beast is a two-tier spur-pruned system (developed in NZ at a place called Te Kauwhata). In effect you end up with two VSP systems (albeit with very short leaf-walls) growing one above the other. Not used widely – although I have seen some in Gisborne. Also known as TK2T.

VSP: Vertically Shoot Positioned. General term used to describe any pruning system (cane or spur-pruned) where the annual canes are trained vertically and attached to wires. Very common and used worldwide in all climates. Requires more canopy management than most, but gives the best quality crop.

Tendone trained vines in the Alto Adige.

yields are possible, low-density spur-pruned systems are usually appropriate.

Materials used in trellising, training and pruning systems

There are a very wide variety of materials used for trellising and training vines. For each individual vine, the choices range from just a piece of string tied to the vine itself and up to the first wire, a short bamboo cane, a plastic or metal stake or a small wooden post either round or sawn square. Each vine ideally needs support until it gets to the stage where its trunk is self-supporting which is generally in three to five years after planting.

For vineyard support posts, the choice is huge. These range from a cleft oak or other hardwood stake to which an individual vine will be tied (such as with basic bush-trained vines) which might with luck last 10-15 years, through to pre-formed galvanised steel posts, complete with built-in hooks to take wires, which have a 30 year guarantee, but will effectively last as long as the vines can be expected to crop.

Timber is probably still the most common material for support posts (although steel is making strong inroads). Untreated stakes made from a hardwood such as oak, acacia or sweet-chestnut (*Castanea sativa*), are commonly seen. These might last as long as 15 or even 20 years, but would require replacing at least once during the life of the vineyard. For narrow-row systems where overall trellis heights are not more than say 1.25 m, posts of 1.75 m will be quite adequate (although how much of a stake needs burying in the ground will depend very much on soil conditions, length of row and whether the site is exposed to sidewinds or not.) An alternative, where longer, more robust supports are required, would be round (as opposed to cleft) posts made from pressure-treated softwood – usually pine of some sort – which, if the timber has been properly kiln-dried and correctly treated, should last 15–20 years. Again, these would require replacing during the life of the vineyard. For systems with overall trellis heights of 1.50 or more requiring posts of between 2 m and 3 m long, pressure-treated softwood is probably the favourite, most cost-effective choice. The durability of a wooden post – natural or treated – is directly related to the amount of durable and rot-proof heartwood in the centre of the post. The heartwood expands with the cross-sectional area of the post, rather than its diameter and a post with a diameter of 75 mm has approximately twice the strength (breaking force) of one with a diameter of 50 mm, owing to the much greater volume of heartwood it contains. One should also know that the strength (by which one generally means the resistance to lateral pressure) of a post, is determined by the depth of post in the ground and that an additional 100 mm in the ground – say 750 mm rather than 650 mm – increases this strength much more than it would appear at face value.

In vineyards with long rows, where the horizontal strength of the system is mainly a function of the tension under which the connecting wires are held, the end-posts

and anchors need to be very good and the distance between intermediate posts not too far apart – about 6 m is the maximum. The greater the distance the intermediate posts are apart, the more the wires will sag and the more downward pressure there will be placed upon the wires. This will result in more strain being exerted upon the end-posts and anchors and will often lead to the end-posts starting to lean in. It often makes for a better trellising system if the inter-post distance is slightly less (say 4 vines rather than 5) which allows one to use a slightly smaller diameter and shorter length post, rather than having a greater inter-post distance which puts more downward pressure on the wires.

Posts required for end-posts, which need to be a little bit longer (as they are generally put in the ground at a 20°–40° angle which in effect shortens their vertical height), are usually at least 50 per cent if not 100 per cent larger in diameter than the posts used as intermediates. A really good end-post and anchor system, with wires kept well tensioned, will often extend the life of weaker intermediates for many years as those intermediates are less subject to side-ways movement which tends to weaken and eventually snap them. Old railway sleepers used to be a favourite for end-posts when they were readily (and cheaply) available

and local supplies of other types of timber are often seen.

Timber posts drive into the ground well and in most soils, perhaps excluding soils with a lot of stones, flints or rocks, instal-ling them does not present a problem. This is despite the fact that a post of say 200 mm diameter, driven into the soil by 800 mm will be displacing a considerable volume of earth. Timber is of course easy to nail into and knocking in staples and hooks to secure and/or hold wires just requires a hammer (although on a large scale, battery or air-as-sisted nail-guns are more popular). By the same token, as timber dries out with age, nails and staples tend to come loose and in established vineyards trellised with wooden posts, replacing nails (and of course posts) is one of the regular winter tasks.

In some regions, posts made of re-cycled plastic are quite popular, the reason often given is that they are less likely to be struck by lightning than metal posts (which personally I have always found an uncon-vincing reason). These come in a variety of wood-shades, as well as black and white and sometimes even less-natural colours. They cost midway between timber and steel and are moulded with notches to take lateral wires. They are usually guaranteed against deterioration (from ultra violet light) and should last 20+ years. Apart from looking

Strong end-post assemblies are essential to the strength of a good trellising system.

claiming that their's is the best at withstanding side-winds, best at not twisting when being driven, longest lasting etc) and they all come pre-notched to take wires and other trellis accessories. Steel posts tend to be more expensive than timber, but should last the life of the vineyard, require no nails or staples, and drive into the ground relatively easily, except for the stoniest of sites. As they do not displace much soil as they are driven in, they perhaps need to be in the ground a touch deeper than wooden ones. This either means buying longer posts, having a lower bottom wire or a shorter overall canopy height. Steel posts are also preferred in vineyards which are machine harvested as modern harvesters quite often shake the nails and staples out of wooden posts which is annoying as they have to be replaced, but doubly annoying if they get into a pump or into a pneumatic press, puncturing the airbag.

Occasionally one will also see old-railway rails, odd pieces of H-section beams, girders and RSJ[55] used as end-posts, but these are generally one-offs. I have also sometimes seen solid granite and slate endposts (up the Douro for instance) and in some parts of the world, reinforced concrete seems quite popular. Quite why this last material is used, I have never been sure, as they generally seem to crack and weaken at ground level, requiring an additional (usually wooden) post to keep them upright. I guess they must be cheap enough to start with – either that or they are subsidised in an attempt to keep a local cement works open!

Wires used in vineyards are almost always of galvanised steel, although even within that description there are a whole host of alternatives (soft steel, high-tensile steel, spring-steel etc). What you need to know about your wire is to what pressure it can be subjected before it starts to stretch, rather than simply tighten. If you attempt to strain it past this point, the wire elon-

slightly out of place in a natural setting, their only real drawback is that in stony or very compact ground (solid chalk for instance), they tend to shatter rather than drive into the soil.

If metal is your material of choice, steel, both natural and galvanised, can be seen all over the world. In drier climates, bare steel is quite often seen and the rust that inevitably coats the posts appears not to affect the vines in any way (although I have heard that it can sometimes increase the iron content in wines when grapes are machine harvested). Angle-iron, notched on each face to hold wires, is a staple of many French vineyards and where only short posts are required (say up to 1.50 m out of the ground), these are probably as good a choice as any. A 30 mm x 30 mm angle-iron post can be very easily driven into the ground (as it displaces very little soil) and will probably last as long as the vine if the steel is sufficiently thick enough. For longer posts, manufacturers make them in a wide variety of proprietary shapes (each

55 Rolled Steel Joists aka girders

gates and is thereby weakened. Stainless steel wire is also an option, albeit an expensive one, although wires can be much thinner (and therefore lighter) for the same tensile strength. Most specialist vineyard wire is of the 'zinc-alu' type which has a zinc-aluminium coating and is lighter per metre run than standard galvanised wire, thus reducing the load on the trellising.

Some vineyards use a filament made from nylon (or a similar synthetic material) instead of training wires, as this has a large amount of elasticity and can be both strained very tight, yet still pulled out and away from the vines during the tucking-in process. In my experience however, they are far too easy to cut with secateurs whilst pruning and the constant strain placed upon the end posts and anchors by the ever-taught 'wires' tends to pull out all but the firmest of anchors.

End anchors also come in all shapes and sizes. Large lumps of rock, concrete blocks or lengths of timber buried in the ground around which an anchor wire can be wrapped will usually suffice if buried deep enough and if the rows are not too long. There are also anchors that can be driven one way into the ground and cannot be pulled out, and disc anchors that can be screwed into the ground using a hydraulic device akin to a large cork-screw.

For systems such as GDC, Lyre and a few others, various types of proprietary frameworks, Y bars and spreader bars are available, which hold and locate the wires upon which the vines will be trained.

Chapter 8
The annual cycle of the vine

The annual cycle of the vine

For the purposes of this chapter, with regard to timings, I shall only deal with vines in the northern hemisphere. Southern hemisphere timings can be arrived at by adding (or subtracting) about six months. In warmer regions, spring will naturally start earlier and all subsequent timings will be earlier. In very early regions and in early years, the harvest can start at the beginning of August. In cooler regions and in late years, normal harvesting will continue well into November. Icewines can be harvested as late as February or March the following year although they will always bear the vintage of the year in which they started the season. There will also be some overlapping in timings which will be weather, site and

Double Guyot trained vine after tying down the canes.

variety dependent. In the southern hemisphere, harvesting in very warm regions will start in early January (sometimes even in late December) and in cooler regions not finish until mid-May.

January–February–March

The vine starts the year in a dormant state. The green canes that grew in the summer will have turned brown and become woody (lignified), the buds on the canes will have been sealed against the winter and are said to 'ripen'. When all the leaves have fallen and the weather has turned cold, the vine is dormant. Any carbohydrates produced in the vine will now be fixed in the plant and migration of these within the plant will have ceased. Pruning can then begin. In reality, growers who have been busy in their wineries will wait until they have their wines settled and Christmas is over. For European growers, the feast day of the patron saint of winegrowers, St. Vincent, which is on January 22nd, is deemed a suitable day to start pruning.

In many vineyards however, for purely practical manpower reasons, pruning needs to start as early as possible as the task of pruning, including cane removal and tying down of canes (in systems where canes are tied down), make up much of the winter work. Where some of the pruning can be mechanised (some spur-pruned systems allow for pre-pruning machines to be used) the pressure to get the work done is lessened. Pruning should be completed and all canes cleaned up and secured to the fruiting wires (in cane-pruned systems) well before bud-burst (March/April in Europe). The only exception to this timing is where, as has already been mentioned, spring frost might be a problem and additional canes are left in case of frost damage which can be removed once the danger of spring frost is over.

Apart from pre-pruning – of which more later – all pruning is carried out with secateurs which can be either manual or powered. As has already been mentioned in the previous chapter, electric, pneumatic and hydraulic secateurs are fairly common and both speed up the pruning process and cause far less strain to worker's hands and wrists. For large cuts, a saw may be necessary, although powered secateurs will cope with wood up to 50 mm in diameter. There are also a variety of powered pruning gantries or rigs, under which pruners can be serenaded with music if they so wish and, more importantly, can be sheltered from the elements as they prune. Standing around in 150 mm (6") of snow whilst trying to remain cheerful and concentrate on the task in hand is far from easy in the middle of winter. For very low-trained vines, small wheeled seating platforms, often battery-powered, upon which pruners can sit and move themselves along the rows, are a common sight in France.

Pruning itself can be considered as a four or three-part process, depending on whether the vines are cane or spur-pruned. In cane pruning, there is firstly the selection of the fruiting canes required for the coming year; secondly the cleaning up and trimming to length of those canes; thirdly the cutting out and removal from the trelliswork of the unwanted wood, known as 'pulling out'; and fourthly the pruning process is completed by the securing of the fruiting canes to the wires, the so-called

Vines pruned with prunings neatly laid down the middle of the rows.

Battery-powered seating platform for pruning

'tying down'. The selection of the fruiting canes requires a degree of expertise, although in many vineyards, the selection follows a fairly strict formula which can be repeated from one vine to another. The wood to be selected must be well positioned in order to provide the maximum amount of fruiting area and come from a point on the trunk that ensures that the crown of the vine remains in the right place, which is usually below the fruiting wire (the lowest wire). If the crown gets too high, the area of fruiting space on the vine will be reduced as the canes will be shorter. In older vines it is sometimes necessary to make quite drastic decisions about cutting out older wood and making a fresh start from a position lower down the vine towards the ground. Large (and sometimes not so large) pruning wounds are often painted with an anti-

Chariot de feu

56 Pollarding is the action of removing all the annual growth
from a mature tree so that a
multitude of shoots is produced in the next season. Many
trees in towns and cities (London plane trees are an
example) are pollarded every or
every other year in order to
keep them to a manageable
size.

of the annual canes. In bent-cane systems (many types of Guyot, Pendlebogen etc) canes are trained over one wire and attached to a lower wire. This bending may be left until the sap starts to move in the vine and the canes become more flexible. A variety of materials are used to secure the canes to the wires ranging from simple paper-covered wire twists to semi-automatic tying systems that use plastic tape, wire or cord. In some parts of Europe, pollarded[56] willows are grown by the sides of vineyards and the thin red or yellow shoots they produce are cut off, soaked in water to make them pliable and then used for this purpose.

In spur-pruned vineyards the vines may well be pre-pruned using a tractor mounted mechanical device which will cut off the majority of the annual wood and chop it into small pieces which will fall to the ground. Manual pruning will then be confined to selecting those shoots which are to become spurs and trimming these back to the required length. Apart from combination systems such as *Sylvoz* pruning, spur-pruned systems do not require bending over or tying down and this, coupled with the ability to carry out pre-pruning, makes them much cheaper systems to operate.

Ideally all pruning should be completed well before the sap starts to rise, although growers in regions where spring frosts can be a problem will delay it as long as possible. Pruning late will slightly delay budburst so that frost damage can be minimised. Other work in the vineyard at this stage may well include repairs to trelliswork, planting new vines in regions where spring frost is not a problem and the distribution of fertiliser and manure when the ground is dry enough to get tractors on to it (although it can also be done when the ground is frozen).

fungal paint to keep out diseases such as *Esca* and *Eutypa lata*.

Once the fruiting canes have been chosen, any unwanted canes around them will be removed, thus making it obvious which canes are to be retained. In many vineyards, more experienced staff will be used for this phase of the pruning operation, with less specialist workers following behind, cutting out and removing the remainder of the unwanted wood and cleaning up the canes to be retained. In most vineyards, the unwanted wood will be laid in the centre of the rows and will be chopped up (mulched) by a tractor-mounted flail-mower or pulveriser at a later stage. Alternatively, the wood can be bundled up and removed from the vineyard for burning or composting. I have also seen machines which can in effect hoover up the wood, spitting it out the back in compressed logs, ready to go straight onto the barbeque. In some French vineyards a *chariot de feu* (usually half an oil drum, perforated with a few holes and welded onto an old wheelbarrow frame) will be employed to burn the prunings *in situ* (and keep the pruners warm) although this is becoming a rarer sight.

The final phase of the cane-pruning process is the bending over and/or tying down

April–May

As the weather warms up, so does the soil temperature and several things start to happen in the vineyard. The cut ends of the canes will start to bleed (produce sap) and the vine starts to come out of dormancy. A vine can produce a very large volume of sap and although one thinks that this must in some way weaken the vine, research has shown that it does not. The winter buds will start to expand and turn woolly and eventually the young shoots will emerge and start to grow. This is known as bud-burst. In cooler regions, rises in soil temperatures are important in promoting bud-burst (soils at 200 mm depth need to rise to 8°C–10°C before vines start to grow) and soils that are wet will warm more slowly. On the floor of the vineyard, weeds and grasses will start to grow and will need to be dealt with.

In many vineyards, especially those where yield restrictions are in place or where experience has shown that there is usually an excess of shoots, some bud-rubbing or shoot-removal will be needed. Taking out excess buds/shoots will allow those remaining to grow in more open conditions, remove competition and promote fruit-bud development on the canes which will produce next year's fruit. Shoot removal in this manner is often practiced in high quality spur-pruned vineyards, less often in cane-pruned ones.

The care of the surface area of the vineyard can be divided into two parts: the area directly beneath the vines and the area in-between the rows (the alleyways). Directly beneath the vines and in a band of around 250 mm - 300 mm either side of the centre line of the vines (so around 500–600 mm overall), it is normal to keep the soil free of weeds or grass. Apart from the desire not to have tall weeds and grasses growing up and interfering with the crop, keeping the soil clear removes competition for nutrients and

Pinot noir about two weeks after bud-burst

moisture from the immediate area of the vine's roots and allows the soil to dry out quickly thus reducing the chance of fungal diseases developing. There are several ways in which a clean under-vine area can be achieved and these have already been dealt with in **Chapter 6 – Vineyard establishment – weed control.**

The vineyard alleyways can also be looked after in a number of ways: they can be cultivated using harrows of various types – disc, spring-tine or powered; they can be grassed down and mown; they can be planted with certain plants (green manuring) which produce valuable amounts of green matter which can be cut and returned to the soil to increase humus levels; or they can be kept weed free with herbicides. The decision about which route to take will depend on practical issues, local traditions and the general philosophy of the grower. Cultivating has its problems, not least of which is that in wet harvests, cultivated soil is not always ideal for the passage of pickers and tractors or of heavy harvesting machines. In some instances, growers will cultivate every other row, confining picking machines or grape-trailers to the non-cultivated rows. Mowing and green manuring are simple and effective methods, but in dry regions, may well deprive the vine of

Shoot showing two large flowers (inflorescences).

57 Diseases and pests of vines are dealt with in Chapters 11 to 13.

58 The harvest interval is the minimum number of days that must elapse between the last application of the chemical and before grapes can be harvested. See Chapter 11 – Diseases and viruses of grapevines, including trunk diseases for more detail.

Inflorescence about half-way through flowering. Caps off and pollen stamens working

methods used, the soil under the vine will need to be kept clean, and the alleyways looked after, for the whole of the growing season.

As the vine starts to grow and young fresh leaves appear, the question of pest and disease control arises. In most vineyards, early sprays will be needed to control diseases such as *Oidium* and Downy Mildew, with *Botrytis* control starting slightly later in the season[57]. Pest and disease control will continue throughout the growing season (although in dry seasons, the frequency of sprays will be reduced) and only end when the harvest is in sight. All chemicals used in agriculture must be cleared for use by law and each has what is known as a harvest interval[58] which will differ from material to material. Apart from this legal requirement, many chemicals, if residues remain on the grapes, will have a negative effect upon yeast growth in the must, something to be avoided if prompt fermentations are to be achieved.

In regions and on sites where experience has shown that spring frost can be a danger – just pre-budburst and just after is the most likely time – measures are often taken to protect the vines and their coming crop. These have been dealt with in **Chapter 6 – Vineyard establishment** in the section on frost protection.

June–July

With many pruning systems (especially VSP systems whether cane or spur-pruned), as the annual shoots grow, the majority will grow up between the wires and their tendrils will help support and guide the canes as they grow. Inevitably, some shoots will fall outside the wires and will need what is known as tucking-in. Various techniques of coping with this problem exist: moveable catch-wires that can be moved up to trap the foliage as it grows; spreader arms that keep the catch-wires apart and help trap the

moisture or increase the use of valuable irrigation water. The use of herbicides to keep alleyways clear is less widespread than it once was owing to an understandable wish to reduce herbicide use. However, if herbicides are used to keep alleyways weed-free, then usually they would also be used beneath the vines. This is known as a 'total herbicide' technique. Whatever the growing shoots; and even machines that handle the whole job mechanically. In some spur-pruned systems (GDC, Blondin, *Sylvoz*, etc) where the annual growth is allowed to hang down from the winter canes unaided, tucking-in is not needed. However, even with these systems, some element of cane positioning may be needed in order to open up the centres of the leaf-wall, allowing light to penetrate the canopy.

During this period, the flowering of the vine will normally take place[59]. Once the annual shoots have grown to (very approximately) 1 m in length, the flower caps will spring off, the flower clusters will open, viable pollen will be produced and pollination (or fertilisation) will take place. Successful flowering is dependent on having a healthy vine with fecund flowers, warm, dry weather and hopefully a light breeze to encourage pollen to migrate from the stamens down via the style to the ovary (the female part of the flower). Although insects – bees, beetles and flies – will often visit vine flowers during pollination, their presence is not generally considered necessary for successful flowering. Likewise, wind is not a factor in the pollination of hermaphrodite varieties of vines as the distance between the stamens and the ovary is extremely short, only a very few millimetres.

The average five-stamened vine-flower will contain about 20,000 grains of pollen, far more than are needed for successful pollination, but able to scent the vineyard with a unique light honey-and-citrus perfume. A cold, wet period at this time will prevent the flower caps from fully coming off and will hamper both the growth of pollen and its transfer from stamen to ovary. This is the most important time of the growth cycle for the coming crop: an early, quick, even and successful flowering will result in a full crop that will ripen evenly and make the prediction of a harvest date that much easier; a cold, damp, delayed and extended flowering will result in a lower (or even a non-existent)

Double-sided leaf trimmer

Single-sided leaf stripper

[59] The exact time of flowering is very climate, weather and variety dependent and in warm parts of Europe, in early years and with precocious varieties, April flowering is not unknown.

crop and one that will ripen unevenly and result in grapes of different ripeness levels ending up in the winery. The problem of an extended flowering which results in uneven pollination and therefore uneven ripening is exacerbated by the use of picking machines which cannot differentiate between ripe and less-ripe bunches. In addition, flowering that has taken place under adverse conditions will result in flowers with incompletely shed flower-caps which may become embedded within the bunch and in tight-bunched varieties lead to a greater risk of *Botrytis*-induced bunch rot.

The success of flowering depends very much upon the quality of the flowers, something which is determined by the growing conditions in the preceding year. What is known as the 'initiation' of the flowers takes place between 15 and 17 months before harvest. That is to say in the May-July of the preceding year for an October harvested crop. Many different factors are at work when the flowers are formed and heat and light levels, the overall health of the vine, whether it is under stress of one sort or another and imbalances of minerals all play their part in determining whether a vine is amply supplied with viable flowers and pollen, or not. Some varieties and certain clones of varieties also have low pollen viability levels and this may well account for poor crops. Good flowering is also very weather dependent and warm, dry, still conditions favour transfer of pollen onto the ovary. At around 15°C, flowers open from time to time, at 17°C they open normally and at 20°C–25°C they open very quickly. Wet and/or humid conditions will both slow pollen growth down and make transfer of the pollen from stamen to ovary less certain and almost inevitably lead to *coulure* and/or *millerandage*[60].

It is at flowering time that some growers will trim (or tip) the shoots of their vines in order to help with the flowering process. It has been shown in many studies that trimming of the shoots at this stage, when flowering is about 30–50 per cent completed, results in heavier crops and increases in yield of up to 25 per cent have been recorded over un-trimmed vines.

In many table grape vineyards, another technique used to improve yields is that of girdling where a small ring of bark is cut off the fruit-bearing arm just prior to flowering. This interrupts the flow of certain nutrients and hormones from the roots to the flowers and in effect tricks the flowers into better pollination. The circle of bark soon grows back and no permanent damage is done. Also, in table grape vineyards, the spraying of vines with gibberellins[61] around three weeks before flowering will reduce compactness in bunches, thus making individual grapes larger, a plus-point for table grapes. Another chemical used to help flowering is a growth retardant based upon a chemical called chlormequat (known as Cycocel or CCC) which reduces shoot elongation and has a similar effect to shoot tipping. In some regions, a product called

Regalis Plus is allowed to be sprayed at flowering time to 'improve bunch architecture' i.e. open up the bunch, to aid *Botrytis* control. See Chapter 11 for more detail.

Immediately after flowering, some growers may also pass through their vines with their sprayers empty of liquid, but with the air fan running in order to blow away any flowering residues – caps and stamens – that are still lingering there. It has been shown in many studies that *Botrytis* often starts on the flower debris trapped inside the bunch. As the bunch expands and gets to 'bunch close', getting fungicide into the centre of the bunch is not possible. Once flowering is completely over and the small berries start to swell and expand to around peppercorn size, many growers will start both trimming (hedging) their vines as well as leaf removal. Trimming after flowering, which falls under the term 'summer pruning', is used in many vineyards to keep the foliage under control, to remove unruly side-shoots and generally maintain a thin, open canopy. This will help keep the alleyways open so that tractors and machinery can pass without pulling off bunch-carrying shoots that have fallen out of the canopy. The leaves of the vine are net-users of carbohydrates until they reach 50–80 per cent of their maximum size, at which point they start to contribute to the accumulation of sugars in the plant. Once they reach their maximum size, their contribution to the accumulation of sugars starts to fall. Trimming therefore, needs to be done carefully so that not too much foliage is removed, but just enough to open up the canopy to allow light and air, plus pesticide sprays, to reach the centre of the leaf-wall. In moderate to high vigour vineyards, tipping may well increase the formation of side-shoots (lateral shoots) which although these may contribute to sugar accumulation, they will also contribute to overcrowding and shading within the leaf-wall. Leaf removal, which can be done by hand or machine, will often also start at around the time that first trimming takes place. Growers will typically remove one third of the leaves in the fruiting zone at the first pass; another third at the second pass; and a final third at the last pass. Of course, in-between passes some leaves will grow back, so the vine is not completely bare in the fruiting zone. In warm to hot climates, leaves may only be removed on the shaded side in order to prevent sunburn of the fruit. Weed control, alleyway management and pest and disease protection will also continue throughout these months.

July–August

During this period – the hottest months of the northern hemisphere's summer – the vine's growth will slow down and shoot extension will not be so rapid. However, some shoots and especially side-shoots may well continue to grow and summer-pruning will continue. The aim of canopy management at this stage is to open up the leaf-wall, allowing light, air and heat into the centre of the canopy, so aiding development of the sugars in the grapes and allowing pest and disease treatments to reach the bunches. This is also the time of *véraison,* the term used to describe when the grapes of red vine varieties start turning from green to red and the ripening process really gets under way with sugars building in the fruit and acids starting to decrease. It is at this stage that 'green harvesting'[62] may be carried out. Green harvesting – bunch or cluster thinning – is an attempt to do two things: remove from the vine those grapes that are the least developed; and to reduce the overall level of the crop. *Véraison* is the ideal time to do this (at least with red wine varieties) because it is evident from the state of the colour change which are the least ripe grapes. These can then be pulled or cut off and discarded.

Although bunch-thinning at this stage will reduce the crop, the overall effect may not be as pronounced as it at first seems. The bunches removed will be the third (and fourth if there is one) on the cane and are typically much smaller than those retained (the first and second on the cane), so removing a third or a half of the bunches numerically, does not reduce the crop by anything like the same percentage. In addition, the vine will attempt (assuming it is well enough supplied with water), to compensate for the lost crop by increasing the size of the remaining bunches and berries. This not only negates the attempt at crop reduction, but can also reduce the quality of the wine, especially with red grapes where the skin to juice ratio is important for wine colour and tannin structure. In order to make a really significant reduction in yield, it is nearly always necessary to remove all but one bunch per cane – something most growers are very reluctant to do.

However, in years when the flowering process has been long and drawn-out, usually due to cool, wet and windy conditions at flowering, there will be uneven levels of ripeness between the first, second and third bunches on the cane, and green harvesting does at least get rid of those bunches that will ripen latest. Where vines are machine picked, green harvesting may well result in quality improvements, harvesting machines lacking the critical faculties to distinguish between ripe and unripe bunches, although of course you then have the additional costs of the green harvesting.

Except in early regions or in very early years (2003 in Europe being a case in point), August will be a time of reduced activity in the vineyard. The weeds should be under control, the canopy should be trimmed and open and pest and disease protection will be at a minimum – a time for *vignerons* to take a break before the harvest.

62 'Green harvesting' is a translation from the French term *'vendange en vert'.*

63 Hang-time is the period when all the viticultural work in the vineyard is finished and wine-makers are waiting for tannins to soften, sugars to rise and fruit flavours to develop. A slightly less generous definition of 'hang time' is given in *The Oxford Companion to Wine*.

64 The entry on physiological ripeness in *The Oxford Companion to Wine* is well worth reading for a fuller definition.

65 In some wineries, red wines are made with the inclusion of stalks, typically 10–20 per cent of the whole, but fermenting 'whole bunch' with all the stalks is not unknown. Where stalks are included, it is even more important that they are fully ripe.

September–October

This is the main harvesting time in Europe. As has already been explained in the section of this book on climate, it was traditionally held that there was an interval of 100 days between the onset of flowering and harvest, but this is no longer the case in most situations. In many parts of the new world the interval between flowering and harvest can be 135–145 days. Certainly, much better pest and disease control, especially of *Botrytis* (due mainly to more effective fungicides, better methods of application and improved canopy management), has meant that growers feel confident enough to extend the period of hang-time[63] for their grapes. The desire to make better wine with greater extract, higher alcohols and riper flavours must also be considered as a contributory factor, as must the use in many vineyards of harvesting machines which can pick in an hour what five people might have achieved in a day. Machine harvesters can also work all day and all night, the latter being an important consideration where daytime temperatures are high. In these regions, harvesting will often start well before first-light and continue until grape temperatures get too high.

The exact time of the harvest will depend on several factors: the condition of the grapes in relation to the type and quality of wine required will be paramount; have the sugars risen enough; are the acids sufficiently low enough (or high enough – it depends on the style of wine); are flavours and colour sufficiently developed? Other factors – not entirely connected to the actual ripeness level of the grapes – will include such practical matters as whether pickers can be hired; is a picking machine available; is there enough tank space in the winery; what is the weather about to do; is there a weekend or a holiday period coming up; is it grandma's birthday at the weekend? Winemakers do have a life away from the winery!

Growers will normally be testing their grapes for sugars, acids and pH in the three to four weeks prior to harvest, although with experience, such things as leaf colour, colour-change of berries, pip condition and the taste of the grapes will give an experienced winegrower a good guide to the date of harvest. Many winemakers will patrol their blocks of vines, tasting individual grapes as they go, in order to get a picture of how the ripening is proceeding. Many winemakers will also discuss the 'physiological ripeness[64] of their grapes in relation to a harvest date. Physiological ripeness is a controversial term and there is no hard-and-fast technique to determine the exact point at which this happens. Parameters such as skin colour and condition, pulp and juice flavour, pip colour and level of pip ripeness (bitterness) and just a general feel for when the grapes are at their optimum to make the best wine possible are all taken into account. In warm and hot climates, grapes harvested at what is considered to be their point of physiological ripeness can be too high in potential alcohol and too low in natural acidity, both of which may well require adjusting if the final wine is to be properly balanced. Much depends on the wine style desired. Of course, in many *appellations* the timing of harvest is down to a local committee of winemakers, growers and state officials who will fix a date for each region and sometimes each sub-region, thus relieving the winemaker of that final decision in the winegrower's year.

One other major consideration in determining a picking date is the physical condition of the grapes. Have they been damaged in some way and is *Botrytis* or another fungal disease likely to invade? Whilst skin finish and condition is not so critical with white grapes (where stalks, skins, pips, pulp etc are discarded at pressing) with red grapes, where, apart from the stalks[65] all other parts of the grape end up in the fermentation tank, grapes damaged with

Botrytis may well lose a lot of their fruit and freshness and even impart a mouldy taint to the wine. In some regions – and especially in isolated vineyards with nearby areas of woodland where birds can roost – some degree of protection against birds will be needed. Regular bird patrols with gunfire and general commotion will scare flocks off and static methods such as automated gas-guns which make a loud bang, firecrackers hung up in strategic locations and various audible and visual warning devices (the distress calls of the species of bird doing the damage are quite popular) will help. Trying to get birds-of-prey to nest nearby is also a good idea and some growers have used birds-of-prey, flown by experienced falconers, to save their grapes. What works one year, may not work the next and if birds are a problem, it usually turns into a short war with the harvest eventually bringing the problem to an end. In parts of the world where vineyards have been established for many years and where vines tend to be the only crop in the area, the annual war against birds has resulted in a much reduced – in many cases a non-existent – bird population and the problem has been largely solved. In newer regions however, overall netting may be the only solution. Netting is expensive and time-consuming, but effective and in New Zealand for instance, around 50 per cent of all vines are bird-netted. Vineyards growing near other fruit crops, especially ones which have already been harvested (such as apples or pears), seem to experience much less bird damage as birds will feed on the riper fallen fruit, rather than relatively acidic, unripe grapes. Apart from the reduction in yield that bird damage can cause, fruit that has been pecked will succumb to bunch-rots of various types. Harvesting early is certainly no answer to a vineyard with a bird problem and another method of protecting the grapes has to be found.

Nets on Lyre-trained vines at Kumeu River Vineyards near Auckland, New Zealand

November–December

Once the harvest is over, there is far less to do in the vineyard. Some growers might apply a clean-up herbicide to burn off any weeds that have grown during the later stages of the growing season. A winter-wash of a copper-based fungicide is sometimes applied to encourage the hardening and ripening of the canes. Growers who cultivate their vineyards, either under the vines or in the alleyways (or both) may give the vineyard one last tidy-up cultivation to open up the soil and let the winter rains soak into the subsoil. In some regions it is traditional to plough close to the base of the vines – called *buttage* in French – so that earth is piled up against the grafts in order to protect them against winter frost damage. (In spring the reverse operation will take place – *debuttage* – to scrape away the soil.)

In vineyards which are spur-pruned,

Vines under nets at Ata Rangi, Martinborough, New Zealand

66 A ton in this instance is the US 2,000 lb ton which equals approx. 907 kg.

pre-pruning machines can make an initial pass through the vines once they are completely dormant and in warm regions, pruning proper can start. Maintenance tasks such as post replacement and repair will be carried out and in warm areas, where the dangers of winter frost are minimal, new vines may well be planted. In many vineyards though, these winter months are ones where nothing much happens and efforts are concentrated in the winery.

Yields and quality – is there a relationship?

A very commonly held view, and one that you will hear repeated time and time again, is that yield is *necessarily* in inverse proportion to quality. In other words, if you reduce the yield, wine quality will always rise. It is true that there are many vineyards where a lower yield will increase wine quality as an individual vine ripening a smaller amount of fruit will have an easier task, all other things being equal. However, is that the only route to increasing wine quality? It might be that by changing the pruning and/or training system of the vineyard, putting a bit more work into canopy manage-

ment (bud-rubbing, shoot-positioning, summer pruning, leaf-removal and perhaps a light bunch-thinning), those vines could have ripened the original crop to the same degree and have produced a wine of equal quality (and in greater quantity).

Most growers will have a view of what crop level their vines will support for the quality of grapes they are trying to produce. That crop level will depend on several factors and a grower selling fruit at say \$587 per ton[66] (average price of all white grapes sold in California in 2017) will have a completely different view to someone achieving \$7,498 per ton (2017 average price) for Napa Cabernet Sauvignon. Growers tied into contracts at fixed prices or taking their chances with the annual spot market may well take the view that the safest way to maximise their incomes is to spend as little on growing the crop as possible and – within the sugar, acidity and yield levels imposed by any contract they might have signed – pick as large a weight of grapes as possible.

Growers who are restricted by *appellation* regulations to a certain yield and who attempt to keep their crops under the set levels by predicting their yields are actually facing a very difficult task. An estimate can be made by test picking say ten vines across a vineyard (something most growers in my experience are very reluctant to do) and then multiplying the average per vine yield by the number of bearing vines in the vineyard (remembering also that in many vineyards, especially older ones, there will be a percentage of under-performing and even missing vines). Inevitably what happens in practice is that once growers have started picking and get a feel for what weight of crop is actually hanging on their vines, they will adjust their picking techniques accordingly. Vineyards with light crops (i.e. under the *appellation* limits) will be stripped of every last bunch; those which look like exceeding the set yield limits will be picked sparingly, with the third (usually the smallest and least-ripe) bunch being left for the birds to harvest (or possibly even a neighbouring grower with a young, low-yielding vineyard to pick). Richard Smart's views on the wisdom of restricting yields to increase quality are well known and he is firmly of the opinion that it is far more cost effective to spend a little bit more on canopy management to help the vine ripen a higher yield of the same quality, than just cut the yield (by hard pruning or vicious *vendange en vert*) and hope for the best.

Picking to the *appellation* yield level and leaving the rest does very little for wine quality and is merely a method of market control. I recall hearing a story about a grower in the Rheinhessen area who picked to the *appellation* limit and gathered in a respectable crop of *Spätlese* quality, leaving behind a considerable quantity of grapes. Three weeks later, after the harvest was over, the grower saw that the grapes he'd left behind had ripened into a fine crop approaching *Beerenauslese* level and decided to pull the plug on the tank of wine he'd already made, pick the grapes, and make a higher quality, more valuable, wine instead!

The relationship between vine age and quality

Whilst in the mood to question a few well-known wine 'facts', a word or two about age of vines in relation to wine quality might be appropriate. Along with *terroir* the idea that the older the vine, the better the wine, is one that suits those who have old vines and have therefore, in marketing terms, a unique attribute that no new entrant to the marketplace can copy. Old vines, with their long-established, deep roots surely are able to produce better wine I hear you say; all those great minerals in the lower layers; all that extensive root structure? Well, yes Lord

Copper[67] – up to a point. In dry weather, older vines with a larger root structure, might well suffer less from drought stress, but so what? Well-watered young vines – and here is the critical factor – bearing the same crop level as their older neighbours, will produce just as good, or as bad, fruit. Many winegrowers will tell you that the first one or two crops from vines – that is to say even as early as their second or third year of growth – will bear excellent quality fruit, undamaged by diseases (which have not yet had time to establish themselves in the vineyard), but – again take note – at low levels of cropping. The MOST critical factor in quality, all other things being equal – is level of yield. Vines, once they get to 20+ years of age, are usually less vigorous, produce lower yields and are therefore better balanced and their fruit is better exposed. It is this factor, and no other, that results in better wine coming from older vines. (But don't let the requirements of a back label or publicity blurb get in the way of a good story!)

As an example, take the red wine that came top in Steven Spurrier's 1976 *Judgement of Paris* tasting. This was the 1973 Stag's Leap Wine Cellars' Cabernet Sauvignon made from vines planted in 1970, so hardly *vielle vignes*. The fabled 1961 vintage in Bordeaux was, at many châteaux on the right bank, in Pomerol and St. Émilion, harvested from vines planted in 1957 and 1958 in the aftermath of the horrific frosts of February 1956 – in other words – from vines of only three and four years old. If old vines are so essential to great wine, the 1961 vintage from these regions would appear to be something of an anomaly. What those young vines did have (as did many of the older vines that survived the frosts, but still had to be severely pruned back to promote the growth of replacement canes) was you guessed it – low yields.

67 If this reference to Lord Copper leaves you perplexed, try reading Scoop by Evelyn Waugh.

Chapter 9
Irrigation

Irrigation

Irrigation of crops is not a new practice and centuries ago it was known to the Babylonians, the Chinese, the Egyptians and many early South American civilisations. The irrigation practiced in these times was simple flood and channel irrigation, techniques still used today, and the basic requirements for any irrigation system have not changed since: a dependable supply of suitable water and a cost-effective and reliable method of getting it onto the land.

Typically, a vine needs between 250 mm and 1,000 mm of water per square metre during the growing season[68]. Thus, for each hectare of vines, up to 10 million litres of water a year might be required. The actual amount of water needed will depend on many factors. The evapotranspiration (ET) rate of the vineyard itself, which is influenced by shading, vegetation cover, soil type and conditions, wind speed, humidity and air temperatures, will be important, as will the rate at which water leaves the vine. This will be affected by the heat and humidity, light levels and wind speeds, and by the stress levels placed upon the plant, especially by the crop. The stress level of the plant can also be raised by keeping the vine undersupplied with water and only giving it water when absolutely necessary. This may be useful in helping control vigour in the vine. Other factors such as the general climate and the amount of natural rainfall will of course also have to be taken into account.

Water sources

Water can come from a number of different sources. It can be taken directly from a natural flowing supply such as a river (which may have been dammed to increase the volume of water available), a canal or from a natural static source such as a pond or lake. In these situations, it is necessary to be sure that enough water will be available from these sources, even in very dry summers, exactly the time when the replenishment of the water is likely to be at its lowest and the demand from the crop the highest. In many areas water extraction regulations may well preclude taking water from natural sources if they fall below set levels. Water can be held in an irrigation lagoon (reservoir), usually man-made, which can be filled from a variety of sources: drained or pumped

68 As a comparison, annual rainfall in most non-irrigated regions would be between 300 mm and 1,000 mm.

Irrigation lagoon at Gallo's Frey Ranch vineyard in Sonoma.

from a river, taken from a convenient spring or filled from a bore-hole. The advantages of using a man-made lagoon are that its size can relate to the amount of water required for the vineyard and that it can be filled during the winter when natural water is usually plentiful. Losses from lagoons by evaporation can be reduced by using floating covers of which there are many different types.

Water can also be drawn directly from a bore-hole and pumps would be needed to bring the water up, sometimes from considerable depths. In this situation, a small buffer lagoon may also be used to overcome fluctuations in supply. The draw-back of relying on a bore-hole is that flows are often irregular, especially during the summer when demand is likely to be at its highest. This can partially be overcome by using irrigation techniques that use an absolute minimum of water, as outlined later in this chapter.

Quality of water

Apart from the rate of the flow of water from the supply, the quality of the water is also an important issue. Factors such as the total dissolved solids, the salinity, and levels of soluble salts of various types will all have a bearing on the water's suitability. Water that is too high in dissolved solids i.e. is too dirty, may well require treating by settling through sand beds and filtering through screens and filters before it can be used. This is especially true in systems where water is used directly from the source. All irrigation systems that use sprinklers or drippers will require clean water if they are not to become blocked, which would lead to uneven watering. Given that there are typically at least one, if not two, drippers per vine, physically inspecting them for blockages is impossible and it is only when vines are visibly stressed that a blockage might be noticed. Water would typically be tested for pH, calcium, magnesium, iron, carbonate and bicarbonate, sulphides, sulphates and in some cases, manganese. Excess levels of any of these may well, in time, cause small aperture systems such as drippers, to block.

Water with high levels of salt (such as chloride, sodium, boron, bicarbonate and nitrates) may well prove unsuitable, even dangerous. Water is taken up by a plant's roots by osmosis, a process by which water passes through a semi-permeable membrane from a solution with low levels of salt (the water in the soil) to one with a higher level of salt (the plant). If this position is reversed, where the water in the soil is higher in salt than the plant, then the direction of osmosis can also be reversed, drying out the plant, rather than watering it. In this situation, the leaves of vines fed with salty water may well start to deteriorate. The use of non-pressurised irrigation techniques such as flood or channel systems can help overcome the problems associated with saline water, as can the practice of applying excessive amounts of water. Rootstocks such as Ramsey, 101–14, Rupestris du Lot and 99R have all proved successful at withstanding moderately salty water and vines growing on their own roots are also able to cope with quite salty water. Research in Israel, where often only saline water is available in desert regions, has produced rootstocks for vines able to cope with high levels of salt. Each time water is used, any salts in it will get concentrated and over time, the levels rise. This is especially the case if the aquifers from which the water is drawn are not being regularly refreshed. In general terms, water with no salt or very low levels of salt is preferable.

Types of irrigation

Once a suitable water supply has been located and the necessary extraction permissions obtained, the question of what system to use to get it onto the vines needs deciding. Systems fall into two broad types:

non-pressurised such as flood and channel; and pressurised such as overhead sprinkler systems and under-vine sprinkler, dripper and leaky-hose types – all of which require a pump to provide pressure.

Flood irrigation is only used where large volumes of water are available and enough manpower to operate sluices and water gates to flood the vineyard evenly. Flood irrigation is usually only practical in level or very nearly level vineyards – for obvious gravitational reasons – and is a very broad-brush approach to the task. However, in regions such as Mendoza in Argentina and many of the Chilean vineyard areas, where ample water from the Andes is available, it is a low-cost and effective technique. As a secondary benefit, vineyards can be planted on their own-roots as the root-living form of *Phylloxera* is drowned by repeated submersion in water. Vineyards would typically be flooded up to six times a season. These systems are however, very wasteful of water.

Channel irrigation (sometimes called furrow irrigation) is similar to flood, but differs in that narrow channels are dug alongside rows of vines and water directed into them from header channels which are supplied from feeder canals which traverse the uphill side of the vineyard. This type of system can be improved by using laser levelling equipment to construct the channels so that they fill up evenly. Erosion of the channels, always a danger when large flows of water are used, can be avoided if the water is supplied through riser tubes. Again, this is quite a broad-brush approach to the task, but one that can be very cost-effective, although as with flood irrigation, sufficient manpower is essential. The disadvantages of channel irrigation are that channels can easily get damaged by tractors and implements and will often fill up with foliage and leaves which have to be removed before they will work effectively. Channel irrigation may also have some effect upon controlling *Phylloxera* but not as much as flood systems.

With both flood and channel systems, the quality of the water is less important and high levels of solids are not usually a problem. Saline water can also be used. As with flood irrigation, this system uses high levels of water.

Travelling overhead sprinklers have their advantages: one sprinkler rig will typically cover a large area; an expensive network of permanent pipes is avoided as they are fed by a flexible hose which unwinds as they travel; and they can be used in several different vineyards in succession. Their main disadvantages are that they use large amounts of water as evaporation levels are high when the water is sprayed through the air before it lands on the crop and the increased humidity levels may exacerbate disease levels. This type of sprinkler, which will throw water in a 30–50 m radius, will never reach 100 per cent of the vineyard surface area and can also deliver uneven results if there are crosswinds.

Fixed overhead sprinklers require an underground system of mains with sprinklers on riser pipes, usually attached to the vineyard posts and spraying above the vines. Again, as with travelling sprinklers, there is bound to be some overlapping and some areas which receive no water. There is also the increased risk of fungal infection. However, this type of sprinkler system can be used for frost protection and this alone may be a deciding factor. Both travelling and fixed overhead sprinklers have relatively large jets and clogging will be less of a problem than with under-vine dripper or sprinkler systems and neither are likely to be damaged by rodents or other animals. They will both need high pressure pumps for them to work effectively.

Under-vine mini-sprinklers are mounted on risers attached to supply pipes – typically one every two to three rows – which are laid on the surface of the vineyard. The sprinklers spray water in a circle of between

2 m and 5 m diameter (the actual area covered will depend on the type of jet and the pressure of the system.) If the system is correctly designed with the sprinklers offset in adjacent rows and close enough together, very few dead spots will occur and almost 100 per cent coverage can be achieved. Mini-sprinklers operate on a fairly low pressure and water cleanliness is less of an issue than with drippers.

Under-vine micro-jets are again carried on risers attached to supply pipes laid on the surface of the vineyard, but in this instance laid in every row. Jets are available in different types: some spray water in a 360° circle, others in a 180° half-circle. As with mini-sprinklers, water cleanliness is not such an issue and pressures are even lower. The supply pipes carrying both mini-sprinklers and micro-jets can be damaged by rodents and other animals as they are very accessible.

Leaky hose is – as the name suggests – a porous hose (usually made from recycled vehicle tyres) through which water can pass as with any other hose, but at certain pressure levels will start to leak water sideways through the walls of the hose. The hoses will be laid along every row of vines, usually at ground, or even slightly below ground, level. They are quite cheap to buy and install, require little maintenance and, if buried underground, will be less easily damaged by rodents and other animals.

Dripper systems are the most commonly found irrigation systems in vineyards. Supply pipes will be laid in each row, typically attached to the lowest wire (the fruiting wire) of the trelliswork, with drippers (sometimes called emitters) fitted at appropriate intervals. Sometimes a separate wire to carry the drippers is installed below the fruiting wire. Usually there will be two drippers per vine, suitably positioned either side of the vine. It is important that the drippers are not positioned directly beside the vine as this may lead to localised wet-

ting and therefore localised root growth and distribution. Drippers need to be far enough away from the vine for its roots to seek the water and spread out. The advantages of this type of system are: economy of water use, a high level of control over individual rows or blocks of vines, a low labour requirement and the ability to work with relatively saline water. Their supply pipes, being around 600 mm–900 mm off the ground, are less open to damage from small rodents than other types of system, although larger animals, rabbits, hares, foxes, coyotes and even deer, have been known to chew on plastic pipes either to get to the

(top) Dripper irrigation systems are the most commonly used in viticulture.

(bottom) Leaky hose irrigation can be laid on the soil's surface or buried beneath it.

Irrigated vines in the Douro Valley, Portugal.

water, or in the case of deer, just because they seem to like chewing plastic (they chew plastic vine-ties quite happily). Most pressurised types of irrigation system can also be used for supplying fertiliser to the vines (so-called fertigation) whereby liquid fertiliser is added to the water supply via a dosing pump. This is a very effective and direct way of getting nutrients to the vine.

Disadvantages of dripper systems include a high capital cost, the requirement for very clean water and patrolling of the drippers if blockages are to be avoided. As has been explained above, water with high levels of certain minerals and salts will, in time, cause the small apertures of drippers to block. Other problems with drippers include blockages caused by algae and bacterial slimes, and flushing with chlorine (or other materials) from time to time may well be necessary. Sub-surface systems might require flushing with a weak herbicide to prevent roots from blocking drippers.

Monitoring the water requirements in the vineyard

With any irrigation system, it is important, both from the needs of the plant and in the interests of economy and water conservation, to know both when the plant needs water, as well as how much it needs. The simplest methods, although perhaps not the most scientific, are by observation of the vines and the condition of the soil. An experienced viticulturist, who knows his or her sites and soils, will often be able to tell

enough from looking at these two factors. Other useful indicators include the weather conditions – wind-speed, temperature and humidity levels and whether there has been recent rain – and the condition of the vineyard floor – is it covered with vegetation, does it have smooth bare earth or has it been recently cultivated? These will all have a bearing on the evaporation rate of water from the vineyard.

Vines that lack water will show less vigorous growth. Their shoots will be less upright and will have reduced internode lengths, their leaves which start to cup and curl especially at the hottest part of the day, and the leaf colour will be less green and vibrant than of vines well supplied with water. In many vineyards, the soil itself will also give a good clue as to its water holding state, although different types of soils will show markedly different states for the same level of moisture. Soil taken from 100-150 mm below surface level and which cannot be balled i.e. easily pressed into a ball which stays intact in one lump, will often indicate a soil that is water deficient (although sandy soils may not ball so easily). Samples taken with an auger from around 500 mm – the level where most of the vine's feeder roots will be located in an irrigated vineyard – will need to be assessed for their level of water holding. Again, seeing to what degree they will ball and hold together is another good (and quick) indicator.

Many irrigation systems will either be completely or partially controlled by machinery and/or computers, which rely on instruments to measure accurately the water state of the vineyard. Instruments such as: a tensiometer, a device buried in the soil which measures the differences in pressure between wet and dry soils; gypsum moisture blocks which measure the electrical resistance of the soil; and neutron probes can all be used to give readings which will indicate the level of water in the soil. All instruments need to be located at levels where the roots are concentrated and will often be located at two or even three different levels to give a spread of readings. Over time and with experience, a pattern will emerge for each type of soil and each block of vines, making interpretation an easier task.

Vine leaves can also be tested for their water-holding capacity with the use of a 'pressure bomb', a portable instrument which, when a leaf is inserted into it and gas pressure applied, will measure the LWP (leaf water potential) of the leaf (also known as the 'turgor' pressure) by seeing at what pressure moisture can be forced from the leaf petiole (stalk). Results will depend upon several factors – the weather conditions, the time of day, state of the vine, where on the vine the leaf was taken from – and a fair degree of experience is required to interpret the results. Some vineyards also use a band dendrometer attached to the trunk of the vine which measures the minute changes in the circumference of the vine as it expands and contracts due to changes in the water demand and supply. Dendrometers can be remotely accessed, giving a real-time picture of a vine's water needs.

The measurement of an individual vine's water status is becoming more scientific as sensors are developed that can measure almost any parameter of the vine. Advanced measuring systems may well have artificial leaves that hang on a target vine, mimicking real leaves but from which readings of light absorption and leaf temperature can be taken. Couple these to data from tensiometers, soil moisture probes and dendrometers and an overall picture can quickly be built up. When fed into a computer and analysed, these can be used to switch on pumps and irrigate vines to the required level.

How much water to apply?

The field capacity of any soil is usually taken to be the amount of water remaining in the soil 24 hrs after complete saturation. The soil is then said to be at its upper limit or at 100 per cent. Once the plants have used all the available water and are showing signs of wilting, the soil is at its lowest limit. The difference between the upper and lower limits is the field's capacity to hold water. Soils will differ in their field capacity according to their type: coarse sand can hold around 35 mm of water per metre of soil, fine sandy loam around 160 mm and very fine sandy clay up to 200 mm. However, soils are rarely uniform to the depth that vines root and in addition, some soils release their water more easily, making the calculation of how much water to add, for any given site, soil and growth pattern, as much an art as a science.

The question of water supply and vine yield is one that much exercises viticulturalists and winemakers. At what level of yield – in warm and hot regions yield is very strongly correlated to water availability – does quality start to diminish? Is it possible to say in any given situation that had the yield been reduced, the quality would have been better or, conversely, could the yield have been increased without loss of quality? With growers who sell their fruit and whose

Without irrigation, viticulture would be impossible at Chard Farm in the Gibbston Valley, Central Otago, New Zealand.

Channel irrigation in a vineyard in Colchagua, Chile.

income is usually (but certainly by no-means always) dependent on the level of crop, the temptation to increase the yield through liberal applications of water is always present. Water is usually more valuable when sold as grape juice than when it remains in the river as water! To overcome this temptation, many grape-purchase contracts will stipulate maximum yield levels or even be calculated on an area basis (per hectare or acre), subject to minimum and maximum yield limits and will certainly include some quality parameters in the payments schedule.

Many growers will also use water supply as an additional tool in their bid to get their canopy management right. A vine that is kept at a threshold level of water availability that is just under that needed for maximum growth will be less vigorous, tend to produce less leaf area and fewer side-shoots in the latter half of the growing season. This will lead to the vine having a more open, and therefore more beneficial, canopy. This technique is known as regulated deficit irrigation (RDI). The vine must also be encouraged to send out roots in search of water and keeping it under-watered can help achieve this.

Another consideration is the cost of water. In areas where water is not restricted and abstraction licence fees are not based upon actual usage but levied per hectare or acre whether water is used sparingly or liberally, the temptation to use it liberally is always there. Conversely, where water is metered and charged per litre or cubic metre, growers are much more likely to be inventive with their water use and concentrate on water retention techniques and ways of maximising water usage.

Partial Rootzone Drying (PRD)

Partial rootzone drying (PRD) is a technique of irrigation developed in Australia for grapevines, but also now extended to top-fruit (apples and pears), stone-fruit (plums, peaches etc) and citrus. With the correct arrangement of irrigation channels, drippers or sprinklers, it has been found that if one side of a plant's root system is wetted, yet the other kept dry, and this pattern alternated in 10–15 day cycles, the plant's roots are confused into thinking that they are under drought-stress and they send a plant hormone called abscisic (sometimes spelt abcissic) acid (ABA) to the vine. ABA tells the vine to close the small pores (stomata) on the leaves which reduces transpiration i.e. stops water escaping. The benefits are severalfold: water use (and therefore water cost) is cut by between 30-50 per cent; shoot growth is reduced; canopies are more open; and the fruit and buds are better exposed. There is therefore less work in the vineyard. Care has to be taken with PRD, especially in very hot regions, that the fruit does not become over-exposed and – as with most viticultural techniques and practices – an element of human intervention is needed to fine-tune the process.

Irrigation – a summary

Irrigation is a powerful tool in the hands of the viticulturalist and makes growing grapes possible and financially rewarding in regions where without it, crops would either be non-existent or too sparse to be economically viable. Not only can irrigation be used to increase yields, but it can also be used to achieve the much-desired state of balance in an otherwise too-vigorous canopy.

In regions which either have sufficient natural water or where dry-farmed grapes command a sufficient premium to make reduced crops acceptable, the bias against irrigation (except perhaps on young vines to aid establishment) still persists. In the European Union, the basic regulation governing the production of Quality Wines still forbids irrigation, unless it is specifically permitted. However, as global warming leads to drier summers and, perhaps more importantly, as traditional old-world producers see their markets being taken by new world producers, most of whom can irrigate without restriction, this bias is being eroded and now, irrigated vineyards are much more common in the drier parts of France, Spain, Portugal and Italy. German winegrowers have also started to install irrigation, much to the dismay of the authorities who tried to prevent it. However, the growers (quite rightly) pointed out that as vineyards in warmer regions were being irrigating (in many regions without a maximum yield limit), whereas they had a yield restriction of 10,500 kg/ha (about 75 hl-ha), then as long as they did not breach this, they ought to be allowed to use it. They were!

Chapter 10
Organic and Biodynamic viticulture

Organic and Biodynamic viticulture

Organic and Biodynamic viticulture (they are not the same, although I will deal with them in the same chapter) are systems of growing grapes that place less reliance (and in some instances almost no reliance) on chemical intervention to guard against pests, diseases and other viticultural problems and more reliance on the vine's ability, given the right encouragement, to look after itself. Whether this ability is innate and present in all vines, or only in those that receive the stimulus of organic and/or Biodynamic practices, is an interesting question and one that remains central to those who question the philosophy behind this branch of agriculture.

All organic and Biodynamic growers (or at least, all, those who wish to label their produce as being organic or Biodynamic), must be inspected by a certification body officially recognised (usually by the national ministry of agriculture) in their country. The inspection will look to see that the land has been free of weedkillers or other banned substances for three years before it can be certified as organic. There is usually more than one certification body in each country and although standards differ, with some appearing to be less stringent than others, at the heart of certification they all have similar rules: no chemically synthesised fungicides, insecticides, pesticides or weed-

69 The word 'Biodynamic' is a registered trademark belonging to Demeter.

killers and no genetically modified organisms (or at least none above a very small threshold). However, many organic and Biodynamic growers will use naturally occurring materials such as copper (subject to strict volume limits – see later) and sulphur, so not totally without recourse to what most laymen would consider 'chemicals'. The standards for Biodynamic growers (as opposed to merely organic) are monitored by the Demeter[69] organisation which operates worldwide, and are stricter than even the strictest organic standards. For instance, because 'Biodynamic agriculture works with the dynamics of subtle forces', crops grown under power lines have to be treated with 'extra applications of the full complement of the Biodynamic preparations' in order to negate the EMF (elector magnetic forces) coming from the power lines.

Rudolf Steiner

The organic and Biodynamic movements owe their origins to the teachings of Rudolf Steiner who was born in 1861 in what is now Croatia, but was then part of the Austro-Hungarian Empire. Steiner was a controversial figure (often accused, with a degree of justification, of being a crank, a racist and a neo-Nazi) and his ideas were not universally liked or admired. His theory of Anthroposophy (from the Greek *anthropo* meaning human and *sophia* meaning wisdom) covered several disciplines: education,

Rudolf Steiner 1861–1925

Many organic and Biodynamic vineyards plough using horsepower.

medicine and agriculture being the best known. In June 1924, only 8 months before he died, he was invited to Schloss Kober-witz (then in German controlled Silesia, now part of Poland) to give a series of lectures and host some discussions (only eight of the former and four of the latter) on a new, non-chemical (Steiner never actually used the term Biodynamic) way forward for agriculture. These lectures were published under the title *Spiritual Foundations for the Renewal of Agriculture* and resulted in the formation of a group of farmers who wished to put his theoretical teachings into practice. By 1928, there were sixty-six farms working in the region, all using the Biodynamic preparations that are at the heart of the system and the Demeter symbol was introduced to guarantee the authenticity of their produce.

For a 'crank', some of Steiner's ideas seem remarkably persistent. Biodynamic agriculture has never been stronger and the public is starting to understand the difference between products farmed conventionally and those coming from organically and/or Biodynamically managed farms. In education, there are now about 1,200 schools (known as Waldorf or Waldorf-Steiner schools) and 2,000 kindergartens in 60 different countries that follow his teachings and 'anthroposophical medicine' is a

small, but important, branch of homeopathic medicine.

Organic and Biodynamic practices

In the EU, up until 1 August 2012, there was no such thing as organic or Biodynamic wine only 'wine made from organic [or Biodynamic] grapes'. However, from that date, Regulation 203/2012 came into force allowing winemakers who adhered to the rules to label their wines as organic or Biodynamic. The rules covered all aspects of wine production including: the type of tank (cannot be plastic or fibreglass), type of yeasts (cannot be genetically engineered and must be natural in the case of Biodynamic wines), sources of materials used in winemaking (must be organic/Biodynamic) and a whole host of other matters.

Organic and Biodynamic growers believe in high standards of soil management, in manures and composts that add 'vitality' back to their soils and, in the case of Biodynamic growers, in various 'preparations' that enhance the manures and composts they use and help the vineyard ecosystem function more naturally. These 'preps' are, if you want to put them into a human context, similar to probiotics which help restore and develop beneficial bacteria in the human digestive system. The preparations are used as starters for the composting process and – according to the claims of Biodynamic growers – result in composts with a higher humus content than those made conventionally. Some of these preparations are akin to human homeopathic medicines and rely on water retaining a 'memory' which transmits a message to the plant. Biodynamic growers also believe that noxious weeds and harmful pests can be warded off by spraying the weeds or plants with the burnt ashes of the weed seeds or animal remains (wild boars, rabbits or starlings for instance, all of which can harm vineyards and their crops) to send a kind of 'don't come back here anymore' message as a form of vineyard protection. This practice is known as 'ashing'. (I still recall spending an evening with James and Annie Millton, noted organic and Biodynamic wine producers from Gisborne, New Zealand, during which we went out into their vineyard to collect dock and thistle seeds so that James could 'ash' a vineyard against these noxious weeds. I remember vividly his care at not throwing a cigarette end onto the dying embers of the barbecue as this was to be where the weeds seeds were to be cremated. Unfortunately, I have never returned to find out if it worked or not.)

Organic and especially Biodynamic growers (and winemakers) also believe that both vineyard and winery operations are optimised by paying attention to solar, lunar, planetary and stellar cycles or rhythms. This is because Biodynamics is not only about using substances such as composts instead of chemical fertilisers, but also about *life forces* and *processes* which make the vineyard soils receptive to cosmic cycles and energies. However, while some cycles, such as pruning under a moon waning from full to new, allow two weeks per month of optimal work time, other cycles, such as picking when the moon stands in front of a so-called 'fire' constellation (such as Leo, Sagittarius or Aries) which are all fa-

vourable to fruit crops like wine grapes, only allow on average one day in four of optimal work time. Bigger vineyards thus have to make some compromises when working according to a celestial calendar.

The most famous modern Biodynamic gardening and farming calendar dates from 1963 and was originally produced by German agriculturalist Maria Thun who died in 2012. Her son Mathias, now publishes *The Maria Thun Biodynamic Calendar* showing which days are most suitable for certain tasks: ploughing, for instance, when the moon stands in front of an earth or root constellation such as Virgo, Taurus, or Capricorn, promotes deeper rooting; racking wines when the moon is descending (getting lower in height) in the sky minimises cloudiness (in the wine that is!). This aspect of organic and Biodynamic viticulture is one of the most controversial and one that conventional growers find least convincing. However, many conventional growers, when asked closely, will admit to remembering that '*my grandfather used to prune according to lunar cycles*', so this is hardly a new philosophy.

Scepticism about growing and making wine according to the planets is also far from new. In my oldest viticulture book, the wonderfully titled '*The Compleat Vineyard: or an Excellent Way for the Planting of Vines according to the German and French Manner and long practiced in England*' written by W. Hughes and published in 1670, the author states:

> 'I finde that in some Countries they are so curious in the time of gathering their Grapes, as to observe in what Signe or Degree the Moon is in, to chuse, if it be possible (as they Suppose) the best time, which (say they) is the moon being in Cancer, Leo, Scorpio, and Capricorn; but these are niceties not worth the taking notice of; only the time best to gather is when we can have them most ripe'.

Some things, it seems, never change!

However, my own experience in the cellar is that wines can taste different at different times. During the winemaking process one is often tasting wines from the same tank or barrel that one knows for certain has not been disturbed or touched between one tasting and the next. Yet, one finds that from day to day, week to week, month to month, they DO taste different! Whether this is cosmic cycles, the moon's phases, the atmospheric pressure (which I am sure affects taste), or the garlic-laden meal of the night before – who knows? The moon certainly has a huge influence on various natural occurrences – the word 'lunatic' is not used without some justification – and having been to Novia Scotia and seen the tides in Fundy Bay where the moon manages to move 115 billion tonnes of water up and down by 17 meters in 12 hours, one realises that it is a powerful object. If it can move this much water in the seas, what effect is it having on the water inside a plant?

Organic and Biodynamic does not mean 'not sprayed'

The aim of organic and Biodynamic vinegrowers is to grow vines in such a way that the plant's natural resistance to pests and diseases is increased. They do this by using natural fertilisers and composts – manure of animal origin often plays a part – and spraying their vines with unadulterated 'naturally occurring' chemicals, as well as *tisanes* (plant teas) and *purins* (liquid manures) made by soaking various herbs, weeds and plants in water. For vinegrowers, this restriction to naturally occurring chemicals usually means a reliance on such things as sulphur, copper, certain oils, soft-soaps, plus commercially available extracts of certain plants (such as rotenone derived from the Derris plant) which can be sprayed onto vines[70]. A quite widely used spray is a *tisane* made from a weed called Common Horsetail (*Equisetum*

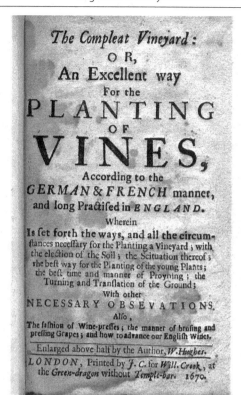

The Compleat Vineyard: OR, An Excellent way For the PLANTING OF VINES, According to the GERMAN & FRENCH manner, and long Practised in ENGLAND. Wherein Is set forth the ways, and all the circumstances necessary for the Planting a Vineyard; with the election of the Soil; the Scituation thereof; the best way for the Planting of the young Plants; the best time and manner of Proyning; the Turning and Translation of the Ground; With other NECESSARY OBSEVATIONS. Also, The fashion of Wine-presses; the manner of brusing and pressing Grapes; and how to advance our English Wines. Enlarged above half by the Author, *W. Hughes*. LONDON, Printed by *J. C.* for *Will. Crook*, at the *Green-dragon* without *Temple-bar*. 1670.

arvense) which is said to ward off fungal diseases. There are also some more controversial field preparations, such as Horn Manure 500, which is said to stimulate humus formation in the soil and thus promote deeper vine rooting. This is made by stuffing fresh cow manure into a cow's horn and burying it in the soil throughout the winter. Likewise, there is also Horn Silica 501 which is used to stimulate the vine's relationship with the sun. This is made by stuffing another cow horn with ground quartz (silica) and burying it for six months. Both preparations are made by taking the contents from the horn (after exhumation from the ground), diluting it and then stirring it into water in a counter rotating process (this is known as dynamising) before application to the soil or the crops.

For a Biodynamic compost pile to be effective it must have six Biodynamic compost preparations inserted into it. These are made from ground oak bark, stinging nettles, and the flowers of chamo-

70 Not all 'naturally occurring' products are that benign. I well remember on taking over a fruit farm in the mid-1970s having to dispose of several cans of nicotine (as well as tar-oil and soft soap) which the former owner had been happily using on his hops and which would certainly not be allowed today.

Biodynamic flowform for dynamising preparations.

Sheep keeping weeds and grasses down in a vineyard in the Alto Adige.

Costs of production in organic and Biodynamic vineyards

Whatever one's views of the effectiveness of growing grapes organically or Biodynamically, there is no doubt that to do so increases the cost of production. One of the major problems is weed-control and with conventional herbicides most decidedly not available, other measures have to be taken. Growers in warm and hot climates, especially where there is little or no rainfall during the bulk of the growing season, may find that the mow-and-throw technique, where grass and weeds mown from the centre of the alleyways are mechanically thrown underneath the vines to act as natural mulch, keeps weeds down to an acceptable level. Other mulches can also be used: chipped bark, composted household waste and straw are examples, but they do have to be certified organic to be used by organic growers. In damper climates, under-vine ploughs, cultivators and even weed-flamers might be used. These are usually considered to be more expensive ways to keep vines weed-free than with herbicides, if only because of the increase in the number of times a tractor and driver has to pass through the vineyard. Other measures include the use of naturally occurring chemicals such as soap, clove oil or acetic acid which have some effect upon suppressing weeds, but would need several treatments during the season to achieve good weed control. Some growers have tried sheep or goats, but for summer weed control (as opposed to winter cleaning-up services) sheep and goats give mixed results. Unless they are penned into quite tight areas, they will graze selectively and will start to nibble leaves and shoots, and have annoying habits like rubbing up against vines and posts and breaking the weaker ones. 'Weeder Geese' have also been used – 4 per acre are advised – to keep down both grass in the alleyways and weeds beneath the vines (and you can eat/sell them

mile, yarrow, dandelion and valerian (the latter pressed to make a liquid extract). Some of these compost preparations are pre-fermented using animal organs such as sheaths (bladders of red deer, cattle intestines, animal skulls and cow's peritoneum) as a means, it is said, of 'enhancing their capacity to sensitise the compost', and thus the farm soil onto which it is spread. There is little wonder that non-believers often talk about the muck-and-mystery approach of organic and Biodynamic growers.

afterwards). A lot of these slightly unusual ways of weed control look better in press releases and publicity shots than they actually perform in reality (although that's not to say that's a bad thing in itself.)

Undoubtedly pest and disease control in organic and Biodynamic vineyards is another area where costs are increased. The natural chemicals and products available to growers are generally less effective than their non-organic counterparts, will be contact and not systemic[71] and will almost always have to be applied more frequently to achieve adequate protection of the vines. They may also have longer harvest intervals. Although this may have little practical effect in dry regions as far as fungal diseases are concerned, pest control may prove particularly difficult. Natural insecticides such as pyrethrins (derived from chrysanthemum flowers) and barrier methods such as various oils and soaps, may well prove ineffective when faced with a concerted attack from pests. Damage to the fruit and lower yields will be the result. Crop quality in terms of pest and disease damage is often lower than with conventionally farmed grapes and this fact, coupled with the condition of fruiting buds and disease problems during flowering, may all reduce yields. Copper-containing sprays have been the main weapon against Downy Mildew for most organic and Biodynamic vinegrowers, but because copper persists in soil and builds up in the earthworm population and in other soil-borne organisms (slowly killing them), the amount of copper that can be sprayed by organic and Biodynamic vinegrowers has recently been reduced. It is now down to 4 kg a year for organic growers and only 3 kg a year for Biodynamic growers, both averaged over 5 years i.e. if you use 5 kg in one year (as an organic grower) you have to reduce your use in subsequent years, keeping under the 4 kg a year average. There was a proposal to make the average over 7 years, but this was rejected by the EU.

Are organic and Biodynamic wines better than conventional ones?

As has been pointed out, many organic and Biodynamic growers use some chemicals in their vineyards – something promotional literature and back labels often fail to publicise – and therefore if the wines produced from them possess special qualities, it does not come from being grown without some form of non-natural intervention. The evidence that wines produced from organic and Biodynamic grapes taste better *because they are organic and Biodynamic* is fairly hard to find. They may well taste better because they come from vines that are less heavily cropped and better tended, but this option is open to conventional growers as well[72]. They may come from vines where the human input in both management terms and physical work terms is higher and where such practices as canopy management, green-harvesting (crop thinning) and pre-harvest de-leafing are carried out manually and with attention to detail. Again, these practices are not unique to organic and Biodynamic viticulturalists and the fact that better wines may result is NOT the product of any adherence to the teachings of Steiner. It is interesting to note that relatively few of the world's really top wines are currently made from grapes grown organically or Biodynamically, although all of them restrict yields, many use manures of animal origin and their labour inputs are of the highest level.

Organic and Biodynamic viticulture – a summary

The commercial attractions of producing crops that are more 'natural' and 'unadulterated' and which have an appeal to those who seek less chemically-grown food and

71 Contact sprays are those that sit on the outside of the plant and provide a barrier against diseases. They will deteriorate in the sunshine and can be washed off by rain. Systemic sprays are those that are taken up by the plant, mainly through its leaves, and work from the inside out. They usually only require 30 minutes dry weather to be absorbed.

72 Organic and Biodynamic growers in other branches of agriculture and horticulture who use varieties of fruit and vegetables which are known to have better flavours than their modern counterparts (most of which have been bred for maximum yields, perfect skin finish, uniform size and better disease resistance) may well grow better tasting crops than conventional growers, albeit at lower yield levels. Vine growers do not have this option if they want to use standard 'international' varieties.

and winery waste, using natural manures, achieving open, balanced canopies through irrigation control and managing the alleyways and under-vine areas in a way that produces a more harmonious vineyard, are all sound viticultural practices with which they agree. The cry from organic and Biodynamic growers is often one of 'sustainability' and the assumption is that theirs is the true path. There is a lot of talk about how conventional agriculture leads to soil that is 'damaged' or 'degraded' without ever explaining how this can be measured. However, in my experience, most conventional farmers, and especially grape growers, farm in a way which does seemingly no harm to their land and all of them wish their land to remain in good heart so that it can be handed on to future generations. There is an old saying in agriculture that 'the best fertiliser is the farmer's footstep' meaning that farmers who get out amongst their crops and *notice* what's going on – what stage the crop is at and whether their plants are looking well or not – are always going to know when to take pre-emptive measures against pests and diseases, when to cultivate or not or whether to trim. These growers will always produce better crops than those whose attention to detail is not so thorough.

drink and for which a premium can be charged, has seen the number of organic and Biodynamic vinegrowers increase in recent years. Accurate figures are hard to obtain, but globally it seems that somewhere around 3 per cent of the world's wines are currently organic or Biodynamic. Small that maybe, but it has massively increased over the last ten years and judging by the way things are going, is set to continue to increase. However, vineyards are usually run as commercial enterprises and they still need to show a positive balance of output against input. As James Millton said at a recent Master of Wine seminar about farming organically 'you can't be in the red and be green'. The additional costs of farming organically and Biodynamically make this, in many regions, a difficult, even impossible task. It is also quite common today to hear and read about vineyards that are run 'along organic lines' although not actually taking the trouble to sign up to the full schemes. There is a suspicion that their motives are partly presentational and done in an attempt to climb aboard the band-wagon and grab some of the price-premium that (they think) these wines achieve.

Many conventional winegrowers have little quarrel with their organic and Biodynamic brothers and sisters. Reducing levels of chemical inputs, composting vineyard

Organic and Biodynamic practices are often faulted for having a weak scientific basis. However, this is really not surprising. There is little money to be made into proving that Biodynamic compost beats oil-based fertilisers or that a nettle-tea is cheaper than and just as effective as a slickly marketed chemical spray. I also have no doubt that there is also a strong placebo effect at work in all organic and Biodynamic vineyards. How this is possible I have no idea and I certainly have no proof to back this statement up – it just seems as likely to be true as most of the other claims made by organic and Biodynamic growers. Prince Charles was once derided for talking to his plants but I have a sneaky feeling that he had a point. However, when influences and topics such as 'geo-acupuncture, dynamised preparations, viticultural homeopathy and sensitive crystallisation' start cropping up in relation to growing grapes, I am afraid I start to wonder what it is all about. Having said that, I do believe that we are nowhere near fully (or even partially) understanding how the whole eco-system works in relation to agriculture and if it is possible to train plants to defend themselves against pests, diseases, drought and stress, then the world would be a better place.

It would be a poor farmer who would argue against the idea that a reduction of chemical inputs, an increase in the use of naturally derived composts and fertilisers and an attention to detail in the vineyard were anything other than beneficial. But one always has to remember that farming has to have an economic basis and many farmers cannot afford to experiment too much and prefer to stick with their (completely legal) conventional practices, and let others do the research into alternative methods of crop production. As far as vineyards go, there is the added dimension of the consumer who (of course) likes the idea of their wines being produced more 'naturally', more 'sustainably' and without the chance of pesticide residues. However, one thing is certain, it is not pesticide or fungicide residues in conventional wines that pose a threat to health. Customers buying organic and Biodynamic wines because they are fearful that conventional wines might poison them should take a look at the labels – it's the alcohol in the bottle that's the killer!

Chapter 11

Diseases and viruses of grapevines, including trunk diseases

Note: (1) Product names used in this chapter are those used in the UK. Other countries may use different product names for the same active ingredient. Application rates and harvest intervals may also differ from country to country.

(2) The term 'pesticide' in law means any product used in agriculture to control pests or diseases. This would include: fungicides, insecticides, acaricides (against mites), molluscicides (against slugs and snails), and herbicides, plus any products used to deter animals, birds or other predators from damaging the crop. It would not include fertilisers, plant stimulants and mineral oils (stickers and wetters) used to make pesticides more effective.

Diseases and viruses of grapevines, including trunk diseases

As with any intensive agricultural or horticultural crop, there are a large number of diseases (as well as pests, viruses and other viticultural problems) that can damage vines and, left untreated, make the production of economically viable crops difficult. Over the last few decades however, several factors have made the care of vines in this respect easier and today's vineyard owners and managers have a better armoury of defences against the regularly occurring problems.

Clones of both rootstock and scion varieties are better than ever and disease resistance and absence of viruses are both high on the list of attributes when selecting material for cloning. The introduction of an EU wide plant passport system in the early 1990s, with its concomitant source inspections and ELISA[73] testing for viruses, has increased the quality of grafted vines. Better

73 ELISA stands for Enzyme-Linked ImmunoSorbent Assay and is test for viruses in many different areas: plants, food and human tissu

74 The smaller the droplet size, the greater is the overall surface area of contact between the chemical contained in the droplets and the plant (mainly the leaf). This means that less product can be used, but to greater effect and the amount lost to 'run-off' (i.e. dripping) is also less.

hygiene in rootstock vineyards, scion mother-gardens and vine nurseries has also lessened the chance of viruses and diseases being transmitted to destination vineyards, although as the incidence of trunk diseases (dealt with later in this chapter) shows, hardwood diseases have by no means disappeared. However, nothing in nature stands still for long and the discovery in California in 2008 of what was thought to be a variant of leafroll virus, but turned out to be a new virus, now known as Red Blotch, shows that vigilance is still required when inspecting vineyards.

Better trellising and training methods – ones more suited to mechanisation – mean that much of the work in vineyards can now be carried out from the seat of a tractor and regular spraying, in regions where this is required, can be done promptly and efficiently. Tractors and spraying equipment are more advanced than ever, with four-wheel drive and air-conditioned comfort-cabs standard on most new tractors. GPS guided tractors (common in arable and horticulture) both manned and unmanned, are starting to make an appearance on fruit farms and vineyards. Improvements in spraying equipment such as nozzles which produce much smaller, evenly-sized droplets[74] are a vast improvement over the old 'spray to run-off' type of sprayers used in the past. Low-volume and recirculation sprayers (which catch, filter and recirculate spray that misses the target) mean that more hectares can be sprayed for any given tank size and productivity is greatly increased. Recirculation sprayers also use up to 50 per cent less spray than normal sprayers, costs of chemicals used are also halved and less is lost to the environment. There is also a much greater realisation that canopy management can play an important part in helping overcome diseases. Heat, light and air are all enemies of fungal disease and if the vineyard canopy is open, with no more than 3–4 leaf layers, has good air drainage through, and especially beneath it, then the vines will dry out more quickly and fungal problems kept to a minimum. Implements such as mechanical trimmers and leaf strippers, which facilitate timely canopy management, are now commonplace.

The spectrum of pests, diseases and other viticultural problems that a vineyard owner will have to deal with will be dependent on many factors: whereabouts in the world the vineyard is, what the climate is, what the weather in the year in question is like and which variety, clone and rootstock is being grown. Economics will also play a part, as will wine style and quality. Every grower would like to bring 100 per cent clean, undamaged grapes into the winery – that much is obvious – but sometimes there is a trade-off between cost and reward and consideration has to be given to the economics of production. The increased use of machine harvesters also means that growers have to have very clean crops if they are not to be penalised at the winery door. You can tell your pickers to pick only the clean grapes; such instructions do not work that well with a machine harvester! Annual differences will also be very noticeable and will be dependent on rainfall, sunshine and heat levels. Some diseases are carried from plant to plant by insects (known as vectors) and control of these vectors (spraying with insecticide and habitat reduction) may well play a part in controlling seemingly uncon-

Double-sided recirculation sprayer working in a UK vineyard.

nected maladies. Other factors such as exposure to prevailing winds, vineyard-floor treatment and prevalence of natural predators (in the case of pests) will also play a part. There is also today more emphasis on monitoring to gauge the pressure of both diseases and pests, with targeted traps, some fitted with remote cameras that record the number of trap-visits per 24 hours, starting to appear in vineyards. Small weather stations which record a wide range of parameters are also becoming much more common in vineyards. The data from these can then be used to predict different 'disease events' and sprays timed accordingly.

Integrated Pest Management (IPM)

There is no doubt that in the past many crops were over-treated with sprays of pesticides and much land has been too liberally sprayed with herbicides. Over the last 25 years however, a combination of factors has moved farmers and growers away from a 'spray first – ask questions afterwards' mentality towards one of trying to understand how problems arise, doing everything possible to mitigate the problem through non-invasive, non-chemical methods and then, as a final resort, using the least possible

Solar-powered mini weather station in a Mornington Peninsular vineyard.

75 Strobilurins are sprays developed from a species of toadstool called *Strobilurus tenacellus*.

amount of chemical to protect their crops. Of course, this is not all altruism. Chemicals are expensive to buy and apply – they typically rank second (behind labour) in terms of cost of production – and their use is tightly controlled by legal restrictions. There is also a much greater awareness by the public that over-sprayed foodstuffs are to be avoided and an increased understanding by farmers and growers that they are custodians of the land they farm and that sustainability must be part-and-parcel of their agricultural operations. The organic and Biodynamic movements have also done their bit to create awareness that it is possible to farm using fewer chemical inputs. Taken together, these factors have made everyone involved with pest, disease and weed control think about ways of minimising chemical inputs to the benefit of the environment, wildlife, the land, the public and farmers and growers.

Integrated Pest Management (IPM) has been around for several decades now and in France is known as *lutte raisonée* or *lutte intégrale*. Wherever it is practiced its aims are much the same: to know what causes the problem; to monitor the situation (usually the weather) to know whether the problem is likely to arise; and to take timely preventative measures instead of (usually) more costly curative measures. IPM also uses natural predators wherever possible, be they parasitic wasps whose larvae destroy certain caterpillars or the strobilurin-based anti-*Oidium* treatment[75]. Some problems – Pierce's Diseases is probably the best known – have proved impossible to control with chemicals, and this one will (hopefully) in time be defeated with a natural predator to the leafhopper insects (the grey-green and glassy winged sharp-shooters) that spread this bacterial disease. Likewise, scientists believe that they may one day find a beneficial nematode that could destroy *Phylloxera* larvae below ground level, thus obviating the need for grafting in some soils. The use of suitable cover crops planted in the middle of vineyard rows, raises the levels of naturally occurring predators in the vineyard, and also helps in preventing soil erosion on sloping sites. However, it may also increase the habitat for disease vectors.

The easiest way to see IPM in action is to look at the University of California's IPM web site (*www.ipm.ucanr.edu*) which covers all crops grown in the state. Look under *agricultural pests* and then *grape* and you can see the array of aids available to a Californian grape grower. Have a look at the Risk Index (RI) pages for diseases such as Powdery Mildew (Oidium). Here you can see, for a variety of sites, the daily risk levels of this disease, based upon the temperature and humidity in the vineyards. From this, growers can assess whether they need to spray or not. Have a look also at the Natural Enemies Gallery to see how many naturally occurring predators there are which could be put to use on the grower's behalf. In France, the Champagne region is probably the one that has done the most to introduce its growers to the *viticulture raisonée* and the CIVC issues an annual *Guide Pratique* for growers to follow. The genesis of the drive in Champagne to get vineyard owners to practice more natural ways of farming seems to have been the criticism of the once widespread practice of using Paris's composted household waste in their vineyards. This led to some very unsightly top-dressings of cut-up plastic bags and bottles which inevitably found their way into the compost, coupled with the almost universal use of total herbicide in the region. The spreading of this compost has now stopped and total herbicide vineyards have disappeared. Growers in Champagne are now using grass and cover-crops in the rows and undervine cultivators for weed control. By 2025, Champagne wants to be herbicide-free.

For many small growers however, IPM is something that is difficult to practice to its fullest extent. Small growers may well rely upon spray recommendations from their chemical suppliers (not perhaps the most independent of advisors), but will always attempt to reduce the concentrations used if only in order to lower costs. Growers who are under contract to wineries to supply grapes or belong to co-operatives will often have to follow the spray programmes provided by the end user of the grapes and therefore their options are also limited. However, all growers will fine-tune their chemical inputs according to their experience with their own vineyards and varieties and cost-saving is a powerful incentive to economise and reduce quantities of materials. Many growers now have small weather stations which give real-time information about the weather in their vineyards and most are plugged in to a reporting system which will give disease predictions, based upon temperature, rainfall and humidity, allowing them to time their spraying more accurately.

Having said all of the above, there is a sneaking feeling that some growers are signing up to sustainability schemes not because they want to, but because they feel they ought to for presentational purposes to both the general public and trade wine-buyers. Woe betide the grower who, when asked by the young thrusting wine-buyer from a major multiple 'what's your sustainability programme' and they answer 'err – we don't have one'. They are toast.

Harvest intervals

All pesticides used in agriculture are rigorously tested before being given clearance to be used and each chemical will have either an 'on-label' or an 'off-label' approval. This will depend on whether the product has been classed for use on a very wide range of crops and situations (on-label) or whether it is for minor crops and certain restricted circumstances (off-label). This approval will detail how the product may be used, what type of sprayer it can be used in, how often it may be sprayed and how many times in a growing season, what amount of product can be used per application and per season, and whether it is compatible and can be tank-mixed with other products. Lastly, in the case of fungicides and insecticides, the approval will also state how many days must elapse between the last treatment and harvest, known as the 'harvest interval'. It will differ from crop to crop and naturally from product to product. Most products used on wine grapes (as opposed to grapes for juice, the table or for drying) have quite long harvest intervals (up to 56 days for some products) as there is a danger, if traces remain on or in the grapes, that yeasts will have difficulty multiplying and fermentation will be affected. All pesticides have a Maximum Residue Level (MRL) which must not be exceeded. Growers therefore looking to apply their last spray, typically against late-season diseases such as *Botrytis*, will have to make an educated guess as to whether they can let the crop stand for the two to three weeks harvest interval if they apply a final spray. Modern residue testing equipment based upon GC-MS (gas chromatography-mass spectrometry) has got more and more accurate, cheaper and easier to use, and can now detect residues as small as 0.01mg/kg which is the equivalent, according to a well-known wine analyst, of 'one grain of salt in 100,000 litres of wine' and is way below all MRLs. Even though growers are using pesticides legally, using the right equipment, the right concentrations and adhering generously to harvest intervals, they may still produce grapes and wines in which there are detectable (but officially not harmful) residues.

Roses and vines

Roses are often planted at the ends of rows of vines and whilst today they are purely decorative, roses did once act as an early warning system against mildew on vines. The same weather conditions that gave rise to mildew on roses (which incidentally was specific to roses and would not transfer to vines), would also be the same conditions that would cause vines to become infected with mildew, but 10–14 days in advance. Vinegrowers would then know that it was time to spray their vines. Today, many modern rose varieties have been cross-bred, hybridised and clonally selected so that they seldom get mildew, black-spot and other ailments, so they serve no practical purpose in vineyards – apart from prompting visitors to ask: *'why do you grow roses at the end of your rows?'* (And making their vineyards look a bit prettier).

Diseases caused by fungi, bacteria and bacteria-like organisms

Worldwide, there are a very large number of different bacterial diseases that affect vines and to list all would be impossible within the scope of this book. I have therefore only selected those that have the most impact. *Botrytis*, Downy Mildew, and *Oidium* are the most geographically widespread and economically damaging and are listed first. The others are dealt with in alphabetical order. Trunk diseases are dealt with in a separate section after other diseases.

Botrytis – Pourriture Gris, Grey Mould, Grey Rot, Bunch Rot, Sour Rot, Stein Rot

Botrytis (*Botrytis cinerea*) is a very common fungus that occurs widely in nature and attacks all manner of vegetable, salad and fruit crops. Lettuces that turn brown and start to liquefy and strawberries and raspberries that subside into a mass of grey/mauve mould are all being attacked by *Botrytis*. It particularly likes wet and damp conditions and thrives where sugar is present – hence its liking for grapes, especially when grown in climates with summer and autumn rain. It is also a problem for table-grape growers if they have to store their grapes and for nurserymen who store wood for grafting. Not only does *Botrytis* lead to physical loss of crop, but also reduces crop quality. If white grapes are heavily infected, some additional SO_2 in the picking bins, better pre-fermentation settling (especially with the addition of bentonite) and a prompt fermentation using a high dose of active yeast, may well produce a wine without any noticeable *Botrytis* taint, but some fruit aromas and flavours will have been lost, the colour may well be a shade darker and more SO_2 will be required in the finished wine in order to achieve a good level of stability. In red wines, where fermentations take place in the presence of skins and pulp, more serious problems may arise including off-flavours and mouldy taints which will need charcoal fining to remove them.

Botrytis is usually present in susceptible vineyards throughout the year. It overwinters in the shape of *sclerotia* (hard, dark-brown encrustations of the dormant fungus) which are present on old wood and on grapes that have not been picked or have fallen to the vineyard floor. As soon as spring conditions are suitable, the *sclerotia* will provide the nucleus for the fungus to infect the young green tissue in the vineyard. In vineyards in regions with summer rainfall and growing varieties known to be susceptible, spraying against *Botrytis* will start when first one or two leaves are expanded to about 25 mm across and may well continue at ten to fourteen day intervals until just before harvest. There will be years when two or three pre-flowering sprays, followed by perhaps one during flowering and two to three after will still be too few; there may on the other hand be years, especially when growing conditions are dry and when the variety in question has a degree of in-built resistance, when two sprays prior to flowering and two after will suffice.

As with many diseases, the damage it can do early in the season, if uncontrolled, will make life much harder later on. *Botrytis* will infect the flowers and in a year with wet flowering conditions especially when the flower caps struggle to detach themselves from the flowers, the disease can remain trapped in the centre of the bunch. As the grapes expand and the bunch closes, the disease will be deep inside and no amount of spraying will penetrate to the centre, although the use of systemic sprays will help. Flower debris remaining in the closed bunch will lead to classic bunch rot and may result in substantial crop loss. Growers in susceptible areas will usually make sure that as flowering finishes they give their vines a good blast with a high-volume air assisted sprayer, loaded with an effective anti-*Botrytis* chemical. This will hopefully do two things: blow out and disperse any fragments of flower caps and stamens left within the bunch and coat the remainder with a protective spray.

Botrytis is also a disease that has a reputation for becoming resistant to certain chemicals. In the 1960s and well into the 1970s, the main products used against *Botrytis* contained an active ingredient called *benzimidazole* (marketed as Benlate or Benomyl) which for many years were very effective. However, growers found that after using them for several years on the same fields, not only did their worm populations start to dwindle, but also the effectiveness of the products fell away and it was realised that their particular strain of *Botrytis* (it has a habit of becoming site specific) had become resistant.

The next generation of anti-*Botrytis* products were based upon active ingredients called *dicarboximides* – Ronilan, Rovral WG and Sumisclex were the three best known – and these proved reliable for a decade or more until, once again, their effectiveness tailed off and resistant strains of *Botrytis* surfaced, although Rovral WG, which has a 14 day HI, can still be used in conjunction with other products up to a maximum of four applications per season. In 1995, a completely new product called Scala, based upon an active ingredient called *pyrimethanil,* was introduced. This is a systemic product (all the previous products are contact only) and its use is restricted to a maximum of only two applications per year. It is, however, one of the most effective materials against *Botrytis*, but it has a 21-day HI in the UK (although outside Europe it only has a 7-day HI). Other products based upon different active ingredients, such as Teldor, Switch and Prolectus (all of which are limited to one or two applications per season), are also permitted for use against *Botrytis*.

In addition to the pesticides listed above, three other products are also permitted for use against *Botrytis* on grapes in the UK. Serenade ASO is a bio-fungicide based upon *Bacillus subtilis* and has no HI, making it useful for the final anti-*Botrytis* spray, although it is one of the most expensive products on the market. Prestop is another bio-fungicide, based upon *Gliocladium catenulatum* which also has a zero-day HI. How effective these bio-products are is open to question and not everyone who has tried them has been totally happy. The third anti-*Botrytis* recommendation is for a growth regulator called Regalis Plus which, if sprayed towards the end of the flowering period, will open up the bunch by reducing the number of berries on the bunch. In years with good flowering conditions, where bunches are expected to be large, and especially with tight-bunched varieties (Chardonnay and some clones of Pinot Noir for instance), this could be considered.

Prudent growers will normally use a combination of different products throughout the growing season so as to reduce the possibility of resistant strains of *Botrytis* building up and to-date, Scala has maintained its reputation as a proven tool in the winegrower's armoury. In my opinion, this one chemical bears a huge responsibility for the ability of growers to produce cleaner crops of riper grapes at higher natural alcohol levels – something few back-labels or winemaker's notes come clean about – owing to the fact that they have much more confidence in the ability of their grapes to ripen without rotting. Increased hang-time is only really possible where your grapes remain healthy until picked.

Botrytis is also a secondary invader and will take advantage of grapes that have been damaged by such things as machinery, hail, insects or birds. In these situations, where the skin of the grape has been split and the pulp exposed, *Botrytis* will develop and gradually infect the whole bunch. It can also just affect the stem of the bunch, causing 'stem rot' which will result in large, even very large, numbers of bunches to fall to the ground. This can be a particular problem in years with large crops, where the stems have been weakened by a general strain on the vine's resources.

Spraying chemicals is not, however, the only technique to control *Botrytis* and good pruning, good trellising and suitable canopy management all help. An open leaf canopy, some shoot and leaf removal in the fruiting zone, and good air movement beneath the vines, will help control the development and spread of the disease. Foliage spreaders can also be used to separate the canes and therefore the bunches. Spores are quickly transmitted from one part of the vine to the other by dripping water, so the quicker the leaves and shoots dry out, the less the disease will spread. An open leaf canopy will also allow chemical sprays to reach their target more easily. In susceptible regions, grape varieties and clones that have smaller leaves, are less vigorous and have an open growth habit with bunches that are less compact (looser) and have a degree of built-in resistance to fungal problems, will be much less prone to *Botrytis* (and of course other fungal diseases) and are to be preferred and will be more rewarding. In Germany (and maybe in other countries as well, although I have not seen it) some Pinot Noir growers practice *traubenteilen* which involves cutting bunches in half at around *véraison*. This technique halves the size of the bunch and causes the shoulders of the bunch to droop, thus loosening the bunch and making access for air, light and sprays easier.

Despite the efforts of vine breeders, *Botrytis* is not a disease that can be easily (if ever) bred out. The problem is that it is a disease which colonises decaying and dead plant material, something common to all plants as they near the end of their existence. However, what can be bred into varieties is something known as 'bunch architecture' which means clones with looser bunches, having larger stalks and more separated berries. There are several loose-berried clones of Pinot Noir for instance, a variety that is fairly *Botrytis* prone. In France these are known as *grappes lache* clones, in German as *lockerbeerige klone* of which the Mariafeld types are a good example. The vine nursery www.sibbus.com has some good information on these.

Botrytis – Noble Rot, Pourriture Noble, Edelfäule

Once grapes reach a potential alcohol level of around 7 per cent, *Botrytis* will affect the grape in a different way. Feeding on the skin of the berry, the fungus will puncture the skin without splitting it and will allow water to leach out. This happens in a slow controlled manner and over time – perhaps up to six weeks – individual grapes on the bunch will shrivel considerably. Such juice as is left in the grape will be much lower in volume, but in terms of sugar content will be much higher. For this to happen several things are necessary: the crop must be clean up until the point where the sugar level rises to the correct level; the weather should be warm, even hot; and humidity is required for the *Botrytis* spores to develop. Early morning mists (as found in Sauternes and Tokaji) are often held to be the secret to good *Botrytis* development. The most suitable grape varieties for this have been found to be: Sémillon and Sauvignon Blanc (Sauternes, Barsac, Montbazillac, Australia), Riesling (German *Trockenbeerenauslese, Beerenauslese, Auslese*), Furmint and Hárslevlú (Tokaji), Chenin Blanc (Loire sweet wines), Gewürztraminer, Muscat, Pinot Gris and Riesling (Alsace's *Vendange Tardive* and *Selection des Grains Nobles*)[76]. In Austria, *Ruster Ausbruch* wines from the region around the town of Rust (which borders the lake called the Neusiedlersee), are made from various *Botrytis*-infected grape var-ieties – Furmint, Welschriesling, Pinot Blanc, Chardonnay and Pinot Gris being the main ones. These are all varieties which have relatively high acid levels and the best sweet wines are those which have enough natural acidity to balance the high levels of residual sugar.

Botrytis affecting a bunch of Riesling grapes

In some warm and dry regions (Australia and California), where *Botrytis* is not a natural phenomenon, attempts are made to induce the disease by keeping the grapes humid with irrigation and spraying them with a liquid infused with active *Botrytis* spores. In the production of sweet wines from *Botrytis* infected grapes, the presence of an antibiotic called *botryticine* (produced by the fungus) inhibits yeast growth and is probably one of the reasons why these wines (a) ferment very slowly and (b) seldom re-ferment, even though copious amounts of residual sugar remain in them.

At their best, wines made from *Botrytis*-affected grapes have a unique balance of sugar and acidity, are rich in glycerol and keep almost indefinitely. Yields can sometimes be ridiculously low. Château d'Yquem averages about 7 hl-ha (one glass per vine) and with *Trockenbeerenauslese* wines, the harvest may well number just a few hundred half-bottles per hectare. The best are justifiably expensive, long-lasting and (in my opinion) worth saving up for.

76 In Alsace, Muscat blanc à petit grains and Muscat Ottonel are allowed to be made into *Vendange Tardive* and *Selection des Grains Nobles* wines.

77 *Mildiou* is the name the French give to Downy Mildew.

Downy Mildew – Peronospora, Mildiou[77]

Downy Mildew (*Plasmopara viticola*), which originated in North America, was first seen in Europe in 1878 and spread quickly throughout all wine regions. It is now endemic and present in a majority of the world's vineyards, although by no means all. Some growers in Oregon say they have never seen it. It overwinters on fallen leaves and, once present in a vineyard, is impossible to eradicate although with regular sprays it can be kept under control. It likes warm, damp conditions and will attack any green part of the vine once the weather warms up in the spring and if allowed to spread unchecked, will destroy flowers and berries, leading to complete crop loss. Grapes, if affected, will turn leathery (hence the German name for the disease *lederbeeren* – leatherberry) and shrivel. If present in sufficient numbers in the harvest, infected grapes will impart a characteristic mouldy taint to the wine. A common pattern to the spread of the disease is that chemical control is gained by the grower in the early part of the year, but as the leaf-wall increases in thickness and density and spray penetration into, and air movement within, the canopy becomes more difficult, late season outbreaks of the disease occur. In these instances, leaves become severely damaged and photosynthesis is reduced, leading to a slowing down of the ripening process.

Control of Downy Mildew is helped by the usual physical ones – opening up the leaf-wall to light, air and drying winds – but these alone will not eradicate the disease and spraying will be necessary. In 1885 it was discovered (by accident[78]) that sprays containing copper were effective against Downy Mildew which led to the development of Bordeaux Mixture, a blend of slaked (or hydrated) lime and copper sulphate, and a very potent protective spray

78 It is said that growers with vineyards alongside a road would spray their grapes with copper sulphate which is both visible and bitter to the taste in order to stop passers-by helping themselves and noticed that these vines did not get Downy Mildew.

against the disease. Its characteristic blue/mauve dusty traces can be seen in vineyards throughout the world. It is very rainfast and if used as a post-harvest, pre-winter spray, will help control the disease through the dormant period. The disadvantages of Bordeaux Mixture are that it needs preparing freshly each time it is used, it isn't stable and cannot be stored for long. It is also only a protectant, not an eradicant. The major issue with its use however, is that it leads to increased levels of copper in the soil which is both toxic to earthworms and other soil flora and fauna. The amount allowed to be used in EU vineyards has slowly been reduced over the past few decades and it currently stands at a maximum of 4 kg of copper per year, averaged over 7 years. Today, Bordeaux Mixture is used far less and other, easier to store, products are available, those containing copper oxychloride and copper hydroxide being the most common. These require no preparation, are stable, can be stored and are less likely to persist in the soil. Luckily there are also many non-copper containing fungicides available for control of Downy Mildew, many developed to control Potato Blight, which is a very similar disease.

Organic and Biodynamic producers are in an especially difficult situation with regard to Downy Mildew. With the quantities of copper allowed being reduced all the time (eventually it is assumed to a point where the amount allowed is no longer effective), organic and Biodynamic grape growing becomes increasingly more problematic. Although some PIWI and older hybrid varieties have a degree of natural protection, there are no mainstream varieties that are resistant to it. It remains to be seen how this challenge will be faced in the future.

Oidium – Powdery Mildew

Oidium tuckerii – now more correctly called *Uncinula necator* – is a fungal disease, native to North America. It was first described there in 1834, but it did not really damage native varieties and caused little excitement. Its first appearance in Europe was, somewhat surprisingly, in Margate on the English north Kent coast in 1845 (the same year as potato blight appeared in Ireland). Here, a Mr. Tucker, gardener to Mr. John Slater, noticed a white powdery discolouration on a few leaves of a vine in a greenhouse under his care. These he sent to a Reverend M. J. Berkeley, an expert on fungi, who wrote an account of the 'new' disease for the *Gardener's Chronicle and Agricultural Gazette* and named it (incorrectly as it happened, as it is not a true Oidium) after gardener Tucker[79].

It soon appeared in France – the keeper of the Versailles grape-forcing houses complained of the new disease in 1846 – and it quickly spread throughout the vineyard regions, causing widespread damage. Tucker had already noticed the physical and visual similarity between 'his' mildew and that of peach mildew which was then (as it still can be today) controlled by sprays of sulphur and it was found that this remedy worked on vines. The vintage of 1854 was the smallest in France since 1788 (a year when French *paysanniere* no doubt had other things on their minds), caused by nationwide attacks of *Oidium*. Only then did growers take to treating their vines with sulphur – sprayed in cooler regions and dusted[80] in warmer ones – which, if used in time, is a very cheap and effective remedy. It was also found that sulphur had the effect of both increasing yields and bringing the harvest forward by 7–10 days, two factors which made the uptake of sulphur as an effective remedy quite rapid. Sulphur also works to a certain extent against other diseases and against mites, so its protection against *Oidium* was but one of a number of benefits. Sulphur applications should not be made either just before or during flowering as scorching of flowers may occur, with

consequent loss of crop. Spraying with sulphur should continue throughout the summer if weather conditions are helpful to the disease.

Oidium is one of the few fungal diseases that are worse in dry years than they are in wet ones and unlike most fungal diseases, it does not require water to convey it from one part of a plant to another. Air with sufficient humidity is enough. It prefers warm, humid weather (20°C–27°C) and still, dry canopies and thrives inside shaded canopies. It overwinters on old wood and given the right conditions, will start producing spores which are spread by the wind and will attack any part of the vine, often early in the season. If early infections are allowed to take place, prevention with sulphur is impossible and other – more expensive – chemicals will have to be employed to eradicate it. *Oidium* attacks the leaves with a characteristic white powdery covering and causes the young berries to split open exposing the seeds. Usually, as Oidium attacks early in the season, damaged berries never reach the point where they ripen and only if there is a large number of damaged berries remaining on the vine when it is (machine) harvested, will there be taints in the juice. Sulphur used to have a harvest interval between 21 and 56 days (depending on the exact formulation) but about a twenty years ago, its legal status changed from that of a pesticide to a fertiliser. This was because since the reduction in the use of coal and coal products for both domestic and industrial heating and energy production, sulphur levels in the atmosphere have fallen considerably, and with that, sulphur levels in soil. Many arable farmers now find that they need to add sulphur to their soils, something which 50 years ago was unheard of. This means that growers can use as much as they like and as often as they like. In some countries there are no harvest intervals for sulphur, but spraying or dusting of sulphur should finish in good time before

79 There is some doubt about this 1845 date as in Archibald Barron's Vines and Vine Culture of 1883, he states that 'in the year 1831 or 1832, the Rev M. J. Berkeley observed the appearance of this mildew in the vinery of Mr. J. Slater, of Margate, which was under the care of Mr. Tucker' and continues by saying that 'an account of this was given by Mr. Tucker to the Kentish Gazette'. I have not been able to verify this.

80 Dusting of sulphur is preferred in warmer regions as it is less likely to cause scalding or russeting of the grape's skin. Dusting is often carried out very early in the morning when there is still dew on the grapes so that the sulphur sticks to the skin, before being absorbed as the skin dries out as the sun rises.

Modern low-volume sprayer spraying three rows at once in a young vineyard

the harvest as if residues are left on the grapes, hydrogen sulphide (H_2S), with its characteristic smell of rotten eggs, may well be produced during fermentation.

Luckily, *Oidium* is one of the easiest diseases to predict and therefore take preventative measures against. Using a combination of temperature, humidity and rainfall readings, it is relatively simple to determine when *Oidium* will be putting out spores and therefore when spraying will be most effective. This forecasting is necessary as *Oidium* is a disease which does not give its presence away visually until it is well into its second generation i.e. too late to take preventative measures. Organic growers – and even some conventional growers – are using a light mineral oil as an alternative to sulphur. This oil, which destroys the cells of the fungus, also has a similar effect on *Botrytis*, as well as some mites and spiders. Apart from sulphur, there are a large number of alternative chemicals and preparations used to control *Oidium* and more recently sprays based upon strobilurins are proving very effective. Sprays of potassium bicarbonate have also been shown to be effective.

Further diseases in alphabetical order

Anthracnose – Bird's Eye Rot, Black Spot

A disease of European origin and one that, before the introduction of Powdery and Downy Mildew, caused considerable loss of crops. It is a disease of damper climates and usually occurs quite early in the season. However, Anthracnose is easily controlled by Bordeaux Mixture and other copper-containing fungicides and it is seldom an isolated problem.

Armillaria Root Rot – Honey Fungus, Oak-Root Fungus

A common problem in woodland and forests, this fungus can attack the roots of vines, especially where vineyards have been established on land that was once wooded. The symptoms are a decline in vigour and eventual wilting of the plant. Often this can be quite sudden and vines will die within a few weeks. Trees growing on the site will usually have shown symptoms of the disease on their roots and is a problem that should be anticipated prior to planting on once-forested land. Control is unfortunately almost impossible except on very localised areas where soil fumigation (usually with methyl bromide) can be undertaken. On large areas this is an impractical solution. The most practical solution, where this fungus is known to be present, is to fallow the land for as long as possible, deep ploughing the land at regular intervals to expose and destroy old tree roots. Although researchers are working on a resistant rootstock, one has yet to be developed.

Bacterial Blight

Bacterial blight is a problem in many parts of the world and although not widespread, when present can cause the abandonment of vineyards as there is no known cure. Infected vines gradually lose their vigour, yields fall and eventually they become un-economic. The only method of control is to remove infected vines and pruners must disinfect their secateurs in-between vines. Copper sprays help with its control and it is worse in regions with summer rainfall than in drier areas.

Black Rot

Black Rot, (known as *Le Black-Rot* in France), is caused by an organism called *Guignardia bidwellii* and impossible to eradicate once present in a vineyard. It is native to North America and was introduced into French vineyards in the 1880s. Control is aided by keeping a clean vineyard, destroying affected material (especially unpicked or fallen grapes) and having an open and airy canopy. However, chemical control will be necessary in most vineyards. Black Rot will start early in the season, as soon as temperature and moisture conditions are right, and sprays need to continue through, and until well after, flowering. Luckily it is controlled by the same spectrum of chemicals used to control the other major fungal diseases (Downy Mildew in particular), so in practical terms it is not a disease that requires singular treatment.

Crown Gall – Black Knot

Caused by a bacterium called *Agrobacterium vitis*, Crown Gall has been known in European vineyards since the mid-1850s. The most common method of distribution is through the grafting process and therefore it is possible for complete batches of vines to be infected. The most common time for vines to become infected is following damage to an established vine after severe winter frost has split the trunk or after mechanical damage (from a hoe, weeder or mower) to the vine. The bacterium, often present in vineyard soils, then takes up residence and causes a large woody gall which swells to the size of a golf-ball (and some-times even larger) and in doing so, often destroys the graft and the vine dies. Ploughing close to the vine so that earth is piled up around and over the graft prior to the winter (*buttage*) can help prevent winter injury to the graft. In the spring the earth has to be ploughed and hoed away from the graft. The disease is known as *Krebs* (Cancer) or *Mauke* in German. In New York State vineyards, growers will train multiple trunks up from the base, so that if one becomes infected, it can be cut off and the vine still remains productive. It is sometimes considered to be one of the numerous trunk diseases.

Grapevine Yellows – *Flavescence Dorée*

Grapevine yellows is a general term for a group of related diseases caused by *phytoplasma* which are small, sometimes microscopically small, organisms similar to bacteria which gain access to the sap of the vine. First discovered in the 1940s in the Armagnac region, *Flavescence Dorée* has spread throughout Europe and is now present in many vineyard regions. It is spread in two main ways: by vectors such as sap-feeding insects (leafhoppers) that can travel from one vine to another; and by using infected material in the vine-grafting process. Infected vines will have curling leaves which turn yellow and ripening and yields are soon affected. There is no known chemical control for the disease and control is confined to: keeping vectors under control and reducing the plants (weeds and grasses) that they live in and on; and better hygiene in vine nurseries. In Australia it was first seen in the mid-1970s, has become present in several vineyard regions and leads to severe crop loss. New vines can be treated by immersing them in hot water at 50°C for 30 minutes before planting which will reduce the incidence of grapevine yellows (as well as several other ailments.) In France those regions with *Flavescence Dorée* must have any new vines heat-treated before they leave the nursery.

Pierce's Disease – PD, Anaheim Disease

Pierce's Disease was first seen in vineyards in Anaheim in southern California in 1892 and has since become widespread throughout North, South and Central America. Its incidence in other parts of the world is rarer, although by no means unknown. Pierce's is a bacterial disease caused by a bacterium called *Xylella fastidiosa* which lives in the xylem of the plant and is spread by various insects. In California, leaf-hoppers – the blue-green sharpshooter and the glassy-winged sharpshooter – are responsible for spreading the bacterium and the control of the disease relies upon controlling the spread of these insects. The first symptoms – usually seen at the end of the first summer of infection – include unusual staining and marking of the leaves. In the second year of infection, the vine is less vigorous, with stunted shoots which carry few viable fruit buds, leading to substantial crop loss. Young vines are more susceptible than older vines and infection usually leads to a financially unviable vineyard. There is no known chemical that can be used against Pierce's Disease and control concentrates on reducing the numbers of sharpshooters in the vineyard and in the vicinity. When the disease first appeared in northern California, it was the blue-green sharpshooter that was largely responsible for its spread. This insect preferred spending its summers in watercourses so keeping these free of weeds and planting vines at some distance from them was helpful. The glassy-winged sharpshooter, however, is a more wide-ranging insect, not confined to river banks and therefore much more difficult to control. Varieties vary in their susceptibility, but Chardonnay and Pinot Noir are easily harmed and therefore the disease is potentially extremely damaging for California. In 2013 it was discovered on olive trees in Puglia in southern Italy and has been slowly creeping northwards affecting both olives and oleander. It has not yet affected vines in Europe, but it surely will at some stage. As global warming raises winter temperatures, sharpshooters might well be able to overwinter and aid the spread of the disease in Europe.

Viruses of grapevines

Since the planting of grafted vines became the norm, viruses have spread throughout the viticultural world. Nurseries taking plant material – for both scions and rootstocks – from virus infected sources, have been the main conduit for the spread of these economically damaging diseases. Once in a vineyard, viruses are then often spread by more natural methods and vectors such as nematodes and insects will transfer them from one plant to another. Since the introduction of mandatory ELISA testing of source material and (at least in the EU) a relatively effective plant passport system which ensures a good degree of traceability, the spread of viruses has been greatly slowed. However, in some parts of the world, especially where nursery hygiene is not so good, where there are less official controls and growers are free to plant (ungrafted) rooted cuttings, viruses are an ever-present hazard. Several viruses are in reality only of concern to those in the nursery business as their presence either makes grafts fail or causes vines to die whilst they are being rooted prior to sale, neither of which is very good for business. For grape growers, the following are the most important.

Corky Bark

Corky bark is one of the most widespread viruses. Infected vines will have red or red/yellow leaves which tend to curl downwards and refuse to drop when the vine enters dormancy or even for a short period after frost. In addition, canes will become grooved and areas on the main stems will expand and turn corky in appearance. The effect is not universal on all species and all varieties and some, especially hybrids and native North American vines, may well be much more damaged than *Viniferas*. As with most viruses, there is no cure and removal and destruction of infected vines the only real solution.

Fanleaf Degeneration – Fanleaf Virus, *Court-noué*

Fanleaf is one of the oldest viruses and has been present in European vineyards for over 200 years. As the name suggests, the virus causes leaves to distort and grow in the shape of a fan and they may also change colour to a mottled green. In addition, growing tips may well split into two or even three different shoots with flat distorted nodes and canes. As the disease progresses into the second and third phases, leaves will become yellow in patches or with yellow veins (known as yellow mosaic and vein-banding) and ultimately yields will fall and eventually stop altogether. As with most viruses, the only cure is one of removal and destruction of infected material, fallowing the site for as long as possible (although the virus can remain in old roots for up to six years) and replanting with virus-free plants. Nematodes are vectors of Fanleaf Virus and therefore planting on nematode resistant rootstocks will aid control.

Leafroll

Leafroll is another widespread virus and probably causes the most economic damage of all viruses. In fact leafroll is caused by more than one individual virus, although as their symptoms are very similar, they are generally referred to as one virus. It is hard to control as symptoms do not appear on all diseased vines especially American root-stocks varieties – and therefore nurseries producing grafted vines need to take extra precautions. As the name suggests, the symptoms are a rolling of the leaves, with slight veining coupled with a colour change, especially in the autumn, from green to bronze and then to red. Many photographs of vineyards showing 'glorious autumn colour' are in fact good examples of heavily leafroll virus infected vines! Infected vines will very quickly have reduced yields, grapes will tend to take longer to ripen – malic acids reduce more slowly – and will not achieve the sugar levels required. Apart from the spread in the grafting process, vectors such as Mealy Bug have been implicated in its spread in New Zealand and South Africa, although this is rare. In South Africa, its presence is unfortunately quite widespread owing to the distribution of infected material during the apartheid years when plant material from overseas was (officially) unavailable and vines were produced by a very few not-very-independent (and not-very-careful) nurseries. This is now changing with infected vineyards being taken out and re-planted with virus-free plants.

Nepoviruses

Nepoviruses are a group of 13 viruses spread by nematodes. They are closely related to fanleaf degeneration, and include tomato ringspot, tobacco ringspot and Arabis mosaic (nepo)virus. Treatments in the nursery include the heat-treatment of cuttings and hot water dipping of grafted vines can also reduce the incidence of these viruses. However, once present in vineyards they are difficult to control and can live in infected plant material for up to ten years. Nepoviruses all share a similar polyhedral[81] structure when looked at under a microscope.

Red Blotch

Only confirmed as a separate virus in 2012 (in California), Red Blotch is causing damage in vineyards across North America. As its name suggests, it presents initially as red patches on leaves, eventually appearing on the grapes. Here it delays ripening, changes the berry colour and shrivels the berry,

81 A polyhedron is 3-dimensional geometric shape having flat faces that meet along straight edges. A dodecahedron, which is bit like a football made up of flat five-sided segments, is one example.

significantly altering the quality and financial worth of the crop. It is carried from vine to vine by a vector, the three-cornered alfalfa tree-hopper, which cannot be controlled with insecticides as it is too widespread. Currently, the only remedy against Red Blotch is to wait until the vineyard is uneconomic and then grub and replant with virus-free vines.

Rugose Wood – Rugose Wood Complex

Rugose wood is a general catch-all term to describe vines affected by several different viruses including Rupestris stem-pitting, Kober stem-grooving, Corky bark and LN33 stem-grooving[82]. As with other viruses, losses in vine nurseries due to poor grafts and deaths whilst the immature vines are in nursery beds make this more of a concern to vine nurseries than grape growers. Also known as *Legno Riccio* in Italy.

Trunk Diseases

Trunk diseases (TDs) are a conglomeration of diseases and vine maladies that in recent decades have become more widespread and more damaging to vines, although many of them have been around for decades and some for over 2,000 years. However, in recent years they have also become more talked about and discussed and achieved a degree of prominence in some regions and with some varieties. 'Young Vine Decline' is a catch-all term that is used to describe problems that have affected many regions with many different varieties and is caused by several different organisms. These damage the woody parts of the vine, often getting into the young grafts, causing graft failure, after which the plant dies. The organisms responsible for TDs are often present in both rootstock plantations and scion mother-gardens and therefore also present throughout all stages of a vine's life: pre-grafting, grafting, planting and establishment. They can be carried from vine to vine

in the vineyard via pruning cuts. They are also wind-blown from vine to vine and given time will spread from one side of a vineyard to the other.

The reasons for the increase in TDs are by no means certain and those given are often disputed by different factions within viticulture. Are nurseries doing enough to stop the spread of TDs? Is it because vines are now less affected by viruses and are therefore more prone to getting TDs? Is it global warming? Are vines more stressed from drought? Are new insects vectoring diseases we never saw before? Nobody is sure. What is certain though is that many hardwood plants have been infected by new diseases in recent decades. In the UK alone we have seen Dutch elm disease, sudden oak death, red band needle blight, horse chestnut bleeding canker, and the latest, ash dieback. It would seem therefore that vines are not alone in seeing and suffering from novel maladies.

It needs underlining that most vines, like most humans, have within them both good germs and bad germs, good gut microflora and bad gut microflora. In normal times, when there is to enough to eat and drink, when our bodies are not stressed mentally or physically and we are getting enough rest and sleep, our bodies cope with the competing elements. But, miss some meals, get thirsty, get short on sleep, and the bad germs and bad microflora start to take over and we fall ill. Vines are very similar. You can test any new vine for TD organisms and usually find a good number of different ones. Cut a new vine in half and some will show the classic staining of TDs such as Bot Canker and Petri Disease. Yet in both these cases, these supposedly 'diseased' vines, will often grow away and thrive. However, not always and in some situations, most commonly when the vines are growing in a stressed environment, they will not thrive and will eventually fail.

There are some basic hygiene rules to try

82 LN33 is a rootstock and the stem-grooving that it can get is not caused by a virus, although the symptoms are similar.

and lessen the impact of TDs. Try not to prune in the wet. Try to prune as late as possible when the weather starts warming up. Paint all large pruning wounds with wound paint. Keep vineyards clean, removing as much of the pruning wood as possible. Avoid training and pruning systems that involve large cordons of old wood.

Below are some of the most commonly found TDs of vines.

Black Foot – *Cylindrocarpon*
Caused by one of many different *Cylindrocarpon* fungi, Black Foot causes reduced vigour in vines, leading to short internodes, stunted shoots and unproductive vines.

Botryosphaeria Canker – Bot Canker, Black Dead Arm
This disease is found in vines both young and old and like almost all TDs, leads to vine death. Cutting through trunk or cordons reveals a tell-tale dark staining, usually V shaped. A failing vine can sometimes be rejuvenated by cutting right back to just above the graft and selecting a convenient 'water-shoot'[83] to create a new trunk and/or cordons.

Esca – Black Measles, Apoplexy
This is caused by one of several different fungal pathogens and is more common in warm to hot regions. Initial damage usually shows up on the leaves with light coloured areas between the veins eventually leading to leaf-edges that become necrotic (turn brown). On the grapes, dark speckling – the so-called black measles – will initially occur, leading to shrivelling and dropping. In severe situations, the vine will suddenly wilt and die. Control is helped by keeping the vineyard clear of old wood, disinfecting large pruning wounds and avoiding pruning systems with large amounts of permanent wood (long cordons, GDC, *Sylvoz* etc). There is also 'Young Esca' or black xylem decline, and caused by *Phaeoacre-*

monium and other fungi and 'Apoplexy' (sudden death of vines) which the French refer to as *folletage* or *tylosis*.

Eutypa – Eutypa Dieback, Eutypiose
Eutypa is widespread throughout the wine-growing world, especially in regions having in excess of 600 mm annual rainfall. It is no respecter of variety or site. The fungus that causes it – *Eutypa lata* – is often introduced into the vineyard via the grafting process. However, it rarely shows up in young vines, but prefers to wait until vines get to around 10 years old, when their vigour starts to lessen. The first signs are usually when spring shoots fail to thrive and remain short and stunted with very short internodes and malformed, chlorotic (yellowing) leaves. This damage is often confined to only one arm (of a spur-pruned vine) and is why the disease is sometimes confusingly known as dead-arm (which is a term more commonly used for Phomopsis, described on the next page). One way of confirming the presence of the disease is to cut through the arm or trunk of a vine that is suspected of being infected. Vines that are infected will have a wedge-shaped portion of the arm or trunk that is dead, often extending to around one-third of the overall area of the arm or trunk. As the vine becomes more and more infected, this area will increase until the vine dies.

There is in practice no immediate or effective long-term cure for Eutypa. Where it is known that Eutypa is present in the vineyard, large pruning wounds can be washed or painted with a suitable paint containing a fungicide. Secateurs have been adapted that will deliver a spray of fungicide as and when each cut is made, although this undoubtedly slows up the pruning process. Painting each cut with fungicide paint is likewise a time-consuming and therefore expensive procedure, although both of these practices slow down the rate of advance of the disease. Pruning later in the

83 A 'water-shoot' is a shoot that grows out from any part of the trunk above the graft and would normally be rubbed off in the early spring unless it was wanted for rejuvenating the vine.

season will also help as pruning wounds heal faster the warmer (within reason) that it is and the natural bleeding of the vine in spring will also afford some protection as this seals the cut surface of the vine.

As Eutypa prefers bodies of old wood, avoiding training systems that have substantial amounts of old wood, such as spur-pruned cordons, in favour of cane-pruned systems will help. Some success in rejuvenating vines infected with Eutypa has been achieved by taking a water-shoot emerging from near the ground (but above the graft) and completely re-training the trunk. Although this practice results in perhaps two years lost crop whilst the vine produces new fruiting wood, it does give the vine another few years of productive life. Removing old wood from the vineyard after pruning and burning it will help stop the spread of Eutypa, although as it is also found in a number of non-*Vitis* species, this is not always successful.

Petri Disease – Black Goo

Another TD that is similar to Black Foot and Bot Canker and starts out life in the rootstock and scion wood. Vines with Petri Disease, when cut in half, will exude small pin-pricks of a black oily substance, hence the colloquial name of Black Goo.

Phomopsis – Phomopsis Cane and Leaf Spot, Dead-Arm, Excoriose

Phomopsis (*Phomopsis viticola*) is another widespread viticultural disease and one that is particularly prevalent in regions with regular summer rainfall. Again, as with Black Rot, it is controlled by chemicals used against Downy Mildew and separate treatments are not usually needed. It can be a problem in nurseries and therefore newly planted vines may require spraying.

Chapter 12

Pests of grapevines

Pests of grapevines

Pests attack vines in many different ways: they can physically damage leaves leading to a loss of photosynthetic ability; they can live on the leaves, not damaging them, but sucking their sap which weakens the whole vine; they can attack the roots leading to a reduction in the vine's capacity to absorb moisture and nutrients; and they can act as vectors, feeding on the vine's sap and carrying diseases, viruses and other ailments from vine to vine. Some insects may physically damage the fruit and must be controlled. Sometimes the damage is really only cosmetic and for wine grapes (as opposed to table grapes) is not financially significant so the insect may not be worth spraying. Most growers will use the absolute minimum of insecticides (to kill insects) and acaricides (to kill mites) as these products will also kill most naturally occurring predators which do the job for free. In many regions, especially where vineyards are relatively isolated from one another and natural predators are at high levels, spraying against pests may not take place at all. In addition, sulphur (and some other chemicals) sprayed to control Powdery Mildew (Oidium) will also control light infestations of many pest species including mites. Monitoring harmful insects to gauge whether populations are high enough to warrant spraying is often done, using sticky-floor traps, coated with the female pheromones of the insect you want to monitor. These traps attract the males which become stuck to the floor of the trap and can then be counted. There are also remote camera traps which emit female pheromones, and visually record (and wirelessly transmit) visits by males. The number often turns out to be many times the number caught on sticky-floor traps.

There are a very wide range of pests which can affect vines and to list and describe them all would require a book many times the size of this one. Many pests will be localised to specific regions or in regions with specific climates and may be completely unknown in other areas. The ones that have been detailed below are therefore those that are most widespread and those that cause the most damage. Other predators which damage vines such as rabbits and deer (to name but two) and birds and other animals which eat grapes, have been dealt with in other chapters.

Beetles

There are a large number of beetles which attack vines. In Europe the beetles known in French as *écrivain (Bromius obscurus)* and *cigarier (Rhynchites betuleti)* both cause damage severe enough for insecticides to be used on a regular basis. There are also species of beetle (known as borers) whose larvae will bore into the woody parts of the vine i.e. the trunks and the cordons of spur-pruned vines. Borers tend to be fairly localised and in places as far apart as California, Oregon and the Hunter Valley, vines are known to suffer damage.

Cutworms

Cutworms are the larvae of moths which live in the soil or under the bark of the vine and emerge at night to feed off the leaves of the vine. Although not in reality a commercial problem on established vines, they can attack newly planted vines and slow down their establishment.

Erinose Mite – Grape Erineum Mite, Grape Leaf Blister Mite

The grapevine is the only known host to the Grape Erineum Mite – *Colomerus vitas* – and although it does little commercial damage, its resemblance to the leaf form of *Phylloxera* means that its appearance often gives viticulturalists a nasty shock. Leaves affected by this mite look very unsightly, being covered with swellings usually with a reddish tinge. Luckily, the mite is usually controlled by sulphur.

Fruit Fly – *Drosophila*, Vinegar Fly, Pomace Fly

Fruit fly, also known as vinegar or pomace fly, is in itself a tiny insect and causes little physical damage. However, it will visit already damaged fruit (perhaps damaged by other insects, wasps, or hail), especially in the later stages of ripening when sugars are high, and spread acetic acid bacteria, so causing what is known as 'sour rot' and raising the volatile acidity (VA) level in wines made from this fruit. Mediterranean fruit-fly (not a *Drosophila* species) is a problem in warm to hot regions (Australia and South Africa) and does similar damage. Vineyards in close proximity to earlier ripening fruit crops such as apricots, peaches and figs, may well experience worse damage than those in regions where grapes are the only crop or where vineyards are isolated. Also see entry for Spotted Wing Drosophila.

Grasshoppers, Locusts

Grasshoppers and locusts (they belong to the same family) can attack vines, eating leaves and reducing the vine's ripening ability. The usual method is to spray when numbers reach damaging levels. Grasshoppers will often migrate from other crops or grassland onto vines, especially when the former become drought affected and the latter remain irrigated and have plenty of green leaf material.

Harlequin Ladybird – Multicoloured Asian Lady Beetle

The Harlequin Ladybird, *Harmonia axyridis* is also known as the Multicoloured Asian Lady Beetle and is a species native to Asia and introduced into the US for biological control of other pests. However, it has now found its way to Europe – once considered too cool for it – where it has already led to spoilt wines. When disturbed, it exudes a substance called 'reflex blood' from its legs which has a foul odour and taste and can taint grapes and wine made from them.

Leafhoppers

Leafhoppers cause damage both directly to the vine, feeding off leaves and destroying them, as well as acting as vectors for more damaging ailments such as Pierce's Disease, *Flavescence Dorée* and some viruses. Spraying insecticides and destroying leafhopper habitat are the main control techniques, but these are not wholly successful. There is a natural predator, a tiny wasp called *Anagrus epos*, which will lay its eggs in the larvae of leafhoppers, but these wasps are susceptible to sulphur sprays.

Leaf-rollers

Leaf-rollers (which have nothing to do with Leafroll Virus), also known as leaf–folders, are insects whose caterpillars damage a vine's leaves, causing them to roll up, thus lowering the leaf area available for photosynthesis. There are several different species of leaf-rollers which are localised to certain vineyard regions and mainly controlled with selective insecticides. In some areas, natural predators may be effective against low levels of attack. When the caterpillars damage the fruit, this may allow other organisms such as *Botrytis* to cause further and greater damage.

Margarodes – Ground Pearls

Margarodes, also known as Ground Pearls, are insects that live in the soil and damage vines in a similar way to *Phylloxera*. They cause stunting of the vine with loss of vigour and eventual death. Margarodes also emit an unpleasant smell and appear to be impervious to most forms of control. There are no rootstocks developed to resist them. Luckily, they appear to be confined to South African vineyards, although there have been occasional appearances in other countries (Chile).

Mealy Bug

There are several different species of mealy bug, a few of which will damage vines. Although they actually do little mechanical damage, what they can do is cover bunches of grapes with a secretion known as honeydew which is attractive to a black sooty mould. This mould will, if taken into the winery, taint the wine made from the grapes. Some species of mealy bug have also been implicated in the spread of viruses, especially Leafroll. The honeydew is also attractive to several species of ant, which, although not damaging to vines, will attack natural predators of both mealy bug and other insect pests. Control of mealy bug is a time-consuming and painstaking business and requires careful monitoring of insect levels and activity before effective insecticide applications are made. Some species of mealy bug are notoriously difficult to control as their eggs overwinter beneath the bark of the vine and are impossible to spray. In greenhouses, stripping the bark off the trunks and cordons of vines and painting them with a fungicide is an annual task in the control of mealy bug.

Mites

Mites are very small insects, often looking like spiders, which colonise and feed on a vine's leaves. Species such as the grapeleaf rust mite, Pacific spider mite, red spider mite and yellow mite all feed on the leaves, reducing the photosynthetic ability of the vine and slowing down the ripening process. In severe infestations, the leaves of vines will turn almost completely red which is often mistaken for natural autumn colouring. Luckily, mite activity is slowed by sulphur used to control Powdery Mildew, but in the case of severe attacks, an acaricide will be sprayed. Growers can also use predatory mites to control the harmful ones, although sulphur sprays tend not to discriminate between the good and the bad.

Moths

There are quite a number of moths that cause damage to vines, although to be more accurate, it is their larvae that cause the damage, burrowing into the immature grapes when the larvae hatch. Although spraying with insecticides against the moths is common, the use of pheromones to cause 'sexual confusion' (*confusion sexuelle*) in the male of the species is now widespread in many countries. The system most commonly seen in vineyards is where the pheromones are contained in small (usually brown) capsules which are hung up on vineyard posts. They work by confusing the male who spends his time being attracted by the capsules, rather than mating with female moths. The only drawback is that all growers in an affected region need to use these capsules, otherwise all the males converge on the only unprotected vineyard(s), mate and then all the egg-laden females

disperse throughout the area. There are also systems which use 'puffers' to puff phero-mones into the atmosphere in the morning and evenings when the male moths are ac-tive. Because the attacks from these moths tend to be sporadic, both pheromone and feeding traps will often be hung up to moni-tor their activity amongst the vines. There are also several species of predator that can be used against moths and all will be con-trolled by a wide range of insecticides. Whilst the damage from the larvae may be actually quite slight, the wounds in the grapes will be ideal for diseases such as *Bot-rytis* to gain a foothold. A few of these moths have occasionally been seen in the UK, but could start making an unwelcome appearance if the climate continues to warm. The following is a list of the most commonly seen moth species:

Cochylis – *Eupoecilia ambiguella* (also
    known as *Traubenwickler*)
Eudemis – European Grape Moth –
    Lobesia botrana
Eulia – *Argyrotaenia pulchellana*
Grape Berry Moth – *Polychrosis viteana*
Grape Vine Moth (NZ) – *Phalaenoides*

glycine
Orange Tortrix Moth – *Argyrotaenia*
    citrana
Pyrale – *Sparganothis pilleriana*

Nematodes

Nematodes, also known as eel-worms, are microscopic worms which live in the soil and can feed on the roots of vines, depriving the vine of both water and nutrients, and weakening the vine so that it becomes prey to other ailments. The root-knot nematode causes knot-like growths on the vine and is one of the most widespread. Other nema-todes serve as vectors for viruses such as Fanleaf. Nematodes are hard to control chemically and in reality cannot easily be eradicated. The use of nematode resistant rootstocks is the most effective method, coupled with better hygiene in nurseries. Dipping rootstocks in hot water at 50°C for 30 minutes prior to planting will kill any ne-matodes present without harming the plants.

Phylloxera
See Chapter 13 – *Phylloxera* and rootstocks

Scale insects

There are a large number of different species of scale insect, all of which feed on the sap of the vine and in doing so, weaken it. Some species also excrete a sticky sub-stance (honeydew) which is attractive to the same black sooty mould found on vines damaged by mealy bug with similar results. Scale insects are controlled by insecticides.

Slugs and Snails

Slugs and snails are not often a problem in mature vines, but in newly planted vine-yards, especially where vines are protected against rabbits and other predators with in-dividual guards, damage can be severe. The warm, often moist atmosphere inside the guards seems attractive to the slugs and snails which will destroy leaves and young

shoots. Sprinkling anti-slug and snail pellets into the guards usually works, although may need repeating depending on the severity of the problem. Snails have also sometimes been seen to damage shoots and leaves on young spring growth on mature vines, but not to the extent that they need treating.

Spotted Wing Drosophila - SWD

Spotted Wing Drosophila (*Drosophila suzuki*), known colloquially as 'SWD' has been attacking all kinds of soft-fruit in Europe – apricots, cherries, blueberries, grapes, nectarines, pears, plums, peaches, raspberries, and strawberries – and causing immense damage. Unlike the common fruit-fly, the larvae of SWD hatch inside the fruits in question, feeding off the pulp, and only emerging when they are fairly well developed – not something consumers want to see as they eat the fresh fruit. When SWD attack wine grapes they cause increased levels of volatile acidity (VA) which is not something one wants in the winery and for growers selling grapes under contract, may well devalue their crops.

Thrips

Thrips, of which there are several different species, are very small black winged insects (also known as thunderbugs) which feed on young shoots causing stunting and on the pollen of vines during flowering. This leads to scarring and russeting of the grapes which may cause splitting later in the year as they expand. Thrips are sometimes held to lead to poor fruit-set, although the evidence for this is scarce. They are more commercially damaging to table grapes than wine grapes (as the damage is more visual than actual).

Western Grapeleaf Skeletonizer

This appropriately named moth does exactly what it says on the tin – turns grapevine leaves into skeletons – although in fact it is the moth larvae that do the harm, not the moths. Either way, it is a pest that if seen requires spraying as, left unchecked, it can completely defoliate a vineyard. Luckily it is fairly localised and mainly confined to the western US grapegrowing regions. Apart from spraying, there are two parasites (one a wasp, the other a fly) which will, in the right conditions, control it and these have been relatively successful in California's San Joaquin Valley.

Chapter 13

Phylloxera and rootstocks

Phylloxera and rootstocks

By far the majority of vines grown in the world are grafted onto rootstocks, the main – but not the only – reason being the presence of the vine louse, *Phylloxera vastatrix* (the devastator). Although commonly known as *Phylloxera*, its correct name is now *Daktulosphaira vitifoliae*.

Phylloxera

Grape *Phylloxera*[84] has its home amongst the wild vines found in the eastern and southern parts of North America, the so-called native American vines. Amongst these wild vines it managed to achieve a symbiosis through co-evolution with its

84 Other species – oak, pecan and hickory – all have their own unique type of Phylloxera.

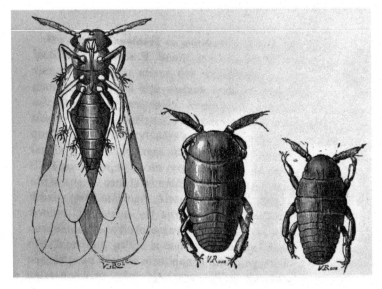

host, living on the leaves and roots of the vines, weakening them sometimes but never killing them. Millennia of existing together produced many species of wild vine whose roots are able to withstand the damage caused by the insect. The American vine's main defence mechanism is that its roots manage to mend the wounds caused by the insect as it feeds, sealing them from invasion by other damaging organisms such as bacteria and fungi which, on *Vitis vinifera* vines, cause the main damage. In addition, the roots of the native American vines contain a sap that is sufficiently unpalatable to the insect for it not to want to spend too long colonising any one particular piece of root. Put (very) simply, the sap clogs up the feeding apparatus of the insect and makes the insect search for a better food source which in turn disrupts, and slows down, its multiplication. There is also evidence to suggest that something in the roots causes juveniles to die or at least not to thrive. In short, the roots of the American vines are an uncomfortable home for the insect from both a feeding and a breeding point-of-view.

On American vines, most of the louse's breeding activity takes place on the leaves during the summer as they find the roots of these species inhospitable. Activity on the roots is therefore minimal. This is different from its behaviour on other species of vine, most notably on *viniferas*, where it avoids the leaves in favour of the roots. Here, below ground level, it can lay its eggs and breed in relative safety, feeding on the roots and weakening them by removing photo-synthates (starches and sugars) and allowing damaging bacteria and fungi to further attack the root structure. At some stage, usually at a moment of stress – perhaps crop or climate related – the vine wilts and slowly dies. *Phylloxera* may be a very slow acting insect – it took decades to cross Europe – but in time, all (or at least, almost all) vinifera vines on their own roots will be damaged.

Grape *Phylloxera* must surely be one of the world's most fascinating living organisms and it is impossible to do it justice in the space available in these pages. Its life cycle has many twists and turns and it can change this life cycle according to its host and environment. This adaptability to its surroundings, its different behaviour in sandy, clay or chalk-rich soils, its dislike of very hot conditions and of wet soils, its ability to differentiate between American species, pure *vinifera* and hybrids, make it a challenging pest to come to terms with, let alone beat. However, its change of habits according to its host species and environment not only made it a devastating problem, but also supplied the secret to its defeat.

The female *Phylloxera*, a small (1 mm) long yellow aphid, is parthenogenetic, that is to say, able to lay fertile eggs without the sexual attentions of a male and, no doubt because of this lack of a need for male companionship, almost all of the eggs laid hatch into females. As if this was not enough to guarantee the survival of the species, a single female can lay up to seven generations in a summer, the first generation laying up to a further six, the second a further five and so on. The multiplication factor is huge and it has been calculated that if all the eggs hatched and no offspring were lost, the weight of aphids would be ten times that of a normal crop of grapes! On native

Phylloxera leaf galls on an American species of vine

American vines, this egg laying takes place mainly on the leaves and an infected vine's leaves will be covered with raised wart-like lumps, which vary in colour between reddish/brown and greenish/white depending on the host species. These are known as galls and look very similar to those sometimes seen on the leaves of oak trees, home to *Phylloxera quercus*. These galls contain the unhatched eggs which in time hatch and the resultant aphids then spend the summer feeding and breeding on the leaves around them until such time as the leaves start to fall and with them, the *Phylloxera's* food source. The aphid then decides to overwinter underground and some of the summer adults turn into crawlers and creep down the trunk to the ground and then through cracks and fissures in the soil to find the roots of the vine nearest to the surface. Here, undisturbed by the weather, by predators – man, birds, other insects – they continue their feeding and breeding, injecting their saliva into the vine's roots, causing what are known as root galls. These galls, as with leaf galls, house the unhatched eggs which they lay.

As temperatures are lower below ground and movement through the soil a bit more difficult, the pace of life is somewhat slower than on the leaves. However, their presence there is no less certain and no less dangerous.

From a single below-ground adult, big colonies of insects will develop, spreading from root to root and from vine to vine. Fertile adults are able to travel a little way by themselves and will emerge from below ground level and crawl across the soil. Some will be carried by man – attached to boots and shoes, tractor tyres, harvesters, picking bins – and in this way can be spread from vineyard to vineyard, even region to region. In some warm climates a winged form exists which can fly for a short distance – about 100 m – and which can lay eggs which produce both male and female offspring. The female offspring of this winged form eventually lays what is known as the winter egg which hatches into a female – similar in a sense to a queen bee or wasp – and known as the *fundatrix* which becomes the mother of a whole new generation in a new location.

Several North American colonies – Virginia and Carolina being examples – were founded with the intention of establishing vineyards. The early settlers saw the abundance of native grapes and attempted to make good wine from them, but without success. The wine made from these indigenous varieties was found to be unpalatable, at least to European palates, although the Native American Indians seemed to relish it. Attempts were then made using *Vinifera* vines, imported no doubt with much hope and enthusiasm. Many tried, but none were successful. In 1773 Thomas Jefferson invited a noted Italian grower, Filippo Mazzei, to establish a vineyard on 162 ha (400 acres) of land adjoining his estate at Monticello in Virginia using European varieties. Despite repeated plantings and re-plantings, either *Phylloxera* or *Oidium* (Powdery Mildew) killed or damaged the vines. Throughout the succeeding years, Jefferson and others discovered that only local varieties would succeed and an industry grew up based upon vines from species such as *V. labrusca* and *V. rotundifolia*. Scuppernong, an un-

likely sounding, but commercially successful *rotundifolia* variety was (and in some states still is), widely grown. Its flavour is (quite kindly) described as 'musky'. Natural hybrids were also produced between American varieties and *viniferas* and plant breeders soon became adept at producing varieties that had good resistance to *Oidium* and limited tolerance of *Phylloxera*. These developments were to prove invaluable when viticulturalists from the Old World came looking for an antidote to *Phylloxera*.

Phylloxera in Europe

The first time *Phylloxera* was seen in Europe was in 1863 and reports vary as to where the first sighting was. George Ordish in his book *The Great Wine Blight* claims that it was in Hammersmith, West London, where a greenhouse vine was suffering from something. *The Gardener's Chronicle's* 'Insect Referee', Professor John Westwood, was sent some damaged leaves and was intrigued. He reported back that he could come to no firm conclusion about the insect 'for want of a knowledge of a male'[85]. Today it seems surprising that anything this interesting, let alone anything to do with vines, should have been found in Hammersmith. In Victorian times however, large mansions with attached 'vineries' were very common in this then very desirable London suburb. There was also an interest in decorative vines such as the Virginia Creeper (a species of *Vitis* and capable of hosting *Phylloxera*) which were being imported from the USA in large quantities and the insect could easily have entered the UK in this way. The first sighting in mainland Europe was, according to Christy Campbell in his fascinating book on the subject *Phylloxera* (HarperCollins, 2004), amongst some vines in a small village called Pujaut a few kilometres north-west of Avignon. Here a local wine merchant, Monsieur Borty, had planted some vines sent to him by 'a friend

85 The French were also confused by the apparent lack of a male – how could this insect possibly breed without any male input? Most un-Gallic!

from America' (some friend!) called M. Carle. These vines, planted in 1861 in ten short rows and labelled according to variety – Clinton, Post-Oak, and Emily – initially thrived, but after two years (1863) some of them started to show signs of attack, but from what, no one knew. The next year, more vines were affected and by 1865, vineyards several kilometres away were suffering. Within five years of the initial attack, many vineyards throughout southern France were being attacked.

At first, it was assumed by the French that the weakening vines and actual deaths were being caused by a disease rather than by an insect. As has already been said, on *Vinifera* vines the insect spends most of its time on the roots and in any event, *Phylloxera* aphids look much like most other aphids to the inexperienced eye. On digging up dead vines all that was found were blackened and rotting roots. No one thought to dig up a healthy vine. Had they done so they would have discovered the cause of the problem. Within a few years, the damage to vines in the region was sufficiently large for the Vaucluse Agricultural Society to establish a commission to look into matters. (The French government also offered a huge reward – 300,000 Francs – to anyone who could rid the country of the insect. This they never actually awarded, claiming that the cure – grafting – never actually got rid of the insect!). One member of the commission was Jules-Emile Planchon, Professor of Botany at the School of Pharmacy in Montpelier, who had been *Keeper of the Herbarium* at Kew Gardens under Sir William Hooker and knew something about diseases of trees. He noticed that the aphids found on the roots of dying vines resembled those of the *Phylloxera quercus* and gave it the name *Phylloxera vastatrix* – the devastator. Once it was realised that it was an insect and not a disease, the answer seemed obvious: kill the insects and the problem

would be solved. But how?

The search for a way to rid vineyards of *Phylloxera* was long, arduous and ultimately, unsuccessful. All kinds of remedies were tried – animal, vegetable, mineral and physical. The injection of Carbon Bisulphide into the soil was tried, but proved more dangerous to the vineyard workers than to the aphids. Many other weird and wonderful remedies were proposed and the longer the problem persisted, the madder became the cures. (Burying a live toad under each vine was one such proposal). One that actually worked, but was only practical on vineyards that were close to a river or canal and on fairly level ground, was to flood the vines for several weeks on end (during the winter) and drown the insects. Schemes to dig a huge network of canals in the Midi were proposed, but foundered on the expense, although even to this day, vineyards with low walls around them (too low to keep out livestock or people) can be seen all over France where once flooding against the insect was practiced.

The realisation that the cure would come from the same place as the problem – North America – wasn't actually that slow in coming, although it took years for vines grafted onto rootstocks to come into general use. In the 1850s, as *Oidium* started to spread through European vineyards (and before the remedy of spraying or dusting sulphur onto the vines was discovered) some growers thought the answer to this very damaging disease lay in planting either native American vines or the recently developed French-American hybrids which were known to be more (or even completely) resistant to the disease. Although these vines proved incapable of producing wine of a high enough quality, it was noticed that they were not damaged by *Phylloxera*. Could it be, that by grafting the varieties which did produce good wine onto rootstocks produced from the vines that were resistant to damage, a solution might be found?

Grafting was of course nothing new – the Romans certainly practiced it – and roses, apples, pears, cherries and many other trees and shrubs were at the time routinely grafted onto rootstocks for a variety of purposes. But to graft noble French varieties onto wild <u>American</u> vines? *Incroyable!* However, such was the desperation of growers that they felt anything was worth trying. Between 1875 and 1879 much development work took place into what rootstocks to use and how best to perform the grafting. The *Cadillac* graft was developed and lessons were given to hundreds of growers and nurserymen in Montpellier. By the time *Phylloxera* reached Champagne, grafted vines were well established in the south and west of the country and suitable rootstocks based on *Vitis berlandieri* had been found (in Texas) for the lime-rich soils of the Charente region where Cognac production was of major importance.

Phylloxera of course, didn't just affect southern France. By 1872 it had reached the Douro in Portugal, parts of Spain two years later, Italy by 1879 and Champagne – the last French vineyard area to be infected – by 1890. In Germany, the first sightings were in 1875 in the south of the country, but, realising the seriousness of the threat, the authorities instigated an immediate grubbing (with compensation) policy. This actually kept *Phylloxera* under control until the 1939-45 war and it was only then, when other matters were of more importance, that it really got a grip on vineyards. The damage caused resulted in a huge replanting programme in the post-war years, all of which were with certified grafted stock, and many of which were of the variety Müller-Thurgau. (The invention of Müller-Thurgau-based *Liebfraumilch*, which arguably did much initially to revive the German wine industry in the 1960s and 1970s, but ultimately led to its debasement in the 1980s and 1990s as a producer of semi-sweet, cheap wines, can therefore also be laid at the feet of this tenacious insect.) Some vineyards managed to hold on to their ungrafted vines for decades after other growers had uprooted theirs and re-planted. The Domaine de la Romanée-Conti's vines in *La Romanée-Conti* itself and *Richebourg* were not grubbed up until 1945 and re-planted two years later with grafted *sélection massale* vines produced using scion wood taken from the old vines.

The destruction caused by *Phylloxera* to two generations of French winegrowers cannot easily be imagined. France of course was not the only country affected. Almost all the winegrowing regions of Europe suffered save only for those places too isolated for the insect to reach, or where the authorities instigated a rigorous grubbing programme (such as they did in Germany). By the turn of the new century most vines on their own roots had been attacked and uprooted and grafted ones planted in their stead. Sadly, these new, highly productive, vineyards, rather than solving the dire economic plight of growers, made it worse as the deluge of wine they produced caused prices to fall dramatically. There were riots in Narbonne in 1907 and in Champagne in 1911, with growers pouring wine into the streets rather than sell it below cost. The army and militia were called in to control the riots and many people were killed. The disruption to the markets caused by the increase in production following *Phylloxera* led directly to the development of the *appellation contrôlée* systems which started in the mid-1920s.

Rootstock development

The early rootstocks were little more than selections of the most common American varieties and French-American hybrids already being tried in France in order to find a vine resistant to *Oidium*[86]. As soon as it was realised that grafting would be successful in beating the problem, nurserymen

86 I was recently told of some old pre-Phylloxera vineyards in the foothills north of Nice in southern France where ungrafted Concord vines are still being grown – albeit only to produce (what I am reliably informed is very undistinguished) wine for home consumption. History lives!

throughout Europe – French, German, Spanish, Italian and Hungarian – all became involved in rootstock development and saw a huge commercial market in prospect. The quest for better and better rootstocks, not only *Phylloxera* tolerant, but also able to counteract a number of other problems and ailments, then started. The names of rootstocks are in themselves a mini-history of viticulture: Couderc, Ganzin, de Grasset, Kober, Millardet, Paulsen, Richter and Teleki are much remembered for the work they did in resurrecting an industry which at one point faced oblivion and their names are still to be found attached to many rootstocks.

It is an interesting debate as to how things would have progressed had nurserymen been able to develop French-American hybrids that were both able to resist *Phylloxera* and produce acceptable, even good, wine. Some observers believe that an unholy alliance between the state, rootstock growers and grafting nurseries effectively put an end to further research down this route as everyone could see a great business in prospect, one where every 30–40 years each vineyard would have to be replanted with fresh stock. (Ungrafted vines will last 80–100 years or even more.) A rump of resistance against grafted vines lingered and the growers of 'direct producers' (*producteurs direct*[87]) attempted to keep the flame alive, but this was snuffed out in the 1930s when hybrids were excluded from Quality Wine production by the *appellation* system.

Today, rootstocks development is based upon science and genetics and is largely in the hands of the state-funded institutions – Geisenheim, Montpelier, Bordeaux, Davis, Cornell – for whom the search for the perfect rootstock variety is ongoing. As new varieties and better clones of old rootstocks varieties are developed, they are licensed to nurserymen who grow them and pay plant-breeder's royalties back to their developers. There are many hundreds of types of rootstocks used in vineyards worldwide and new ones are being developed and introduced all the time.

Types of rootstock

Rootstocks are chosen for a number of reasons. It goes without saying, that *Phylloxera* tolerance is paramount. The most *Phylloxera* tolerant American species are *Vitis riparia*, *Vitis rupestris* and *Vitis berlandieri* and clones of these three, or crossings between members of these species, are the most successful in this respect. Crossings between vines of these species and *viniferas* are also used as rootstocks. *Vinifera x berlandieri* crosses such as 41B and 333EM are sufficiently resistant in suitable soils, although the *vinifera x rupestris* crossing AXR1 (also known as ARG1) has proved an expensive failure in California (see later section in this chapter). One rootstock, Börner (a *riparia x cinerea* cross), can actually resist *Phylloxera* (rather than tolerating it) and although its reception by nurseries has been muted, it does possibly provide a key to the way forward should existing rootstocks prove inadequate.

Rootstocks resistant to nematodes, which either cause damage to the roots (root knot nematode), or spread viruses, can be helpful in regions where nematodes are present. Vines suffering from nematode attack will rarely yield well and although they may not be killed, will seldom thrive. Soils can be fumigated to get rid of nematodes and vines subsequently planted must be on nematode resistant rootstocks. *Vitis* species such as *V. champini* and *V. longii* are the most nematode resistant and crosses with *V. vinifera* in them the least. Dog Ridge, Freedom, Harmony and Ramsey are examples of highly nematode resistant rootstocks.

On soils rich in limestone (such as are found in Champagne, Cognac, Burgundy and in other regions throughout the world),

87 These are hybrid vines that in theory were sufficiently resistant to Phylloxera so that they could be grown without the need for rootstocks.

88 More on chlorosis in Chapter
14 – Nutritional disorders and
other viticultural problems.

vines growing on unsuitable rootstocks will suffer from lime-induced chlorosis[88], a condition where the high active lime (i.e. active calcium carbonate – *calcaire actif*) content in the soil locks up the iron, needed to produce the chlorophyll required for photosynthesis to take place. Rootstocks with a high *Vitis berlandieri* content – SO4, 41B, 333EM and Fercal are all popular – and will help counteract this problem. All rootstocks are categorised according to their ability to withstand the soil's active chalk content which can vary from 10 per cent (relatively low) to 40 per cent (very high) and it is important that soils over pH 7.5 be tested before a rootstock is chosen. It also important to note that whilst total calcium carbonate levels give you an idea of a soil's active calcium carbonate, they are not the same measurement.

Some rootstocks can help vines grow in regions with low levels of rainfall – their roots dig especially deep – and *berlandieri-rupestris* crosses are the best where this is a problem. Rootstocks developed from *V. riparia* and hybrids are worst in this respect. Other rootstocks known for their shallow rooting – 41B and 101–14 Millardet et de Grasset (to give 101–14 its full name) for example – are useful in irrigated vineyards with shallow soils.

Sometimes the only water available for irrigation has high levels of salt. This may be because only chloride-rich water is available or a previously good water source has become salty as more and more water is drawn from the aquifer supplying it. In these instances, rootstocks based upon *V. berlandierii*, *V. champini* (Ramsey) and *viniferas* will help. Vines in soils which are over-vigorous (fresh soils which have not been used for vinegrowing before, especially where vines are irrigated) should be grown on root-stocks which help reduce vigour: Riparia Gloire de Montpelier (RGM), 420A, 41B, 3309C and 101-14 are all examples of *riparia*-based

vigour-reducing rootstocks. Conversely, vines growing on tired or thin soils and which need some encouragement should be grown on rootstocks which promote growth: Rupestris St. George, 99R and 110R, based upon *V. rupestris*, are all vigour inducing rootstocks. Some rootstocks are also said to promote earliness, although other factors (the weather) may have more influence.

In addition to the requirements dictated by soil or climate, certain scion varieties are more successfully grafted onto certain rootstocks – the graft bonds better – and the percentage of graft failures in the nursery is much lower. Also, *appellation* rules must specify which rootstocks are to be used, so in any given area (in the EU at least) most growers will be using a similar spread of rootstocks.

The correct choice of rootstocks is often as important – some would say more important – than the scion variety. If the vine cannot root and thrive, then it will never produce economically viable yields. The same cultivar and clone of a variety, grown on the same site, but on different rootstocks, will often show different characteristics with regard to time of budburst, *véraison* and harvest, yield level and levels of pH, sugar and acidity in the grapes. In short, the choice of the right rootstock for the type, style, quality and quantity of wine to be produced is one of the most important decisions that has be taken if an economically viable vineyard is to be established. Once selected, a rootstock can never be changed, unless the vineyard is grubbed and replanted.

Phylloxera and the Californian experience

As the experience of Californian vinegrowers over the last forty to fifty years has shown, *Phylloxera* is not an insect to disregard lightly. *Phylloxera* first appeared in

California in the 1860s, delivered there probably on American hybrid vines sent from the Eastern seaboard states. Although slow to spread – vigorous vines can often survive a light infestation and a warm climate is not always to the insect's liking – by the turn of the 20th century most ungrafted vines had been killed[89] and new vineyards were being planted with grafted vines. What with the odd earthquake or two, a couple of world wars, Prohibition (1920–1933) and the downturn in the economy between the wars, winegrowing was understandably slow to get going after the 2nd World War. The real expansion of the Californian vineyard area did not take place until the mid-1950s.

Californian growers were then advised to plant on one of two rootstocks: the vigorous Rupestris St. George (RG), ideal for dry-farmed vines where quality was more important than quantity; and AXR1 (see later), the *vinifera* hybrid, which was suitable for irrigated vines where high yields were required. Although warned by the French that AXR1 was not sufficiently resistant to *Phylloxera*, advisors (most notably the University of California's Davis vine and wine section) continued to insist that it was safe to use in Californian conditions. By the start of the 1980s – by which time many vines planted on AXR1 had been happily cropping for over 30 years – it was obvious that vineyards were once again succumbing to *Phylloxera*.

The reasons why *Phylloxera* took so long to reassert itself in California are not altogether clear. There are some in the region who claim that a new biotype (Biotype B) – in effect a variant of the insect brought about by natural mutation – learnt to thrive in the environment (soil, climate and host) of the region and started to breed on AXR1 in sufficient quantities to cause economic damage. Others accept that it was always present and all the while vines were vigorous, irrigated and growing well, they managed to survive.

It was only when the vines got older and less vigorous that the insect was able to get a grip. Whatever the cause, the cure was the old one: graft onto more resistant rootstocks. The cost of doing this has been huge and the financial problems of some of the area's biggest and best-known wineries (Mondavi's for instance) can be traced back to the need to raise funds for replanting.

Vineyards on their own roots

Of course, it is possible to grow vines on their own natural roots and there are many regions in the world – usually those physically isolated from regions with *Phylloxera* – where ungrafted vines thrive. *Vinifera* roots are able to withstand very high levels of active calcium carbonate and chlorosis is never a problem on own-rooted vines. Notable regions where ungrafted vines grow are Chile, where the Andes have proved (so far) to be a barrier to the insect, and many vineyard regions in Australia – the Barossa is an example. Where regions with *Phylloxera* and regions without have to co-exist side by side and where personnel and machinery may have to travel between the two, strict quarantine requirements make sure that no

89 Not all own-rooted vines in California were killed and ungrafted vines of well over 100 years old can still be found.

Movement controls are required in some regions to prevent Phylloxera spreading

plant material (to which *Phylloxera* eggs might adhere) is transported by accident. Grape harvesters, tractors and picking bins would all have to be thoroughly pressure-washed before entering a *Phylloxera*-free zone. Where plant material is transported on purpose i.e. vines or wood for cuttings are imported, they must go through a rigorous inspection system and, if necessary, will be quarantined for up to two (or even more) years to make sure they are clean.

In *Phylloxera*-free regions, where new varieties and new clones cannot easily be introduced, Vine Improvement Programmes (VIPs) ensure that growers and nurseries have access to clean plant material for the production of new vines. Without the necessity to graft, vines can be produced simply by individual growers taking hardwood cuttings from their own or neighbour's vineyards, rooting them and planting them out the following year. The dangers are that any diseases and viruses present in the host vineyard will be transported to the destination vineyard, hence the need for VIPs to provide clean wood. However, many recent plantings in Australia have used rootstocks, not for their anti-*Phylloxera* benefits, but for their other attributes: better yields, nematode resistance, drought resistance and salt tolerance.

Even where *Phylloxera* is present, there are certain conditions where it may be possible to grow vines on their own roots for a considerable period of time, if not for ever. Vineyards where flood irrigation is practiced – and there are many of these in Argentina and Chile – can replicate the old remedy of annual flooding. In New Zealand in the early days of post-war viticulture, growers found that vineyards planted with Müller-Thurgau, which in the right conditions (fresh soils, humid weather and plenty of water) is an exceptionally vigorous variety, it was simpler (and much cheaper) to plant vines on their own roots. Once established and cropping, *Phylloxera* would generally colonise some of the roots, but as this had the effect of lessening the excessive vigour, this was no bad thing. After say ten years of heavy cropping, the vines could be grubbed up and cheaply replanted. Even in parts of Europe where almost all vines are grafted, there are isolated vineyards, perhaps planted on inhospitable soils such as sand or clay, or in very warm regions, where vines can be grown on their own roots.

On the Mosel, the well-known grower Ernst Loosen has vines planted on its slate-covered slopes on their own roots and these have been cropping problem-free for many decades. Here too, replacements are layered, rather than replanted. In the Midi, vines grown on the sandy soils of the Rhône estuary – the *Vin de Sables* – are sometimes ungrafted, the combination of the sandy soil and occasional flooding being enough to keep *Phylloxera* at bay. In Portugal's Douro Valley, *Quinta do Noval* has a 2.5 ha portion of one of their terraced vineyards where the vines are ungrafted and from which the fabled *Nacional* vintage port is produced in most years. Even in Champagne, Bollinger have 0.5 ha of vineyards in Aÿ-Champagne and Bouzy – from which they produce a Champagne called *Vieilles Vignes Françaises* – planted with ungrafted vines. These are planted *en foule,* a system of random planting where replacement vines are layered rather than re-planted with new stock. Vineyards like these are, however, the exception, rather than the rule.

Modern developments in *Phylloxera* control

Geisenheim Viticultural Research Institute (together with a number of other similar institutes), is looking into the possibility of using a naturally occurring soil fungus, *Metarhizium anisopliae*, which infects the soil-borne aphids with a disease that kills them. The fungus – originally isolated from a beetle – is a parasite and has been known about since the 1870s. It has been used for controlling wheat grain beetle, termites, locusts, tsetse flies and several other species and in controlled tests appears to halt the spread of *Phylloxera* although in field-scale trials it has not (yet) proved workable. The use of other types of fungus, together with chemical controls, are also being investigated, but to date, are not commercially successful. Grafting onto rootstocks remains the only currently available control method. The use of genetically modified plant species to counteract threats from insects, diseases and viruses is relatively common in agriculture now, but to date, viticulture has not been touched by this revolution and remains staunchly conventional in this respect. However, research is going on into GM scion varieties which can survive such things as Pierce's Disease, Fanleaf virus and *Phylloxera* and it may be, that in the future, as generations grow up and realise that GM plants are not dangerous to the environment, these might become acceptable.

Pre-*Phylloxera* vines and wines

When wine from European pre-*Phylloxera* ungrafted vines was readily available, it was often claimed that it was far superior to wine from grafted stock. How correct this was is open to debate. With the passage of time, pre-*Phylloxera* wine of European origin has become extremely rare and expensive and few wine drinkers, save perhaps for a few lucky auctioneers who specialise in selling very old wines, now have any experience of these wines. When one looks at the production figures from vineyards that lived through the *Phylloxera* crisis, the one most pertinent difference is the level of production. Before the insect struck, a good yield in a top Bordeaux estate might be around 10–15 hl-ha. After replanting with clonally selected plant material, grafted onto virus-free stock, and re-trellised and trained, average yields might well be around

60–75 hl-ha, with much higher yields possible. This fact alone is probably largely responsible for any quality difference. Although the rootstock and the scion is joined via the graft, there is absolutely no evidence that the flavour of the grapes is in any way affected by the vine's attachment to a non-*vinifera* root system. What is changed however is the growth pattern of the vine and this in turn will affect the way in which the vine grows, its yield level and how it ripens its crop. A grafted vine may well be more vigorous, have a deeper root system and a denser canopy than an own-rooted neighbour and this will of course mean that its grapes, and the wine produced from them, will be different.

Conclusion – *Phylloxera*

Phylloxera vastatrix continues to live up to its name and growers in regions where it is still a possible danger can ill afford to take its threat lightly. In Germany there have been reports of a decline in vigour and cropping of vines grafted onto rootstock 5C in areas where *Phylloxera* is known to be active, a worrying development. The benefits of rootstocks go far beyond their ability to

Own-rooted vines planted en foule in Burgundy.

protect against the insect and the additional cost compared to planting rooted cuttings is small when taken over a vine's long life. Only in very isolated regions are non-grafted vines really secure and even then, in this age of flying winemakers, flying viticulturalists and even flying vineyard visitors, is any wine region that isolated? Growers can also not afford to be complacent. As has been seen in California, *Phylloxera* has the ability to change and adapt to its environment and there is no telling what it might do in the future.

Chapter 14

Nutritional disorders and other viticultural problems

Mineral requirements of vines

This is a complex subject and one that can only be dealt with in brief here. In **Chapter 5 – Soils for vineyards**, the importance of pH in relation to nutrient availability and uptake was discussed and should be borne in mind when reading this chapter.

Major elements

There are three major elements required for plant life – nitrogen, phosphorous and potassium – these are dealt with first, with the minor and trace elements afterwards in alphabetical order.

Nitrogen (N)

Many vines require very little additional nitrogen and gain all they need from that created by the break-down of the shoots, canes and leaves returned to the soil, together with the grasses, plants and weeds growing in-between the rows which will usually be regularly mown. Indeed, excessive nitrogen is more often a problem than a deficiency and can lead to soft, lush growth, shaded canopies and over-vigorous vines prone to fungal diseases. Some plants – legumes such as clover and alfalfa (lucerne) – are able to fix nitrogen taken from the atmosphere on nodules on their roots and if excess nitrogen is likely to be a problem, these plants should be excluded from inter-row plantings. Vines growing on light sandy soils, especially on sites where vines have been cropped for many years, may show a deficiency of nitrogen and this is usually indicated by pale, often yellowing, leaves in extreme situations, and reduced photosynthetic ability. In these instances, small applications of nitrogen, often added as a foliar spray in the form of urea, will be needed. Nitrogen deficiency is not to be confused with what are often called the June Yellows. The month of June (in the northern hemisphere) is the time when the vine is making its maximum growth and making the heaviest demands upon its root structure. If the weather turns cold, the vines' leaves may suddenly turn a lighter shade of green than normal, but the colour usually recovers once warmer weather returns. Some growers will also apply urea post-harvest to the vineyard floor to hasten the breakdown of leaves and shoots which will then be taken down into the soil by worms and other soil microorganisms.

Phosphorous (P)

Although a major element, vines have a low requirement for phosphorous and seldom suffer from a deficiency. Very little is taken out when grapes are harvested and most soils have ample reserves. On soils with very low pHs, low phosphorous levels may lead to chlorosis-like symptoms, but this is rare. If phosphorous is required, it should ideally be added before vines are planted and ploughed in as deeply as possible.

Potassium (K)

Potassium, confusingly indicated in soil sample reports by the initial K (its chemical symbol and from the German for potassium which is *kalium*), is the third of the major elements required by vines (and indeed most plants) for successful growth and fruiting. Vines deficient in potassium will show chlorotic leaf margins, often accompanied by a cupping of the leaves. Vines are more likely to show these symptoms in times of stress – during a drought or when temperatures are low – both of which affect the ability of the roots to take up potassium. Deficiencies can be remedied in the short term by a foliar feed and in the long term by the application of fertilisers containing potash.

Excess potassium in soils is often associated with high pH levels in wine (although the correlation is not always as linear as one might expect) which can lead to flabby wines prone to oxidation and bacterial spoilage. Vines grown on low-vigour rootstocks (Riparia Gloire, 101-14 and 420A for instance) tend to give juice and wine with lower amounts of potassium. Conversely, vines growing on high-vigour rootstocks (5BB, 110R, 5C and 125AA) tend to have high levels of potassium. This is explained because over-vigorous vines tend to have more shaded canopies, and in shaded conditions, potassium migrates to the leaves and thence to the fruit. Canopy management techniques which reduce shading can therefore play a part in bringing wine pH levels into a better balance.

Minor and trace elements

Boron (B)

Boron is a trace element, but deficiencies of it can have a major effect upon vine health, especially on sandy, acidic soils in high rainfall areas. The most noticeable effect is a poor fruit set caused by poor pollen tube growth, followed by irregular sized grapes with an over-abundance of small berries. Shoot growth is also often distorted and irregular, and yields are often severely adversely affected. Excess boron can be a problem where irrigation water contains high concentrations of the element and levels need to be monitored carefully. Boron does not move readily within the plant, so that if a vine shows signs of boron deficiency, the best remedy is a foliar feed.

Calcium (Ca)

Calcium is required for successful vine growth and fruiting and helps protect grapes against attack from microbes. Many vineyard soils are naturally rich in calcium and in these soils a shortage is never a problem. Soils with low pH levels – below 6.0 – will need liming to bring them up to as near neutral (7.0) as possible, but with very acidic soils this may be difficult except with very large inputs of lime and plenty of time.

Copper (Cu)

Copper is a trace element that is required by vines in very small amounts and is seldom in short supply, mainly because copper-containing fungicides are one of the main weapons against Downy Mildew. Situations of excess copper have been known in regions that have continuously used relatively primitive copper sprays, such as Bordeaux Mixture, and vines can become stunted. Earthworm and microbial activity in the soil is also very much reduced when copper is used excessively. Applications of humus and lime, together with green manuring and the use of alternative fungicides, will often correct a situation where there is excess copper.

Iron (Fe)

As has been mentioned before, iron is required for chlorophyll production and deficiencies are normally only associated with very alkaline (high pH) soils. Liquid fertilisers containing chelated iron (iron that has been treated so that it becomes soluble) can be sprayed on vines or injected into the soil as a short-term remedy. In the long term, the correct choice of rootstock must be made for vines growing on highly alkaline soils if lime-induced chlorosis (see later in this chapter) is to be avoided.

Magnesium (Mg)

Although magnesium is a minor element, it is nonetheless an important one in the process of photosynthesis as it is a component of the chlorophyll molecule. Vines deficient in magnesium will show symptoms of chlorosis with yellowing leaves which get more noticeable towards ripening. Magnesium deficiencies are also associated with damage to the stems of bunches (bunch stem necrosis – see later in this chapter) which adversely affects ripening. Soils high in potassium also tend to show symptoms of magnesium deficiency, even though there may well be adequate magnesium in the soil. Some rootstocks (SO4 and Fercal) appear to be poor at taking up magnesium and vines growing on these rootstocks (often used in high pH, chalky soils) will show signs of magnesium deficiencies. Remedies include foliar feeds in the short term (Epsom salts are very effective) and fertilisers in the long-term. Light, sandy soils tend to be more deficient in magnesium than heavier clay or loam soils.

Manganese (Mn)

Manganese is a trace element required by the vine for successful growth, albeit in very small amounts. Deficiencies are indicated by yellow stripes between the veins of the leaves and are most common in alkaline, sandy soils. Prompt foliar feeds are usually effective in providing the vine with sufficient manganese. In acidic soils, excess manganese can sometimes be a problem, leading to stunted growth and crop-loss. Vines in these soils also often suffer from chlorosis and the two problems often go hand-in-hand.

Molybdenum (Mo)

Molybdenum is a metal and found in minute quantities in plants, including vines. Lack of molybdenum has been associated with poor flowering (especially with Merlot in Australia) and given that it costs little to apply it, applications of 'moly' will often be included in pre-flowering sprays as a matter of course. Care should be taken not to raise molybdenum levels too high and soils should be tested on a regular basis.

Sulphur (S)

Sulphur is an important requirement for any plant, but luckily vines seldom suffer deficiencies owing to the use of super-phosphate fertilisers which contain 11 per cent sulphur and the use of sulphur sprays against Powdery Mildew (Oidium).

Zinc (Zn)

Zinc deficiencies are most common in sandy, alkaline soils or in soils with high phosphorous levels. Yellow veining and irregular growth patterns of leaves are the first symptoms of a zinc deficiency, followed by stunted shoot growth and poor fruit set. Vines deficient in zinc are less able to synthesise the plant hormones called auxins which promote cell division. Zinc can be applied as a foliar spray and in susceptible vineyards, it may be applied on a regular basis throughout the growing season.

Other viticultural problems

Bunch Stem Necrosis – BSN

Bunch stem necrosis is caused by a number of factors: poor nutrition (low levels of calcium and magnesium), over-vigorous growth, and cold and wet weather at flowering have all been implicated. The condition causes bunches to shrivel and the berries stop developing, resulting in low sugars and high acids. Yields are also greatly reduced. The problem can also affect vines preflowering when it is known as *Early Bunch Stem Necrosis* or *EBSN*. Apart from addressing the nutritional shortages, there is no real cure for BSN.

Chlorosis – Iron Chlorosis, Lime-Induced Chlorosis

When vines are grown on soils with a high lime content, iron, required by the vine to produce chlorophyll – the green colouring in leaves that is required for photosynthesis to take place – becomes locked in the soil and cannot be taken up by the plant. Soils that have a high lime or chalk content, usually those with pH levels of 7.5 or more, need testing for the percentage of *active* calcium carbonate (*calcaire actif*) *present* in the soil (which is NOT the same thing as the *total* calcium carbonate content). This can range from 0 per cent up to 50 per cent and for levels over 5 per cent, an appropriate lime-tolerant rootstock should be selected.

Coulure

Coulure is the result of poor flowering conditions and/or an imbalance of nutrients in the vine. Either or both of these conditions leads to poor or imperfect pollination resulting in bunches with few berries. This usually means a substantial loss of crop. Some varieties are more prone to *coulure* (although some clones are less susceptible) and techniques such as tip-trimming during flowering may help. In English the condition is also sometimes known as 'shatter'.

Millerandage – Hen and chicken

Millerandage (known as hen and chicken in some countries) is a condition which results in some of the vine's flowers either remaining un-pollinated or forming very small berries that have no seeds. It is caused by adverse weather during flowering – cold or cold and wet – and some varieties and clones (Gewürztraminer and Mendoza clone Chardonnay for instance) are more prone. The small berries will usually grow to full term, ripen very early and will be very sweet. This can sometimes be an advantage with winemakers believing that smaller berries make better wines, although it can also lead to the unwanted attentions of birds and wasps which attack the very small ripe berries before the bulk of the crop is ready for harvesting.

MW Examination questions related to viticulture 1999–2019

1. Examine the principal factors within the direct control of the vineyard manager which affect the quality of the grapes produced. (1999)

2. Mineral deficiencies in the vineyard can lead to numerous problems. Discuss the major elements necessary for healthy vine growth and explain how deficiencies should be corrected. (1999)

3. New owners of a vineyard have put you in overall charge of vineyard management and wine production and have asked you to cultivate their vineyard organically. What are your recommendations, taking into account financial, as well as quality, considerations? (1999)

4. Describe what you understand by the concept of "Terroir" and draw conclusions as to its influence, using examples drawn from both New World and Old World vineyards. (1999)

5. Why are some grape varieties more successful than others in certain vineyard environments? Discuss the principals involved and give examples from both hemispheres. (2000)

6. If vineyard health is essential to good quality wine production, what steps can be taken to ensure that vines produce the quality and quantity of grapes required? (2000)

7. Viticulture is difficult on an acid soil and the grower may need to rectify the pH of the soil itself. What are the consequences and the constraints of an acid soil? (2000)

8. Climate, soil and vine all influence final wine quality. Do you consider any one of these factors to be more significant than the others? Give reasons for your conclusions about their relative importance. (2001)

9. Why is pruning so important? Discuss the different methods in use, the timing of their use and their respective influences on quality. (2001)

10. Consider the question of plant density, giving examples drawn from current practice in both New and Old World vineyards. (2001)

11. Which are the most dangerous pests and diseases that confront the modern vineyard manager? Evaluate recent developments designed to combat the problems. Discuss with particular reference to a) Burgundy and b) California. (2001)

12. Consider the options open to the winemaker seeking to improve the raw material in the vineyard, and the fruit as it enters the winery. (2002)

13. Discuss the factors that influence the choice of rootstock and scion. (2002)

14. Explore the advantages and disadvantages of young and old vines. What are the implications for both yield and quality? (2002)

15. Examine the differences between biodynamic cultivation, organic cultivation, lutte raisonnée, and other forms of minimum intervention, using example from

both Old and New World regions. (2002)

16. How important is the role of soil in producing high quality wine? (2003)

17. When planting a new vineyard, what would you do to eliminate potential disease? (2003)

18. Examine the effects of water and heat on vines. (2003)

19. Examine the reasons for clonal selection, the alternatives and all relevant quality considerations. (2003)

20. Restricted yields have traditionally been an important requirement in the making of high quality wines. Have modern viticultural methods reduced this requirement? (2004)

21. What factors determine the optimum useful life of a vine? (2004)

22. How may sweetness be achieved in a wine? Illustrate your answer with examples from around the world. (2004)

23. Planting densities vary considerably. What impact does this have on wine quality? (2005)

24. Examine the role of water management during the growing season in the production of quality wine around the world. (2005)

25. To what extent is the notion of "terroir" still valid for today's viticulture? (2005)

26. Describe the principal acids present in must and wine. How may the winegrower and winemaker obtain the desired acid balance in wine? (2005)

27. How can a winemaker influence the final alcohol level of a wine, and why might this be required? (2006)

28. How does canopy management influence fruit maturity? (2006)

29. Examine the elements of vine nutrition essential for the production of high quality wine. (2006)

30. Examine the effects of botrytis cinerea. When and why is it desirable or undesirable to produce wines made from botrytis affected grapes? (2006)

31. As a vineyard manager, evaluate the key factors required to produce a wine of outstanding quality. (2007)

31. Examine the different methods of working the soil that can affect the potential yield and quality in a vineyard. (2007)

32. How and why do grape growers prune vines at different times of the year? (2007)

33. What are the benefits and relative costs associated with biodynamic, organic and sustainable (lutte raisonnée) viticulture? Illustrate your answers with examples from the Old World and the New World. (2008)

34. What consequences for viticulture does climate change present globally, and what can viticulturalists do to exploit and moderate its effects? (2008)

35. Identify the major pests and diseases affecting vineyards worldwide. Outline their effects and treatments used to counter them. (2008)

36. What role does water play in viticulture? (2009)

37. Using relevant examples, outline the problems and advantages of 'marginal climate' vineyard sites for quality wine producers. (2009)

38. What impact do the trellising systems chosen have on the yield and health of vines? (2009)

39. What are the advantages and disadvantages of increasing mechanisation in vineyards? (2009)

40. How might alcohol levels in unfortified wines be influenced in both the vineyard and the cellar and why might this be desirable? (2010)

41. How would you manage an established vineyard in a 'hot climate'? (2010)

42. How can vine nutrition be improved through soil management? (2010)

43. What are the vineyard factors that influence the choice of rootstocks? (2011)

44. Examine the differences between phenolic and physiological ripeness and their impact on winemaking? (2011)

45. Compare and contrast the advantages and disadvantages between organic and non-organic viticulture. (2011)

46. How does soil influence wine quality? (2012)

47. Compare and contrast the harvesting options available to a vineyard owner and explain how these options affect wine quality. (2012)

48. What are the roles of tannins in wine and how can a winemaker vary their extraction and presence in wine? (2012)

49. Analyse the ways in which changing the trellising system in a vineyard can have an impact on the yields and health of the vines. (2012)

50. What are the most relevant pests and diseases today? Describe their effects and how they should be combatted. (2013)

51. Many factors can affect flowering and fruit set. Examine what effect these might have on quality and yield. (2013).

52. You are tasked with establishing new vineyard sites to produce Chardonnay in Casablanca Valley, Chile and Champagne, France. What would be your major concerns? (2013)

53. Define the effects Botrytis Cinerea have on wine quality and explain the measures a winery should carry out when both white and red grapes have extensive Botrytis infection on entering the winery. (2013)

54. How can viticultural and winemaking techniques influence aromatic compounds in a wine? Refer to wines made from Riesling, Sauvignon Blanc and Pinot Noir. (2014)

55. Do the highest potential quality wines come from vines planted on a slope? (2014)

56. What are the quantitative and qualitative implications of young and old vines? (2014)

57. How important is the management of the area between the rows? Consider vineyards in both warm and cool climates. (2014)

58. What are the causes of grapevine trunk diseases, such as Esca, and what are the best strategies to combat them? (2015)

59. What nutrients are important to the grapevine for the production of quality grapes, and why? (2015)

60. When and how does frost pose a risk to grape production? Evaluate the different methods of frost protection available to the grape grower. (2015)

61. Which are the most suitable grape varieties for the production of high quality traditional method sparkling wines, and why? (2015)

62. Why does density of vine plantation vary from vineyard to vineyard? Assess the advantages of low and high density plantings. (2015)

63. How might the costs of growing grapes and managing a vineyard affect the price of a bottle of wine? (2015)

64. How can sweetness be achieved in non-fortified wines through viticulture and vinification? (2015)

65. Assess the effectiveness of the options available to organic and biodynamic grape growers to control pests and diseases. (2016)

66. What practical options does a viticulturist have at his or her disposal to address long term changes in climate in an established vineyard? (2016)

67. Can Cabernet Sauvignon and Riesling be successful in the same location? (2016)

68. Compare the main vine training systems used in the following wine regions: (a) Mosel (b) Alsace (c) Marlborough (d) Châteauneuf-du-Pape (2016)

69. What steps can a viticulturist take to provide and maintain proper vine nutrition? (2016)

70. When and how can hail cause damage at various stages of vine growth? What methods are most effective for preventing or responding to such damage? (2016)

71. Temperature is one of the most impactful environmental variables on wine grape growing. How does temperature affect viticulture? (2017)

72. Water availability is increasingly an issue in some wine producing regions. How can a viticulturist best ensure water sustainability when establishing and managing vineyards in drought-prone regions? (2017)

73. Labour supply for vineyard work is decreasing in many parts of the world. If this trend continues, how will this affect viticulture, and how can vineyard managers around the world best prepare for, and handle, a shortage of workers? (2017)

74. Discuss which vine varieties would be most suitable for the production of dessert wines. Explain your choice with specific reference to any climatic requirements. (2017)

75. Does soil preparation affect the potential yield and quality in a vineyard? (2017). What are the principal pests and diseases facing vine growers today, and how can they best be managed? (2017)

76. Many wine regions can produce wines at a wide range of price points. Referencing at least two of such regions, compare and contrast methods of managing vineyards for high priced wines and low-priced wines. (2018)

77. Referencing at least three wine regions, discuss how climate change is influencing grape growers' viticultural practices. (2018)

78. Identify the most important trunk diseases in vineyards around the world. How can they be best controlled and managed? (2018)

79. Is the use of cover crops worthwhile in viticulture? (2018)

80. What is the role of pruning when managing an established vineyard? (2018)

81. Old vines have a mystique to them. What are the practical challenges and solutions to maintaining vineyards of old vines? (2018)

82. Are yield restrictions necessary to produce high-quality wine? (2019)

83. Your company has acquired a vineyard suitable for high-quality wine production that is currently producing grapes for bulk wine. Indicate what steps you would take to convert it. (2019)

84. Assess how drought tolerance can be achieved through viticulture. (2019)

85. Mildews continue to afflict vineyards. What strategies might a vineyard manager employ to reduce the risk? (2019)

86. What are the critical considerations for selecting a rootstock when establishing a new vineyard? (2019)

87. Discuss the role of the following factors in the production of high-quality grapes: aspect, vine density, row orientation. (2019)

Bibliography

Coombe B.G & Dry P.R (Editors) *Viticulture* Volume I: Resources, Winetitles, Adelaide, 2nd Edition. 2005

Coombe B.G & Dry P.R (Editors) *Viticulture* Volume 2: Practices, Winetitles, Adelaide, 1992

Campbell, Christie *Phylloxera*, Harper Collins. London, 2004.

Crossen, Tom *Venture into Viticulture*, Country Wide Press, Australia. 2001

Goode, Jamie *Wine Science*, The Application of Science in Winemaking, Mitchell Beazley, London, 2005.

Iland, Patrick; Dry, Peter; Proffitt, Tony; Tyreman, Steve *The Grapevine* Patrick Iland Wine Promotions, Adelaide, South Australia, 2011.

Jackson, David *Monographs in cool climate viticulture* No. 2: Climate, Daphne Brasell Associates Ltd., Wellington, New Zealand, 2001

Jackson, David *Monographs in cool climate viticulture* No. 1, Pruning 2nd Training', Lincoln University Press, New Zealand, 1997

Maltman, Alex *Vineyards, Rocks and Soils, A Wine Lover's Guide to Geology*, Oxford University Press, Oxford. 2018.

May, Peter *Flowering and Fruitset in Grapevines*, Phylloxera and Grape Industry Board of South Australia with Lythrum Press, Adelaide, 2004.

Mollah, Mahabubur *Practical Aspects of Grapevine Trellising*, Winetitles, Adelaide. 1997

Ordish, George *The Great Wine Blight*, J. M. Dent and Sons Ltd., London. 1971 and 1987

Robinson, Jancis (Editor) *Oxford Companion to Wine*, 4th Edition, Oxford University Press,2015

Smart, Richard and Robinson, Mike Sunlight into Wine - A Handbook for Winegrape Canopy Management, Winetitles, Adelaide, 1991

Waldin, Monty *Biodynamic Wines*, The Infinite Ideas Classic Wine Library, Oxford, 2016

Wilson, James E. Terroir, *The Role of Geology, Climate and Culture in the Making of French Wines*, Mitchell Beazley, London, 1998.

The Author

Stephen Skelton MW has been involved with growing vines and making wine since 1975. He spent two years in Germany, working at Schloss Schönborn in the Rheingau and studying at Geisenheim, the world-renowned college of winegrowing and winemaking, with the late Professor Helmut Becker. In 1977 he returned to the UK to establish the vineyards at Tenterden in Kent (now the home of the UK's largest wine producer, Chapel Down Wines), and made wine there for 22 consecutive vintages. From 1988 to 1991 he was also winemaker and general manager at Lamberhurst Vineyards, at that time the largest winery in the UK. He now works as a consultant to vineyards and wineries in the UK, setting up vineyards for the production of both still and sparkling wines.

In 1986 Stephen started writing and lecturing about wine and has contributed articles to many different publications. In 1989 he wrote (and published) his first book, *The Vineyards of England* and in 2001 his second, *The Wines of Britain and Ireland* (Faber and Faber) which won the André Simon Award for Drinks Book of the Year. This was followed by three editions of the *UK Vineyards Guide* (2008, 2010 and 2016), *Vine Varieties, Clones and Rootstocks for UK Vineyards* (2014) and *Wine Growing in Great Britain* (2014). His latest book is *The Wines of Great Britain* (2019), one of the titles in the *Classic Wine Library* series. The book on his specialist subject, *Viticulture* was first published in 2007 and to date has sold almost 10,000 copies, making it one of the largest selling books on its subject in English. It has been sold worldwide and has recently been translated into Japanese and Chinese. He was for many years the English and Welsh vineyards contributor for the annual wine guides written by Hugh Johnson, Oz Clarke and Tom Stevenson and still writes the section on English and Welsh wines in Jancis Robinson's *Oxford Companion to Wine* and in Hugh Johnson and Jancis Robinson's *World Atlas of Wine*.

Stephen was a director of the English Vineyards Association (EVA) from 1982 to 1995 and of its successor organisation, the United Kingdom Vineyards Association

(UKVA) from 1995–2003. He was Chairman of the UKVA from 1999–2003. He currently is a member of the WineGB Management Advisory Committee (MAC) and is Chairman of the Viticulture Working Group (VWG). He was also at various times between 1982 and 1986, Treasurer, Secretary and Chairman of the South East Vineyards Association, Secretary of the Circle of Wine Writers between 1990 and 1997 and has served on various EU committees in Brussels representing UK winegrowers. In 1999 he took three years off from the viticulture business to do a BSc in Multimedia Technology and Design at Brunel University. Whilst at Brunel, Stephen was awarded the *Ede and Ravenscroft Prize* for his final year project, a touch-screen wine selector and in 2011 was awarded an Honorary Doctorate in Business Administration from Anglia-Ruskin University. In 2013 he completed an MA in Life Writing (Biography) at the Creative Writing Department of the University of East Anglia.

In 2003, Stephen became a Master of Wine, winning the prestigious *Robert Mondavi Trophy* for gaining the highest marks in the Theory section of the examination. He was a member of the MW Education Committee from 2003–9 and served as education course wine coordinator for that period. In 2005 he won the *AXA Millésimes Communicator of the Year Award* for services to the MW education programme. He was a member of the MW Council from 2009–17 and Vice Chairman from 2014–17. He is currently Chairman of the Research Paper Examination Committee. Stephen has judged for the *International Wine Challenge*, the *International Wine and Spirit Competition*, the *Japan Wine Challenge* and the *Veritas Wine Awards* and has been UK Panel Chair for *The Decanter World Wine Awards* since 2008.

Other books by Stephen Skelton MW – Details on www.englishwine.com

THE WINES OF
GREAT BRITAIN

STEPHEN SKELTON MW

UK Vineyards Guide

A directory of vineyards in Great Britain,
Ireland and the Channel Isles

By Stephen Skelton MW

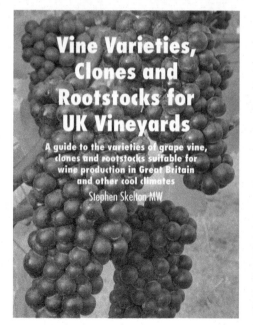

Vine Varieties,
Clones and
Rootstocks for
UK Vineyards

A guide to the varieties of grape vine,
clones and rootstocks suitable for
wine production in Great Britain
and other cool climates

Stephen Skelton MW

WINE GROWING
IN GREAT BRITAIN

A complete guide to growing grapes for wine
production in cool climates

STEPHEN SKELTON MW

Index

abcissic (abscisic) acid, 102
abiotic factors, 16
abscisic (abscisic) acid, 102
acid levels (acidity), 29, 33, 35, 40
    volatile acidity, 130, 133
advection frost, 51–2
age of vine and quality, 95
Agrobacterium vitis, 123
Airén, 33, 34
alcohol levels, 26, 32, 33, 118
    reduction, 26, 33, 34
alkaline soils, 40, 147
alleyways, 87–8
    cover-crops in, 66
    frost protection and, 53
altitude (elevation), 27
Anaheim/Pierce's disease (and *Xylella fastidiosa*), 26,
    114, 124
anchor posts (end-posts/anchors), 55, 81, 82, 83
animals:
    in biodynamic and organic practice, 108–9
    predator, protection, 50–1, 93
annual cycle, 84–95
    canopy management, 66, 91, 92, 94
anthracnose, 122
apoplexy, 127
appellations, 9, 10, 21
    rules and regulations, 21, 26, 33, 62, 67, 78, 94, 140
    terroir and, 42
Argentina, 31, 32
Armillaria root rot, 122
aspect of site, 27–8
aspersion technique, 53
Australia, 31, 32
    minimal pruning, 77
Austria, noble rot, 119
autumn (September/October/November in northern
    hemisphere), 92–4
AXR1 (ARG1) rootstock, 139, 141

bacteria (and bacteria-like organisms) causing
    disease, 114, 122–3, 124
Ballerina (training system), 78
bark girdling, 90
Basket (training system), 78

Becker, Helmut, 14
beetles, 129–30, 130
benzimidazole, 117
biodynamic viticulture, 14, 104–11, 114, 120
bio-fungicides (incl. naturally occurring fungicides),
    18
    Botrytis, 117–18
birds, 93
bird's eye rot, 122
black dead arm, 127
black foot, 127
black goo, 128
black knot, 123
black measles, 127
black rot, 123
black spot, 122
blight, bacterial, 122–3
Blodin (training system), 53, 78, 89
Bordeaux, 23–4
    terroire, 43
Bordeaux Mixture, 120, 122, 146
bore-hole, 97
borers (beetles), 129–30
Börner rootstock, 139
boron, 146
Botryosphaeria canker (bot canker), 127
botryticine, 119
Botrytis (pourriture gris; grey mould; grey rot; bunch
    rot; sour rot), 116–20
    control, 25, 88, 89, 117–18
    flowering and, 90
buds (nodes), 3, 4
    bud-burst, 87
        delayed, 6, 53, 86
    density and, 66
    fruiting:
        cane-pruning and, 74
        spur-pruning and, 75, 76
    in training/trellising/pruning, 66, 70, 73, 74, 75, 76
bunch rot, 116–19
bunch stem necrosis, 148
bunch-thinning (crop-thinning; green harvesting),
    64, 65, 91, 94, 109
burners, 52
Bush (training system), 78

Viticulture is particularly good on the practicalities of viticulture. Definitely useful for those with vines to plant and/or exams to take.

Jancis Robinson MW

The in-depth text ... covers the entire process of viticulture in great detail. There is no doubt it will be a useful learning and reference tool

Wine and Spirit Magazine

Wonderful little book ...
good book on the subject

Bo Simons, Wayward Tendrils Magazine

Recommended by the Wine and Spirit EducationTrust for the Diploma course

ISBN 978-0-9931-2357-3

9 780993 123573

VITICULTURE

An introduction to commercial grape growing

Stephen Skelton MW

VITICULTURE

An introduction to commercial grape growing for wine production

Stephen Skelton MW

2nd edition, revised and updated 2020